Praise for *The French House*

"On a tiny French island, a couple of American dreamers redefine their lives by restoring a ruin—which in this lovely, shimmering story becomes a parable of a saner, greener, more sustainable path that we all can follow if we will but listen to the wisdom of the villagers the way the Wallaces did. *The French House* moves to a soulful, very funny rhythm all its own."

—*Meryl Streep*

"*The French House* is a brave, insightful, and very amusing memoir about a fantasy that many of us have had but not dared to attempt. The only problem with it is that now I want to adopt myself into the Wallace family."

—*Jane Smiley*

"In this beautifully written, rich, moving story of a fabulous, resourceful, and utterly original family, Don Wallace has crafted a delicious French bonbon of a book. *The French House* is full of humor, hope, and, I daresay, lessons on how to live a life full of meaning. I loved it."

—*Dani Shapiro, bestselling author of* Devotion *and* Still Writing

"*The French House* isn't a memoir. It's a vacation. Charming, gorgeous, perceptive, it is peppered with unforgettable characters and steeped in the deep red wine of long-term friendship, showing us how a remarkable place can make a life worth living. You will never want to leave Belle Île or Don Wallace's inspiring tale of holding on to a dream despite overwhelming adversity."

—*Jennie Fields, international bestselling author of* The Age of Desire

THE
FRENCH HOUSE

An American Family, a Ruined *Maison*,
and the Village That Restored Them All

DON WALLACE

 sourcebooks

Published by Sourcebooks, Inc.
P.O. Box 4410, Naperville, Illinois 60567-4410
(630) 961-3900
Fax: (630) 961-2168
www.sourcebooks.com

Library of Congress Cataloging-in-Publication data is on file with the publisher.

Printed and bound in the United States of America.
VP 10 9 8 7 6 5 4 3

Contents

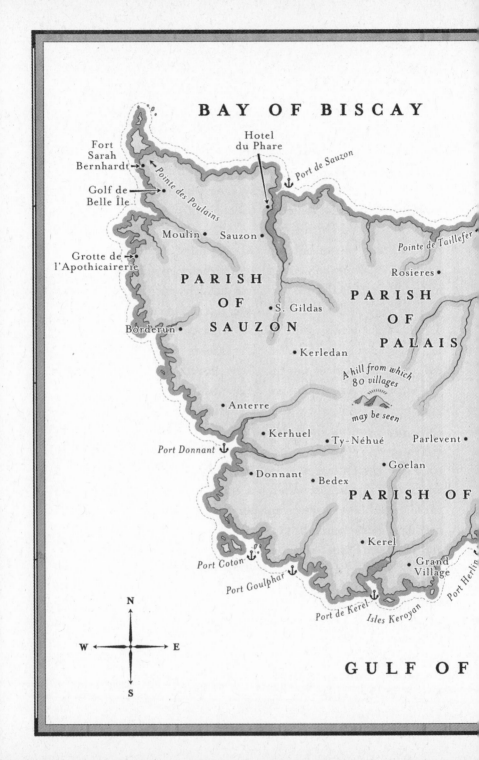

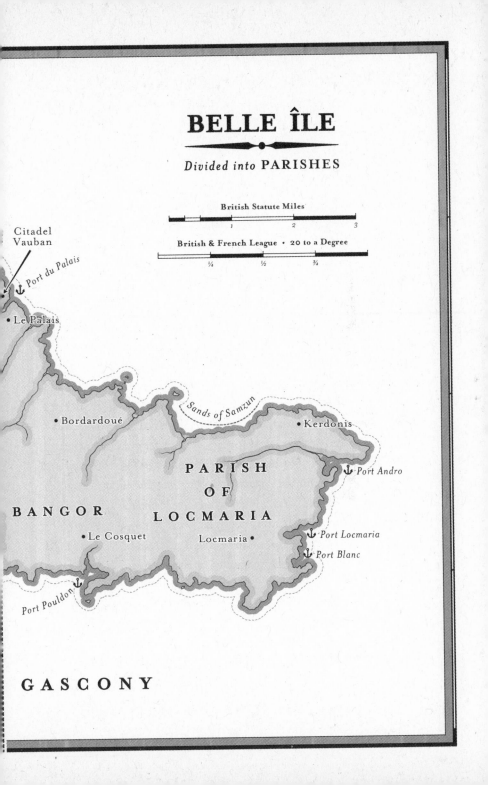

BELLE ÎLE

Divided into PARISHES

British Statute Miles

| | 1 | 2 | 3 |

British & French League • 20 to a Degree

| ¼ | ½ | ¾ |

Citadel
Vauban

⚓ *Port du Palais*

• Le Palais

• Bordardoué

Sands of Samzun

• Kerdonis

⚓ *Port Andro*

PARISH
OF
LOCMARIA

BANGOR

• Le Cosquet

Locmaria •

⚓ *Port Locmaria*

⚓ *Port Blanc*

⚓

Port Pouldon

GASCONY

To Mindy and Rory

*Any one of us
can tell our story
in terms of fate,
in terms of luck,
or in terms of choice,
and never know
with exact certitude
what is working.*

—Sheena Iyengar, *The Art of Choosing*

Top Ten Facts
about Belle Île

1. It swims offshore like a fat sole fried in butter, but its bones are blue-green granite.
2. It is located ten miles out in the Atlantic from the coast of Brittany, in what is called the Bay of Biscay.
3. Its golden fields are held aloft by sharp-toothed, bone-shattering cliffs, like an offering to older gods.
4. One hundred fifty-two little villages, most amounting to only a half dozen houses, bask in valleys cut by trickling creeks or huddle in the lee of low knolls.
5. Each village has its own personality and schedule and history. Each has a cow. Each has a mystery. (*Who owns that cow?*)
6. Each village also shares a daily rhythm with everything else here, because of the way the island breathes with the tides. All of it, farm and beach and rockbound coast, drawbridge and fishing boat and mud-burrowing clam, the wiggling sardines soon to become the daily special on the chalkboard outside the *crêperie* Guerveur, even the lines of wobbling tourist cyclists clogging the island lanes—all seem to wax and wane, rise and fall, along with the sea's inhalation and exhalation, those sweeping tides that come twice a day, twice at night.
7. It's beautiful here, often dramatically so.
8. But, as always, beauty comes at a cost. There are too many tourists in July and August, although they're good for the local economy. There is pressure to build on open farmland to accommodate development. Pollution is a problem, mostly from outmoded septic

systems. Young people can't find jobs to suit their education level and feel they must move to the Continent. As my wife, Mindy, knows from leaving her native Hawaii, this can be painful: it's never quite the same after you go away.

9. There is an ancient and unresolved drama revolving around the island. It looks postcard-pretty upon arrival at Le Palais, the walled port on the protected side that faces the French mainland. It presents a brave face on its western coast, too, the aptly named Côte Sauvage. But it is trapped in an abusive relationship with the treacherous Bay of Biscay, taking the brunt of whatever mood the sea is in. Cliffs crumble, dark masses of seaweed cover the beaches, rows of cypresses fall, ripping up the earth with their roots. Fishermen and tourists are washed away to become crab bait. Early in the morning after a storm, the island tries to convince you that its bruises mean nothing, calling your attention instead to the sun-kissed mists and drifts of spume, taller than a man, that collect in the coves and creeks. The shadow of violence in her eyes haunts you, however. *Never turn your back on the sea.*

10. But the island is also gentled by the warming tickle of the tail end of the Gulf Stream. It gets a lot of sunshine, less rain than the Continent, and periods of scintillating glassy calm that, in summer, occasionally peak in what the local *Bellilois* call *beau temps*: a day or two of warm, windless clarity and peace, almost psychedelic in nature, when orb spiders weave tapestries of bedewed diamonds along the valley path, shiny green lizards dart underfoot, and people talk in whispers out of an instinctive awe and reverence.

In other words, it is called Belle Île for a reason.

Instructions
Opening the House

B onjour et bienvenue—
　　　There are a few things that have to be done immediately when you open the house. *Please read ALL these points carefully.* First, however, apologies if the ocean was rough on the ferry ride over. We hope nobody got seasick. If somebody did, please check, and clean, the soles of their (not yours, I hope) shoes.

　Note: do not start to unpack or have that stiff drink, however well-deserved, or chase after cats and lizards and movie starlets, no matter how adorable, until after you have completed all the opening tasks. Otherwise, there may be a small disaster, such as not having hot water for your bath, or a bigger one, such as open faucets flooding the upstairs.

　But perhaps you're not here yet. Perhaps you're reading ahead (recommended) or else, like us thirty years ago, you've arrived to find yourself standing in the middle of a rural village without any idea of where you are and searching for a cottage you must locate without a street sign or house number in sight. If the latter, here's hoping you stashed these instructions in a place where they can easily be found. Because you'll need them.

Finding the House

Imagine the village as a bicycle lying on its side in the cornfields. Our first dusty intersection is the rear wheel hub, the spokes of which form four shady lanes. Follow the right-hand lane uphill.

The first house you pass will look on the verge of collapse or abandonment. Its windows are without glass, and the drystone walls are covered in vines that might be the only thing holding them together. You may see feminine underwear hanging on various bushes. You may see kittens. You will probably not see Suzanne, especially if she has sensed your arrival, or that of any stranger, but this is her house.

Next up, in the middle of our row of three, is a small, narrow cottage painted a gleaming white with pink and green trim under the eaves and around the windows and door. Everybody exclaims at how pretty and perfect it is, so go right ahead, squeal: *"It's so cute!"* We're used to it.

The date of its construction is chiseled over the lintel: MDCCCXLII. We guess this goes over well with the tourists, this boast of semiantiquity, but just so you know: this is *not* our house.

Our house is the one next door, up the lane, toward the sky and the sunset. It's older than the cute house with the date—in fact, the second oldest in the village—but what really impresses the locals is that it has never sheltered farm animals. In Belle Île, that's high-class.

In case you were wondering, the house was built over one hundred eighty years ago, and in all that time, only its plank floor and slate roof have needed to be replaced—once each. The stone walls and many of the beams are original. Now consider, as a point of reference, the plywood-and-drywall frame of your average house in an average American development, which begins to delaminate or crumble in about twenty years.

It is our hope that all of this sounds impressive enough to distract your attention from the peeling paint, the exposed wires and bent nails, the cracked glass in the *cabanet*, the rickety furniture that looks like it could collapse any minute, the tar-stained green nylon fishermen's nets strung between rafters like hammocks, the blackened chimney, and so forth. But we know it's hopeless. Nothing takes away from the fact that we basically bought a ruin, one that is still awaiting renovation so many years later. We're just glad we're not here to see your face.

That was supposed to be a joke, by the way. Go ahead and laugh—at the joke, at the house, at us. We're used to it.

The Key...

...Is with Suzanne. Yes, the owner of the *other* ruin in our row of houses. She is our elderly Breton friend and a former cowherd, always chic in a blue dress and blue floral apron. Her black hair may look as if it has never seen the interior of the Elle-Lui Salon du Coiffeur in Le Palais, but you'd be wrong. She gets it done maybe four times a year. Suzanne is about eighty years old. She's a wonderful gardener—those are her flowers all over the village. She wanders around with cuttings in her blue apron pockets, fitting them into the chinks in the stone walls and gaps in the shrubbery. I think she talks to them. (At least her lips move.)

We're pretty sure she's a secret Druid, Veneti, Celt, or whatever you would call the remnant culture going back to the pre-Christian era. That's when the Romans under Julius Caesar conquered Gaul and Britain and squeezed the fleeing Celtic Britons and Bretons together into a cul-de-sac of a French peninsula called Brittany. Suzanne is descended from these mystical ancestors and has spent her entire life within three miles of our village here. Brittany's coast is only ten miles away by ferry from Belle Île, but to Suzanne it might as well be ten thousand, for all the times she's visited.

The village of Kerbordardoué has always been a beauty, but it was under wraps when we first came. Since Suzanne moved in twenty years ago, though, the center lane from her drystone shed to our house has become a miniature Hanging Garden of Babylon, with giant bobbing hydrangeas, tiny red-slippered and yellow-bloomed things, boldly blushing roses, purple-belled hyacinths, daisies, and lately, taking advantage of sodden spots where we wash off our surfboards and wet suits every evening, delicate violet-and-white lilies transplanted from the marshy places and hidden springs Suzanne visits on her rounds.

About Suzanne: she is shy. She speaks through her flowers, her fragile one-toothed smile, and her lace. When we first met her, or rather glimpsed her, Suzanne was literally afraid to be seen. She darted in and out of the village, too fast to catch, much less detain for a conversation. Everyone called her *La Femme Sauvage* for a while.

I agree, an unfortunate nickname. We stopped using it after we glimpsed Suzanne as we sat at an outdoor garden table at Gwened's place up the lane. Among the guests were some rather supercilious Parisians, renters of the MDCCCXLII house adjoining ours. One of them made a show of sneaking around back and ambushing Suzanne, who was peering shyly through a hedge. "*La Femme Sauvage!*" they hooted at the sight of her leaping over a ditch with petticoats flying, like a large, elderly bunny woman, to flee into the fields. I don't think I've been more ashamed of myself, just to have been sitting there and to have said nothing.

I do believe those Parisians were the reason it took a year for Suzanne to be coaxed back into village life. Le Vicomte, the village's gruff old patriarch, did the coaxing. I hope you get a chance to meet him. Aristocratic yet democratic in his tattered black sweater, "Le Vic" has a sly way of sniffing "*trop snob*" whenever his fancier visitors put on airs— which many do, under the impression that's what a *vicomte* (or viscount, as we would say if we were English) would prefer.

He treats Suzanne with light but loving consideration, recognizing, I think, that they are two of a vanishing species—the village lord and the cowherd—who have more in common with each other than with the more recent arrivals. That's his house at the bottom of the lane, adjacent to a ruin that is as carefully preserved in its ruination by Le Vic; his wife, Yvonne; and their children, Thierry and Philippe, as their own whitewashed house is immaculate.

By the way, Suzanne knitted the lace over our windows, the real stuff. When you greet her, she will blush like an eighty-year-old teenager. So if your French is shaky or you're nervous or tired from the long trip and it's late at night, don't worry. Being shy herself, Suzanne is fluent in tongue-tied.

But while she shies away from company, finding her shouldn't be a problem. She is usually around. If she isn't at her shed at the head of the lane, try the farmhouse whose turnoff is in the middle of the first tree tunnel you drove through. Suzanne visits there regularly with Madame Morgane, her best friend since girlhood.

Madame Morgane is the cornerstone of our village, not so much for being active, like Le Vic tending to his ruins or Suzanne to her flowers, but for her status as the last of the village *Bellilois* to have been born here and lived here and worked here all her life (except for four years on the Continent during the Nazi occupation). Her word carries weight among the rest of us. Her presence lends gravity to a chance meeting; her approval matters. Warning: her disapproval devastates.

A farmer's widow, she bears a popular and powerful family name and is, with Suzanne, Kerbordardoué's last link to the Breton agrarian tradition. (That's a mouthful, I know, but the clichéd term, "peasantry," would be insulting and inaccurate. These folks are the owners and shapers of their lives.) Madame Morgane owns the surrounding fields and, at the time we came here, a dozen cows. She also married, unlike Suzanne, and has children and grandchildren. For all this, then, she is always Madame while Suzanne is Mademoiselle.

To find the key to our house, "*Je cherche a Suzanne pour la clé du maison Wallace*" is the lingua franca. It literally means "I'm looking for Suzanne for the key to the Wallace house."

Go ahead and say it: "*Jay. Share-shay. Lay clay. Duh may-zone Wall-Ass.*" Please, try not to giggle.

Oh, Mindy says that my French is incorrect, once again. The proper phrase is… Great, now she won't tell me!

꙾

Among ourselves we like to call the house Chez Jeannie, after the last of the original family to live here. Jeannie (Guer'ch) Morgane was aunt or mother or grandmother to many of the villagers, including Madame

Morgane. She exuded spirit and joy, it is said. But the villagers, unsentimental in the way of country people everywhere (or so I've read in books by sentimental city people), surprised us by not going along with our little gesture, no matter how well-meant. To them the house is ours, and so I've heard it spoken of as "Duh May-Zone Wall-Ass." Doesn't quite flatter us, I agree.

Okay, you've found it. Here's the drill:

1. **Electric**. When you open the door, there is a *cabanet* to your right. This is where the *electric* switches are and the *water* line.
2. **Water**. In the same *cabanet*, *at the bottom*, is a water line with a cutoff valve. Turn the valve all the way open. *Important*: we leave the taps open during the winter so they won't freeze. Please, go immediately upstairs and check the bathtub and sink faucets in case you are the first user of the new year, in which case they will sputter and then begin to gush.
3. **Water heater**. To turn on the water for the water heater, *go to the closet across from the cabanet*. It is full of sporty stuff (tennis rackets, golf clubs, swim fins, masks and snorkels, spear guns, wet suits, Frisbees, bocce balls, all of which you may use *after* you complete every step of these instructions).

   You want to get water going into the heater. To do this, peer behind the water tank—at the base near the wall you will see a *black switch*. Turn it *parallel* to the floor. You should hear a clunk. *Note:* **do not touch the red faucet.** Nobody knows what it does. We think it connects to the secret core of hot magma that lies under the island and, if thrown, will result in worldwide catastrophe.

   You will have hot water in about three to four hours. And it *will* be hot. Very! Be careful not to scald yourself. If there are many of you, take "shower-baths" with the telephone-shaped hand nozzle connected to the faucet by a hose. You will have noted the lack of a shower curtain, so do this while sitting in the tub, please. Otherwise, the water you spray all over the bathroom will most assuredly worm its way through a crack in the floorboards, collect on the ceiling below, and eventually land—*plop!*—on the dining table at the exact moment you have placed the salad, *sole meunière*, and lemon tart before your eager dinner guests.

There is usually enough water in a tank for 3.5 good consecutive shower-baths at the end of the day, after the beach, when you really need it. The water reheats quickly, too. Still, whoever gets the 0.5 is going to feel shortchanged, so we find it helps to rotate "first bath"—as in, "David gets first bath tonight! Rory had it last night." That way nobody gets frozen, and the inevitable bathroom hog can be taught moderation.

(Attention, siblings, cousins, and parents of bathroom hogs: when you hear the bath taps running, you may find it desirable to start doing the dishes, using plenty of hot water.)

4. **Bathroom**. Go upstairs to the bathroom. By the toilet you will see boxes of the septic tank chemical that will keep everything smelling sweet. Put two packets in the bowl and flush.

Despite this, you may notice a sort of sickly odor that rises like a miasma at night when the entire village is humming behind closed doors and windows are fogged from all the shower-baths taken in succession. This odor should be ignored; taking notice of it will only encourage it.

For Women Only: You will note that there is only one tiny mirror in the bathroom and no mirrors anywhere else in the house. This is deliberate and done for your own well-being. Of course, you *can* wash your face and comb your hair in the morning and after the beach, but other than that, we recommend cultivating the Belle Île look of bohemian-athletic-seaside dishevelment to go with that Coco Chanel suntan you're working on. The same goes for clothes.

You're never going to surpass the Frenchwomen in Paris, but here everyone is taking a break from trying too hard. That resort thing you do—changing into a new outfit three times a day—can be safely retired until back on the Continent. And please, lose the heels. There's a reason traditional Breton women wore wooden sabots. You don't want to become mired in the mud by the stiletto heels of your Manolo Blahniks. It's a style, this dishevelment: *le sportif.*

Oh, Mindy says I'm out of my mind if I think Frenchwomen aren't working it overtime. Well, I'll be doggoned… Now she's pointing out that she hasn't forgotten the summer our neighbor the movie starlet threw her towel down next to mine, yanked off her punk rock T-shirt, and unveiled her nasty black bikini. Okay, okay—I didn't realize what was going on until it was, you know, going on… (And I didn't realize you were watching, honeybunch.)

For Men Only: If you have any male children, it may be wise to have Daddy demonstrate how the toilet lid works, or fails to, if you're attempting to take a whiz while standing up. Just when you least expect it—*bang!*—the lid falls like a guillotine.

Don't worry if you botch this demonstration. Even if your son starts wetting the bed because you nearly amputated your own unit, you're in luck—not for nothing is Belle Île known as "the island of psychiatrists." There are two in Kerbordardoué, another three in adjoining villages, and they all sit down at the beach together, which makes an informal consultation easy to arrange.

5. **Stove/Oven**: France uses propane for cooking, which is interesting if you think of her distinguished pedigree for cuisine and how, in America, a propane tank is associated with backyard barbecue or football tailgating.

Under the sink is a blue bottle with a *round disk valve* on top. Turn this all the way open. Wait a minute and turn on a burner and light a match to test it. *Note*: we turn off the blue gas bottle at night. (Just our neurotic American ways, I guess, but once you read about the oven you will understand.)

Important oven note: sadly, the oven has become so unpredictable we have to say: *try to avoid using it.* The dials mean nothing, so you may think you have turned it off and it is merrily filling with gas.

There's a reason the knobs are unreliable. One afternoon our son Rory's older cousin Devo filled the stove with gas before lighting the oven. The resulting explosion removed his eyebrows and budding soul patch. It also blew the knobs across the room. In his defense, Devo was only trying to improvise a puff pastry pizza that Rory had demanded.

Rory knew how to work the stove but was too lazy to get up off *le ef-ef* (a shorthand we've adopted for *the fucking fauteuil*, which is a doll-sized sofa the boys fight over Every. Single. Day.). And so Rory dictated the correct instructions to Devo while lying on *le ef-ef* like some preteen Caligula, but he just happened to leave off the part about lighting the match immediately until a couple of minutes had elapsed.

Mindy and I were, of course, then blamed by the kids for going out surfing and not cooking, as we were supposed to be doing, under the Universal Parental Penal Code. I think one knob is still embedded in the wall. The others dangle on the stove, looking deceptively functional.

(Look, we've tried to get the oven fixed for three years now, but repairmen always seem to have other things on their mind—like the movie starlet, famous for assassinating tough guys while wearing shiny black vinyl culottes, who haunts the ghostly white château behind the village.)

Oh, and the recipe for chorizo pizza using supermarket dough (not puff pastry—Devo was improvising) is in the knife drawer. The recipes for Mindy's famous chocolate football and Madame Morgane's *crêpes* are in the drawer with the tinfoil and the corkscrew. *Note*: the insufferably hot, jolting, rickety little train you took earlier today out to the tip of the peninsula to the ferry port? It's called *le tire-bouchon*. The corkscrew. Clever, huh?

There are no other recipes, no cookbook. Just buy good local ingredients and cook. Use butter with eggs and sole, olive oil with everything else, animal, vegetable, or mineral. And if someone drops a sack of fresh sardines off on the doorstep, don't ask any questions—head straight for the barbecue.

6. **The fireplace:** Works well. When we bought the place it was just about the only positive in the eyes of our neighbor Franck. Anyway, just keep fires small, especially at first, so the smoke has a chance to draw up the chimney and dry it out after the long winter. A fire after a day at the beach is a nice thing. Don't be afraid to try it. Unlike propane, wood burns at a predictable and uneventful rate.

P.S. The barbecue in the fireplace goes outside, to the right, where our house's white wall meets the rough stone wall of the shed. That's where we grill those sardines you found on the doorstep, as well as island lamb chops, striped bass, mackerel, merguez, and chipolata sausages, all summer long. You can do it, too!

P.P.S. The bicycle in the chimney is also to be removed before starting any fires. If you can get the chain to stay on, feel free to ride it. Don't ask why it's there. That's a story for another time.

Attractive Hazards

This is a wild and rugged island, and that is part of its allure. We're not 'fraidy cats, but we do give a wide berth to certain places, situations, tides, and ocean conditions. That big, beautiful beach, for instance: Donnant has twenty-foot tides and, when a swell is running, pumps out epic surf that should only be tackled by experts—a child or weak swimmer may have trouble. People drown there. As for the giant, three-hundred-foot-deep sea cave on all the tourist maps, the Grotto of the Apothecary, it has earned its postcard reputation for the sublime—and for swallowing up a tourist or two every year.

The moors are dense with gorse and thistles and can tear your ankles to shreds. Just like in *The Hound of the Baskervilles*, there are a couple of sinkholes, including one a hundred feet deep, Le Trou de Vazen. The cliffs on the Côte Sauvage are very steep and sharp. Because there are so many coves and grottos that beckon from above, it's easy to imagine that you can just scramble down those rocky ribs and have a romantic picnic by yourselves. Well, some places you can, and some you can't. So guard your children at the edges of the Côte Sauvage. And don't lose your own good judgment in raptures over its dizzying overlooks; that's a long drop at your feet.

What other attractive hazards lie in store? Wives, you've picked up my hint about the movie starlet. Men, eyes front. Close that slack mouth and suck in that gut. Don't offer her your domestic assistance. Gals? If you need to extract a little revenge, try a flirtation *à la Française*. They say Johnny Depp comes here and I'm sure his girlfriend will look the other way. (She's French, isn't she?) For romantic advice, you can ask that gypsy-looking woman who roams the village lanes at twilight, all aswirl in pastel veils like a senior citizen version of Stevie Nicks. She was the lover of Marlon Brando. Really.

I also ought to mention the bulls. It seems that the farmers of France have gotten a bit competitive, or insecure, about their status and have started buying stud bulls instead of relying on *l'insémination artificielle*. The thing is, these same farmers can be a bit lax about keeping up their mildly electrified fences, which are often weak single-strand affairs charged by a car battery.

I know this sounds far-fetched, but if a large snorting beast with sharp horns appears to be taking an active interest in you or your red windbreaker, as once happened to me, it may be wise to run away like a mo-fo while stripping off aforesaid windbreaker and throwing it over a bush as you leap into a deep ravine filled with thorny blackberry vines. I lived to tell the tale, and you might, too.

Let's see—have I forgotten anything?

Oh, yes… The lane above our house makes a left turn into a tunnel of trees and a leaf-strewn drive. As you walk up the lane between tall, gappy hedges, no doubt a bit bedazzled and jet-lagged, drawn by the sunset or, in the early morning, nudged gently by the shimmering warm palm of a rising sun at your back, be on the lookout for a red cord. If you should find your way blocked by such a red cord, stay put.

Somewhere in your vicinity there is a Zen archer taking aim with her eleven-foot kyudo composite bow. She is dressed all in white, with a black sash and a red headband. She has been meditating for forty minutes on a single arrow. She does not see you or hear you; she only has eyes for the tiny, white paper bull's-eye pinned up forty yards away.

Wait.

Wait.

Wait for the *thwack!* of a hit. Or the *whooshhhh* of an arrow flying past.

Then you may go. Don't stop to introduce yourself. Gwened is in the midst of her war against cancer, and it is a very serious thing, literally a matter of life and death. She has one more arrow to draw and shoot on this day, your first in Kerbordardoué. Believe me, you don't want to get in Gwened's way.

Emergencies

Police. It is not strictly true that there are no police on Belle Île. In summer, two or three gendarmes are always zipping around the Le Palais roundabout in their blue Land Rovers, writing tickets and checking for pollution stickers and registrations. Do wear your seat belts—that's a guaranteed write-up. There is no mercy in the *Code Napoléon* for seat-belt violations.

There really is no need for police on Belle Île, since there is no crime. Okay, a sneak thief took my barbecue charcoal not once but twice a couple of summers ago. Now there's an Agatha Christie plot!

But real crime? Not much. Oh, of course we all have our stories of favorite murders, both solved and unsolved, but that's storytelling and island gossip. (In particular, the rumor that tourists come here to murder their mothers is unproved. The legion of psychiatrists who summer on the island thinks it is more likely that the idea occurs after arrival, possibly after they've seen the menu at the witch's hat château by the sea and realized they cannot *both* afford to order the lobster.)

There is also an unseen but apparently very active smuggling network that uses go-fast boats running up and down the coast from Portugal to Cornwall, swapping loads of ecstasy, hashish, and cocaine while dropping off illegal immigrants from northern Africa. What I know about this, and how, is best saved for another occasion and told over a pint in a loud sailors' bar down on the Le Palais waterfront. (After which, while staggering home, we shall disappear. Bystanders will hear a loud splash but see nothing, and our bodies will never be recovered.) So all in all, you won't need the police. Ideally.

Fire Department. If you have an emergency, on the other hand, call the fire department, or *Les Pompiers*. They do everything, including calling in the ER, the lifeguards, or the medivac helicopter. If someone blows up the house with the propane stove, falls in the well, breaks a leg, or gets trapped in a blackberry ravine, call *Les Pompiers*.

Do I have their number? No. We don't have a phone.

About Phones. Remember, you came here to get away, but if you really need to make a call on your cell, you will have to drive or bicycle or walk back to the main road, position yourself by the two menhirs, standing stones from 3,500 BC, and shake your fist (holding your cell phone, of course) at the sky while cursing. This seems to work well enough for the Parisians.

Oh, and remember to face east—not because of any mystical or religious reason, but because that's where the nearest cell tower is.

Medical. Docteur Pleybien, whom we have patronized in the main town, Le Palais, is a brisk and vibrant spirit with an intellectual and erotic appetite that may have been a little constrained by such a small island. I say this because, alas, she has packed it in to sail away on a fifty-five-foot sloop with a harem of potential boyfriends. I suspect she leaves behind a trail of broken hearts and wobbly marriages.

Anyway, if you need to see a doctor, ask at the pharmacy in town. I think I can promise that you will find the French healthcare system a revelation.

Oh, and if you need a psychiatrist? Just knock on any door in the village. Odds are you'll find one. Or even better, find a villager just waiting to invite someone in for a coffee and a nice, long chat. This can be very soothing, even if you don't speak French. I didn't, not much, for a long time—and look at me now. Why, it's easily been a couple of years since I've offered to cut off someone's penis while under the impression that I was offering to mow their lawn…

So, with all that said, welcome to Kerbordardoué, the most beautiful village on the magical island of Belle Île! Just don't touch the red handle on the hot water heater.

Chapter One

Far Breton

I t's another day in Kerbordardoué.

Up at eight, before the others. The sun doesn't set until nine thirty or ten during summer at this latitude, so it feels early. Treasuring the quiet, moving like a French Country Ninja, I put on the water, light the gas stove, quietly clean off the wineglasses, dessert plates, and empty bottles from last night. I ease open the window facing the dining table. A giant flowering bush pushes inside. It has to be pushed back outside every evening, like a last inebriated guest. I inhale herb-scented air, listen to the buzz of the bees. The square is empty, the village silent, the sky pink from sun diffused through a cottony marine haze.

With a faint crunch of gravel underfoot, Suzanne strolls into view, hands clasped behind her back, trailed by a kitten. She's in her usual blue apron over her usual blue-black shirtdress, the same outfit she's worn every day for the last ten years, and probably every adult day of her life. The kitten dances with her heels and boxes the hem of her dress.

Suzanne moseys over to the well in the wall. Terraced sides of uneven stones form a veritable Hanging Garden of Babylon with the clippings she has inserted into the moist crevices. Her fingers fuss, tamping and fixing. She plucks a few live shoots to tuck into her apron pockets and transplant elsewhere. Then, hands clasped behind her back, she continues her promenade up the lane, past our door, eyes sweeping the flowers and shrubs along our thin verge of garden, most of which she's planted and tended when we're away, back in the States. If she were to raise her eyes, she'd see me. But like most older *Bellilois*, she tries not to look into windows or open doorways. Or at least if she does, to not get caught.

A hiss from water spitting from the pot breaks the spell, sends me back to the stove. She probably knows I'm watching, anyway.

Tap-tap-tap. Work has started somewhere. Peering out through the lace curtains on our door's window, hand-knitted by Suzanne, I spot a close-cropped head rising above the tile roofline of the tall A-framed cowshed across the square. Rolling a dozen nails between his lips, Loup slides slates into place and *tap-tap-taps.* Another slate down, nine thousand to go.

A well-muscled guy with a large tattoo of his German shepherd on his bicep, Loup is single-handedly rehabbing the long, narrow building. He's restored the exterior walls to simple drystone glory, a seventeenth-century skill he had to teach himself. He's ripped out the cow stalls and laid a floor of antique salvage oak, then an upper story where once swallows nested and shat. I've seen the future of the cowshed and it's gorgeous: a building that sat ignored and decaying for forty years will soon be mistaken for an elegant village relic. Parisian women will set their snares for Loup, only to find themselves flustered and outsmarted by his first love, work. Meanwhile, one more blackened tooth in Kerbordardoué's crooked smile will be restored.

Clad in chic powder blue running togs, the blond wife of the Unforgiving Couple steps out into the square and does a quick set of bends and stretches. Fifteen years ago, the couple bought the empty lot across from us, a field of weeds spanned by rusted arches of iron that formerly supported the roof of a barn. Mindy and I took the loss of our view—a blue line of sea—stoically. One day the arches would be attractive hazards for our son and the village children, we thought.

But before we could meet the couple, they submitted plans for a three-story McMansion to the Mairie de Sauzon, or mayor's office. Once enough people had taken a look and gagged, Gwened the Archer led a charm offensive. The couple blew her off. Gwened took our protest to the Mairie de Sauzon, who dismissed her as a mere second-home owner, even though her grandfather was from Belle Île and she had been coming here her whole life.

When she informed him about the regulations on the books and how they forbade a third story, he patronized her. That did it. Gwened went door to door with a petition, the first, some said, in island history. About half of the second-home owners signed it, but not us—Gwened felt having *un étranger Américain* would backfire. The *Bellilois* elected not to sign: such is the strength of feeling here about imposing one's opinions on others. When Gwened returned to the Mairie, he shrugged. *Madame, we have never been presented with a petition and this is not the time to start.*

That left the fate of that lot to our village's widowed matriarch, owner of the surrounding fields. No way the stern and reserved Madame Morgane would sign anything so forward as a petition, but she agreed to go to the post office, which was next door to the Mairie de Sauzon, who happened to be in, with his door wide open to the street. Naturally he greeted her. A conversation took place. The subject almost didn't come up. Then he scoffed at *all this foolishness.* She replied that the new house would be "too tall."

Too tall? The Mairie frowned. The first plan was rejected. A second came in with two stories—but enormous glass walls. This was actually easier for the Mairie to reject. There *are* laws against that sort of thing. Belle Île enjoys national heritage status, which specifically covers home construction and renovation.

The couple responded by building a house without any windows facing the square, which was fine with us once some ivy grew up the blank white wall. In fifteen years, I can't remember them once waving hello. It's really too bad.

Oh, well. They don't come from here. They don't even come from some*body*, as the political machine hacks say in Chicago.

At least we come from "somebody"—and gratefully. *Gwened.* She lured us here—invited us to Belle Île when we were reeling around Europe fifteen years ago, our dream of living and writing in Paris having come undone. Mindy had been her student long before, in the campus abroad program where Gwened taught. Gwened had offered us her house and ended up changing our life.

The wife runs off, hippity-hop, classic *le jogging* style. Spooning out black mounds of cheap supermarket coffee, as good and aromatic as any of the expensive beans I noisily grind in our kitchen back in New York, I pour the boiling water into a cone filter wobbling atop a brown pot hand-thrown by our Scandinavian potter neighbor. Suddenly a voice echoes in my head: *My very own randy Dane up the lane…*

It's my sister's joke, from her visit a year ago, and a bit unfair—though the potter certainly did trail Anne around his atelier in the fields. What a view to a seduction he had: fat yellow heads of buckwheat bending to the breeze, then a dark dense green windbreak of cypresses, and after that, the wide, glittering blue-steel sea. The Atlantic. Pure horizon.

His tanned fingers kneading Anne's arm, finding more muscle than expected, he cried out in English: "But you are strong!" Excited, as if imagining her churning butter on his Viking homestead, walking behind the plow, a baby crooked in each arm.

"*Merci,*" she said, mustering all her French. With a flutter of her eyelashes she pulled away. "Unfortunately, we *really* must be going."

"Just think," Anne sighed that day, after we rode away on our rickety bikes, the potter waving forlornly to our backs. "If I ran away with him, we could live in adjoining villages and pay each other visits at teatime."

"That would be nice," said Mindy.

"We could have Earl Grey in cups made by my very own randy Dane up the lane."

"Anne!" Mindy shrieked. *Et voilà!* The quip attached itself to the pot like a superfluous handle.

Mindy always says Anne is the sister she never had. They laugh together, joke together, surf Huntington Beach's Chair 16 together. But we don't see enough of her. Since at different hours of the day Anne is a mother, a wife, a stepmother, a daughter, a schoolteacher, a golf teacher, and a writer, I'm sure nobody sees enough of her. Living on opposite coasts doesn't help, which is our fault for moving to New York City.

As I sat there, watching the coffee drip into the brown potter's cups, I missed my sister and considered how hard that trip must have been for her. Getting Anne over here is a project of ours. She's chafed at living in our hometown all her life. Once or twice she almost left, but for some reason at the city limits, life always pulled a U-turn.

The first time she was about to make her escape from Long Beach, on a yearlong surf safari down to Mexico and South America with her boyfriend, the car broke down on the freeway on-ramp. Our parents came down hard on the guy, and they broke up. Before I even heard about any of this, she was engaged to the son of our father's business partner, who proposed, I think, on the golf course. Anne had two young kids before the marriage went bad. She might have gone south to make a new start, but in the same week she was diagnosed with stage IV throat cancer. Divorced and healed up after miracle surgery and radiation, she found a man. He wouldn't commit.

Then the current one came along, a carpenter who surfed and read *The New Yorker*. Ideal, right? She married him. But already there were strains. Anne's teenaged daughter was acting out big-time. And, underlying everything, a deeper tension rattled my sister's confidence. She'd confided to me that she'd glimpsed the pattern of her life and vowed that, no matter what, she'd bust out one day, if only to Seal Beach, just across the county line.

As I was helping Anne to engineer her escape to Belle Île, I fed her air routes and plans for her whole family to come. Circumstances combined to whittle it down to just her and her son. When she hesitated, I supplied rationales for a vacation from the tempestuous daughter, the teaching job, the old dog, cat, and plants—oh, yes, and from her husband's three kids on alternate weekends. She definitely needed a break, I argued. And successfully.

But what I didn't realize was how selfish that was. All these people loved her and had legitimate claims on her. I was beginning to see I really wanted her to validate Belle Île for me. I wanted to see Belle Île through her eyes. And to watch her fall in love with it. After so much family criticism over our coming here, of all places, rather than closer to home in California, I wanted to see her pick up on the way the island was like all those idyllic Pacific coves and beaches we knew when we were children, before the bulldozers and housing tracts. Like those places, but better. I wanted to give Anne this, and then surely she'd do as we'd done—make every effort to return every year.

Belle Île was already Mindy's and my alternative base from home, established over the protests of our families. Now, like every breakaway republic, we were recruiting, and because Anne was the shining light, the radiant one, among the Wallaces, I'd introduced a conflict of loyalties, forcing her to choose between us and the rest of the family. She saw it. I didn't, not yet.

Once I got my wish and she was here, of course Anne *would* be Anne. On her third day here last summer, she watched me prepare for a picnic with the kids at the Hidden Grotto of Swimming Lizards. "I want to play that thirteen-hole golf course," she said. "Sarah Bernhardt's golf course. The first course started by a woman. I can sell a story about that to *Golf for Women* and pay most of my expenses here." She tossed her head back and laughed, as if feeling the fingers of the wind coursing through her hair. "You can write one, too, Donny. And you, Mindy. We can make so much money and expense dinners at the Hôtel du Fart."

"Du Phare," corrected Mindy, laughing at Anne's wicked mispronunciation of our island's most picturesque restaurant. "Pronounced *far*, meaning lighthouse."

"Wait! Then what's that dessert we had at Hôtel du *Pharrrrt?*"

"Far Breton."

"Lighthouse cake?"

"Noooo…"

Anne was having such a good time mangling the language that it actually made me jealous. Normally that was my gig. At dinner at the Hôtel du Phare she'd feigned confusion at every menu choice, *fruites des mer* becoming "fruit of a female horse" instead of a seafood plate and so forth, ending with the rubbery egg and prune concoction called "Far Breton."

"Wait—how can *phare* be a lighthouse and *far* a cake?"

"One word is French, the other Breton," I explained.

"Well, I think that for you, Far Breton means 'sweet distance,'" she replied curtly.

Snark from Anne was a surprise. "Meaning?"

"You didn't just go for the Far Breton," she said mock accusatively. "You went for the Far, *Far* Breton."

"Look, I *like* Long Beach." Our hometown.

"Funny way to show it, going ten thousand miles away."

"Only five. Look at Mindy. Hawaii's even farther."

"Far, far, far." Anne shook her head. Message delivered: we were too far away. Though I still didn't know from whom, I could guess: Mom.

But, being Anne, she immediately deflected the point of the barb toward herself. "And I *still* can't get out of Long Beach."

This actually caused a pang of remorse. I felt she'd read my mind, that she thought that I thought she'd missed out on life. Stuck in the old hometown, repeating herself. I couldn't reply.

⚘

My morning reverie comes to an end when our eleven-year-old, Rory, and David, Anne's son, tumble downstairs and briefly struggle over which of the deep wicker chairs to sit in. There's no difference, except for a matter of placement. The far end of the table is the prize. Mumbling good morning, they attack their waiting cups of hot cocoa and Krispy Rolls "Suedoise"—a kind of Swedish hardtack.

But all is repetition here, too, I should've protested to Anne. If only she had come this year, too—but, instead, she sent her giant teenager to

21

eat us out of house and home. Fortunately, we love Devo, a six-foot-four high schooler. Even better, he came bearing an envelope of cash with "Feed Me" written on it.

Mindy has been upstairs for a while, writing in her journal. Now she comes for her coffee and Krispy Rolls. We have only a few scrapes of blackberry jam left in the jar but plenty of butter. Only in France do we put butter on bread. There's no point in trying it in the States; I've tried, and it doesn't taste anything like the incomparable beauty of French *beurre*.

Crunching and sipping, the boys lean over the chessboard and begin setting up the pieces.

"No!" shouts Mindy. "No chess until you make a surf check." Mindy can't plan her day unless she knows whether there are waves.

"Hmm," says Devo. "No surf check until checkmate." He moves his pawn.

"No lunch unless you make surf check. Chop-chop! Now!" Mindy claps her hands loudly. Yesterday the boys started playing a game and didn't leave the house until early afternoon. This plays hell with our schedule, such as it is. The threat of no lunch usually works. When it doesn't, and we abandon the boys to their own devices, there is a definite danger that the house won't be there when we return, due to the combination of Devo's appetite and the stove, knobless after several explosions.

"Your move."

"I'll make you an omelet if you check surf now," Mindy pleads.

"Hmm. What kind of omelet?"

"Chorizo and tomatoes and Gruyere."

"Okay." Devo looks at Rory. Then, with a crash, both shove their chairs back and race for the door. There's a struggle at the handle that Rory loses, being a foot shorter and seventy pounds lighter than his older cousin. But he's faster and arrives first at the bikes leaning against Gwened's barn. One bike's chain slips; the other doesn't. Another struggle begins.

"Peace at last," I murmur. "More coffee?"

"Sure. And an omelet."

"Hey!"

"I want to write while it's quiet. Everything is so noisy here."

This is a slight exaggeration, considering that in New York City, garbage trucks groan and drunks sing and clubbers fight and hookers hook and then swear at each other under our windows from midnight to dawn. But everything is relative. I understand that.

Through the window I see the boys whiz past down the rutted lane. I grit my teeth and wait for the crash at the bottom turn. Nothing happens. Good.

A surf check means we have at least twenty-four minutes of peace—nine for the boys to pedal madly up the road, take the shortcut across the fields, descend the treacherous dirt lane to the paved road, pedal madly up to the turn to the village of Kerhuel, pedal madly through Kerhuel dodging free-range chickens and sleeping dogs and one-eyed cats, then pedal madly to the cliff and the overlook. You can't do an honest surf check from where the road ends, so they'll have to run to the cliff edge, which takes three minutes. We've charged them with providing specific answers to our questions, so that means at least two minutes watching, though we'd prefer ten. The return trip is a bit faster, involving less uphill.

"Maybe we have time?" Mindy nods at the stairs and arches an eyebrow.

"Well..." I check my watch. "Twenty minutes." We look at each other, counting off the seconds. Once the boys made it back in nineteen. We trade glances: too risky. Not relaxing.

"Okay," Mindy says. "Make sure they rinse their feet at the door."

Back to the stove I go. Chop garlic and onion, slice rounds of hard Spanish chorizo, the Don Moroni brand that I smuggle back to the United States each year. Diced green peppers and tomatoes also go into the skillet. While they're cooking, I crack six eggs into a bowl, add some milk, and stir.

Spatula in hand, I drift over to the front door, open it, and stand barefoot on the concrete stoop, worn by weather and summer feet. Pushing through the billowing hydrangeas that mask her patio and front entrance from the square, Gwened emerges holding a paper high in the air.

"Oh, Don! I have a letter from Daniel!" She's wearing a simple floral frock with a scooped neck that shows off her deep tan, cleavage, and a gold orb on a chain that dangles there. On her feet are the rope espadrilles that Gene Kelly and Bridget Bardot made famous. You can always rely on Gwened for a fabulous entrance.

She switches into French for my daily grammar workout. We talk about Daniel, her son who lives in the United States. He's found a job doing art therapy at a hospital. Life is good. His wife is trying her hand at writing articles for a newspaper. Will I correspond with her, pass along advice and encouragement? Of course.

Recalling my duties at the stove, I dash in to slide the sautéed vegetables onto a plate and pour the beaten eggs into the skillet. Gwened waves and moves on down the lane, letter in hand. I suspect she will stop at Suzanne's plain stone house. Then, if Le Vic is out sunning himself while his sons and wife garden, she'll pause at his white picket fence for a chat, then sweep up the road to Madame Morgane's.

That is, if she doesn't do a quick hook around to the house of the Accomplished Academics. Yes, she'll go there. Their daughters are wonderful musicians, budding professionals whose violin and viola sweeten the air all summer. After that, it's on to Celeste and Henry, the village psychiatrists. (Freudian.) Yes, Kerbordardoué is a full-service gossip stop for anyone, but especially empty-nest parents like Gwened. We've got everything you need right here.

As Gwened moves off, letter held high as a flag, I smile. If only my Anne had seen her like this, she wouldn't have been so suspicious. "Tell me more about Gwened," Anne had demanded early in her visit. "That's her house above ours? She's the one? The reason you're here? You said she's a professor. What else?"

"She's a witch," I said.

"*No!* Not really."

"Mom believes she tried to seduce Dad with some kind of potion."

"*What?* I can't believe this! Mindy—Donny's making this up, isn't he?"

"She was doing some kind of witch thing," Mindy confirmed. "Right in front of your mother, she was casting a spell. And he really was falling for it."

"I can't believe it! This is so bizarre! How did she cast a spell?"

"Near the end of the trip, your dad cut his leg in the hotel swimming pool, and it got infected. Gwened noticed when we were having aperitifs. So she went over to her well and pulled out a handful of this slimy green moss and made a poultice out of it. Put it on his shin."

"You're telling a story. You're *both* making this up. Donny? Is Mindy telling the truth?"

"All I can say is, it really did feel strange. I couldn't believe it was happening myself. Gwened was chatting away in this very lulling voice, and Dad had this big smile on his face. He couldn't take his eyes off her."

"He couldn't take his eyes off her boobs, you mean," said Mindy. "She kept bending over right in front of him. She found a way to pop a button."

"You mean he was falling for it? Dad? *Nooooo!*"

"Women have their ways." Mindy looked wise. "French women especially."

"I think she scares me a little," Anne said with a little shiver. "And I *can't wait* for her to come to dinner tomorrow." Laughter. "What will you guys cook?"

"*Lotte*, tomatoes, green beans, chorizo, zucchini, green salad, goat cheese."

"Ooooh. Donny, where did you learn to cook?"

"I always cooked. In Boy Scouts, in college."

"Not like this. I tasted your cooking in Santa Cruz. So where was it?"

"Here."

"Who taught you? Gwened?"

"No…" Anne kept staring at me, so I shifted in my chair and started over. "I guess I started *tasting* food, really tasting, when Mindy first brought me to France. First tasting, then really paying attention to ingredients, then practicing in New York. One month in Belle Île, then the rest of the year trying to duplicate recipes, tastes. You can find anything in New York. Well, almost. I haven't tasted a good American peach for years."

"This is so amazing," Anne said. "You know, it's a whole world you have here. I want to spend more time here. Can I come next year?"

"You'd better!" Already, though, I had my doubts.

The boys are back, pulling up on their bikes to shout through the window: "No surf!"

"You're sure?" I ask. "Who was in the water?"

"Nobody."

"Will you be quiet, please?" calls Mindy from the dormer above.

"Sorry."

"I've been going crazy listening to your mangled French all morning, discussing the most incredible banalities under my window."

"Time to feed the Mommy," I say to the boys, loud enough so Mindy can overhear it. To feed Mindy means dividing the omelet—to Devo's dismay—then cutting bread and setting out little goat cheeses from my friend the cheese lady, who *appreciates* my French. Tomatoes and lettuce, oil and vinegar. At the foot of the staircase I call: "Lunch!" It's only eleven o'clock, but food fuels good humor as well as activity.

And we must have activity.

The boys lay out their spear guns and masks and wet suits, talking of the fish they'll hunt today when we finally head out. They eat, then resume the chess game. Time stops. I grab a book and sit out on the thin ledge of concrete that runs along the base of the foundation, toes in the grass. Bees buzz around. Swallows dip and nip midges. An hour passes. The king is trapped, the game resigned.

"Let's go!" shouts Rory. We fill the bright Duty Free and striped Lancôme gift bags, now redolent of salty fish guts and sand, load a straw bag with towels, a thermos of hot tea, cookies, a Wiffle ball and bat, the *Herald Tribune.*

At the last second, Mindy joins us and insists we strap her surfboard on the roof rack. The old Renault turns over, smoking and shaking. As I work the choke in and out and feather the gas, the bright car of the movie starlet who lives at the top of the lane creeps out from between the hedges. She's got her Garbo goggles on and a Japanese Red Army Faction head scarf, right out of a Godard film (which she hasn't been in). Her blond daughter, Rory's age, is nowhere to be seen, thank heavens. Or maybe that's a bad thing—we have to keep an eye on her. She grew up in Hollywood, and there's a touch of Lindsay Lohan in her tempestuous nature.

Once the movie star is past, I can back up and point the car's nose down the rutted lane. Staggering, blowing blue smoke, we scrape between Suzanne's massed hydrangeas. The blossoms beating against the windows remind me of cheerleaders waving their pom-poms at football players as they emerge from the stadium tunnel.

Twenty feet later, the car stalls in front of Le Vicomte's. "Rick" and Yvonne are sitting under an umbrella playing cards in cardigan sweaters and flannel trousers, while one bare-chested son, Thierry, smokes a cigarette and stuffs weeds into the flaming open hearth of a roofless sixteenth-century ruin. Everyone waves and offers salutations as I try to start the car.

Eventually we crawl up the road through the tunnel of trees. Madame Morgane scuttles away up her drive, her daughter-in-law going the opposite direction to her own house. We exchange nods. At last we're through the gauntlet and into open fields. But here comes an oncoming car. It's Pierre-Louis and Sidonie, another psychiatrist couple—Lacanians—who live ten villages away from us. Stopping alongside, chatting through open windows, reaching out for a handshake, we make plans for an aperitif the following day and drive on. We're getting there.

"God, it takes so much time to do *anything* here!" Mindy shifts irritably in her seat.

We take a left turn and run past the former surf shop, now reverted back to a cottage, the half-pipe gone where skateboarders used to practice roller coasters and rail grabs. We pass the house of the lawyer for the Big Important Newspaper, hidden by a dense palisade of tall straight Norfolk pines.

After a switchback series of turns into and out of dirt lanes and paved roads, passing the estate of the Majestic Madame Who Fought in the Resistance and Survived Auschwitz, we reach the stark "Village of Merde," as we privately call this windswept cluster of houses, and slo-mo slalom around cats, ducks, chickens, a hog, several small children in Wellingtons splashing in lakes of animal shit, and finally a string of horses and Shetland ponies, all saddled up and ready to go. *Poney Bleu à votre service, Monsieur et Madame! Stages, randonnées, promenades…*

"Surf check," Mindy says at the next crossroads. The boys complain, but they sound guilty. They probably blew it off this morning. Then again, boys always sound guilty.

Past some hunched-over whitewashed houses, once again in open fields, we carefully overtake cyclists and the occasional oblivious couple pushing a baby carriage in the middle of nowhere. And there's Dede, pedaling his old clunker. The proprietor of the village, he is a large man in blue overalls and Wellingtons, huge head tucked into a newsboy's cap, tin pail in his hand, going blackberrying on his lunch hour. "What's for lunch?" asks Devo. Because it is, incredibly, lunchtime again.

The road dead-ends at the old ramparts of a fort, either Roman or Celtic, later repurposed by Napoleon and tweaked again by the Germans during the Occupation. Now it's just a grassy ring by a graveled car park. At the cliff's edge, we look down on Donnant, the most changeable beach in creation. After a minute Mindy decides she's staying to see if the tide will bring a bump to the thin, glassy waves. She unstraps her yellow board and shoulders her backpack with towel, wet suit, second lunch. Down the cliff she goes on a narrow rock ledge, sure-footed on her wide-splayed toes—luau feet, they're called in Hawaii. Below on the glitter-green sea a couple of our surf crew float on their boards, talking.

With the mommy gone, the car goes tribal. Devo takes shotgun and slaps the venerable cassette into the car stereo. There's only one song for going spearfishing: "Stand!" by Sly and the Family Stone. Heading down the corrugated dirt road with dust boiling in our wake, we sing at the top of our lungs while I pump the brakes in time.

Today's dive spot is a rocky fjord with a beach of round stones. Ten feet out, a subterranean stream creates an underwater freshwater spring over a sand bottom. Thick kelp stalks swing in the slow pulse of swells. Once the boys signal that the water quality is good, I take off on foot up a narrow trail and follow the shattered cliff edge of the Côte Sauvage back toward Donnant. I bring my swim fins in case there is surf, but one look at Mindy and the crew floating on their boards is enough to keep me high and dry.

Walking back to the cove on a rabbit trail, I feel the sun drawing near and discharging great ripples of heat over the moor. Spongy mossy knobs under my feet sprout little red and blue and white flowers, and the gorse flares yellow. Even the thorns shimmer invitingly. When I reach the cliff overlooking the fjord, the boys are directly below, swimming slowly about a hundred yards from the rocky beach. They dive, cruise deep, surface with snorkels spouting.

Climbing down, I take up a place on a flat shelf of rock that isn't too uncomfortable, lie back on my towel, and open my newspaper. Every few minutes a shout goes up, Rory and Devo devising tactics to drive their quarry into the open. I nap. When I open my eyes again, a fat, lime-green fish impaled on a spear is being thrust at me by a creature wearing a glass mask, with lips blue and teeth chattering. Fish and boy look remarkably alike.

So far the dive at the fjord has resulted in the single *vieille*, a soft-bodied rock cod of no great taste. I'll need to supplement it with another fish, so a visit to Sauzon, our nearest town, is in order. I'll have to fight the crowd at the quay when the boat comes in. The prospect makes me savor the *Herald Tribune*, squeezing every last drop of useless information out of its twenty-two pages. Financial tables, European soccer news, Italian politics—as long as it is in English, I'll read it.

Eventually the boys tire and strip off their wet suits and drape themselves over hot rocks. Then we load the car and shudder up the dirt road, over ruts like small canyons. I drive back to the old ramparts and we head down the cliff, only to find Mindy freezing and ready to leave. The thermos of tea and a slice of bread and cheese revive her. She decides to walk up the valley to the village to warm up and enjoy a quiet house. The boys join a loose gang in kicking a soccer ball over the long, wet sand flat left by the ebbing tide. A game starts.

The French lunch hour is over. People appear at the gap in the sand dunes where *Les Sauveteurs en Mer* have constructed a wooden stair. The families carry folding chairs, tents and sunshades, parasols and rubber boats. Babies cry; young people run, scattering sand. The *tap-tap* of endless paddleball games begins. Lifeguards stroll up and down in their bright emergency orange vests and Speedos, carrying waterproof walkie-talkies and swim fins clamped under one armpit. The elegance is itself reassuring.

It's now or never for me, so I grab my fins and start down to the water, wishing Rory, Devo, and I could rethink our pact to never wear wet suits when bodysurfing. The water temperature is 61 degrees! Oh, the things we do to impress our kids and teach them the proper hardiness…

Of course, I want to impress the French, too. Show them we are true Americans, Californians, Hawaiians, endowed by our creator with a superhuman ocean sense and testicles that shrink to the size of raisins in the icy temps. Mustn't let down the side. With a shudder, I push into the first ankle-high waves and begin the slow slog out to the impact zone a hundred yards offshore.

Forty-eight minutes later, I emerge to find half the village lounging on the hot sand. People leap to their feet to kiss my cheeks (and wince at how cold they are): Celeste and Henry, our village psychiatrists; Sidonie and Pierre-Louis, the psychiatrists from ten villages down; Yvonne, wife of Le Vicomte; and a handful of friends visiting from other villages or Paris. Gwened lies on her towel a discreet thirty yards away—like Mindy, she prefers calm and quiet, less of a *rhubarb*, one of those quaint English words that has never lost the ability to provoke laughter in France.

The soccer game breaks up and the boys of several villages crash the circle of towels, plundering sacks of cookies: Le Petit Ecolier, *Sablés Beurré Nantais*, and the chocolate-and-orange-zest-covered marshmallow domes whose name we never tire of saying: "Goooters." Girls scoot their towels closer, joining the circle. A couple of the older teens light up cigarettes, drawing eye rolls from the adults—except for Sidonie, who turns to a fifteen-year-old.

"May I bum a smoke?" she asks in English, deadpan. Looks at me: "Bum is correct, Don? It eez not ze same as ass, no?"

I nod, but Celeste's husband, Henry, wags a finger. "No, ze bum is ze ass, but only for ze *Anglais*. Yes, Don?"

"No, Henry," I reply. "One must not forget that, *pour les Anglais*, ze ass is ze arse."

Sidonie's husband, Pierre-Louis, smacks his head. "Oh, but of course! Ze arse Anglais."

The kids blush, trying not to look shocked but totally flustered. The cigarette pack goes back into a purse. Score one for the psychiatrists. Everyone cackles, trading double entendres, and an hour passes in beach blanket Babylon: French people trying to speak English, French teenagers practicing American rapper slang with the American boys, and the lone American adult addressing men as women and women as men and referring to himself as both—a psychiatrist's idea of heaven, for sure.

A football comes out and the boys began throwing and catching, moving ever closer to the sea. At their gestures, I heave myself up and join them—activity, we must have more activity! Running brings the heat back into my limbs. Another hour passes.

31

Even at four o'clock the sun is bright, high overhead, but by French rules it's getting late. People pack and drift back through the dunes to the parking lot. Just as I'm wondering what to do about dinner (I've missed the boat at Sauzon), Mindy comes across the sands carrying a straw basket filled with salami, apples, baguettes, beets in vinaigrette, and an oval fresh-baked cake.

"Hmm," says Devo, eyeing the cake. "The chocolate football." Another hour passes. With Mindy here, the conversation switches back to French, too fast and subtle for me to do more than nod and smile.

The crowd at the beach thins out. The twenty or thirty who remain scattered over a half mile of sand and rocky cul-de-sacs are revealed as a class: lovers and beachcombers and a few *Bellilois* come for an after-work plunge. We know quite a few. We are all thankful that, at this hour, discreet waves of the hand may be substituted for the usual getting up, going over, and kissing.

A loud air horn indicates *Les Sauveteurs en Mer* are going off duty. True lords of their domain, they receive salutations as they stroll up to their shed. Henry and Celeste and Sidonie and Pierre-Louis say they must go. We decline offers to join them for an aperitif and they don't press the issue, knowing from long experience and surprisingly earnest debate that at certain tides, we simply will not leave the beach.

Our village rises as one, gathering towels and heading up through the dunes and into the grassy valley. As they go, they pass the next shift arriving: local surfers coming for the evening glass-off. Soloists scramble like goats down the cliff, boards snug under one arm and already in their wet suits. Others with families march up the sandy throat of the canyon loaded down like Bedouin caravans.

It is seven o'clock and I've been outdoors for five hours. Yet this is when the real action begins. The tide is coming up, and the little bump of this morning is now a swell with two distinct lines in the middle, a point break at each side caused by the rock islets that bookend the beach, and even a decent shore break where the kids with bodyboards go wild. The surfers are mostly *Bellilois*, with a few regular summer visitors.

The lifeguards come down and join us, shedding their orange vests. Everybody in the water!

I join Rory and David and Celeste and Henry's son, Marc, in the bare-chested bodysurfing brigade. We duck dive and kick under the onrushing white water. Eight minutes later, we're on the outside looking in, floating on the heaving Atlantic with the cliffs and golden sand dunes glowing in the evening sun. An hour later and we're still there, plus or minus a few friends who've come or gone, giving and taking waves.

The sun sinks slowly, yet I'd swear the water feels warmer. It's because of the waves, of course—our engine rooms are stoked by the constant kicking, diving, stroking, and best of all, the adrenaline rush of sliding down the steep faces. Sluicing along in the concave half-pipe of green sea. Making section after section, passing your friends paddling out, hearing them hoot.

I gather myself at the peak of a large swell. As it starts to topple forward, I slice down on my chest and angle for the heart of the tube. Inside, for a moment, all is quiet and hissing, then the walls implode. The breaking wave takes me into an underwater world that alternates from light to darkness, rolling me and spinning me. My heels strike the sand bottom a good ten feet deep as the wave plunges silently past, like a waterfall. A hard hold-down, followed by a twitchy release from the ocean's coils that says: *Okay, I'm done with you, for now. Just don't try that again.*

Far inshore, on the beach in the advancing shadows, I can just make out specks of people walking the beach. The after-dinner contingent has arrived. And still we linger.

Chapter Two
Le Grand Détour
(*Year Zero*)

I t wasn't always this way. Fifteen years ago, in fact, we had no idea
that Belle Île even existed. But then, in the aftermath of a dream
trip to Paris that turned sour, Gwened threw a net of enchantment over
us. Like Circe in *The Odyssey*, she made us captives of her realm on her
island. We never knew what hit us until it was too late.

🌿

Belle Île hove into view, a low, dark coastline under a moonless night
and fast-moving rain squalls. As the aging diesel ferry *Guenveur* heaved
to the tops of swells and crashed down the other side, sending walls of
green water over bolted-down windows on the main deck, Mindy and
I peered anxiously in search of the bright lights that might indicate a
hotel, an outdoor café, anything resembling life. But there were only a
couple of navigation beacons on a long stone mole against which waves
exploded in curtains of white lace.

It was past nine o'clock on a Friday night in frigid mid-January. No one would be waiting for us at the quay. Gwened had said that in the off-season there were no taxis or buses.

When we'd dragged our bags and battered psyches to Gwened's door in Tours, a medieval town famous for being the gateway to the Loire Valley and its châteaux, we thought we'd settle in for a weekend of absentee mothering, jolly conversation, heavenly food, and delectable wine. The Grand Tour of Europe we'd been saving up for over the previous five years had turned into a train wreck: London a costly disappointment, Paris a disaster, then a panicky flight to Athens that was followed by a howling mistral that canceled ferries and trapped us on the Greek island of Santorini—for six weeks! Six weeks living in a whitewashed cave, eating feta and cabbage…

So we were in crisis. But Gwened was in the midst of dealing with her own crisis. Her teenaged son, Daniel, threw a typewriter out his bedroom window the evening we arrived, after which her elegantly bearded accountant husband abruptly excused himself from the dining table to descend to his wine cave and count out the week's cash receipts. In the morning, Gwened simply handed us a page of directions to her Breton farmhouse on the island where her grandfather had been born. We walked to the train station and, like zombies, headed out to the frigid Atlantic coast of Brittany.

Distracted and brusque, Gwened hadn't supplied a map of the island or even a coherent description of where the village lay. Fortunately a paper place mat from the harbor café where we had our last coffee before boarding the ferry revealed the island's contours. It looked like a sole or flounder lying on its side, a thought that only made us hungry.

Staggering in our backpacks down the gangway, we mounted the wet stone *quai*. We'd made a sign using the place mat, writing "Donnant," the name of a big beach we thought might be close to Gwened's village, and stuck out our thumbs. The few cars on the ferry departed swiftly. It was blustery, cold, dark. Just as we were giving up, a car that had passed us did a U-turn and pulled up. A brother and a sister, older than our parents, were headed for their family's home.

"Donnant is our village, but we don't know you," the man said to Mindy. "And we know *everyone*. Where are you *really* going?"

※

Where are you really going?

Good question. If Mindy had followed the course laid out for her, she'd likely be practicing law in Honolulu, not wandering around a French island with her thumb stuck out. And if I'd followed my birth-right as a third-generation Californian, I'd be on another path, too—probably working some newspaper job that secretly bored me, while boring other people with boasts of how I'd rather be rambling down Mexico way to drink mezcal and warble with mariachis.

Funny how Belle Île would change all that. But first we had to get there. And before that could happen, Mindy and I had to meet, marry, and muddle our way into a cul-de-sac from which we saw no escape. This was easily accomplished by deciding to be writers. While our respective universities were seventy miles apart, once we stepped into that writing river, the current swept us away and eventually deposited us in the same eddy in Iowa City, where as two westerners at the Writers' Workshop, it almost seems inevitable that we would walk into a bar, glare at each other, swap insults, and fall in love.

Just a couple of heedless kids with windblown hair who thought they were going to conquer the world with their portable electric type-writers, Mindy and I then brought our glowing smiles and infuriating self-assurance back to the lands of our mothers. We'd originally decided to marry in a county courthouse in Iowa City, but now there would be a proper Hawaiian wedding in Honolulu.

We stopped for a weekend in Long Beach, where my parents reserved the big table at the country club to show us off. One of our family's oldest friends lurched up and planted his hands on the tablecloth and gave Mindy a long look. "Well," he said, "thank god she isn't black!"

This was a direct shot at me and my father. While in high school and in the throes of the Civil Rights spirit, I'd brought a black friend, Michael, to the club's heretofore unintegrated mixed grill. Next Dad had proposed a black family friend, Bill, as a member. After Bill was rejected, my father was shunned and harassed. Someone actually stole his golf shoes from his locker, but more seriously, his law practice lost clients. This was on par with the treatment my mom had been getting as president of the school board after she imposed busing on the district as a way of balancing racial demographics in the high schools.

For a moment I was too stunned to react to the comment about Mindy. Then I rose and was cocking my fist (something I could barely recall how to do) when family thankfully came between us. I turned to Mindy, who looked shell-shocked. *Welcome to Long Beach, honey.*

Honolulu was much more welcoming. At the reception at The Willows, guest after guest rose to perform an impromptu hula in our honor while the Irmgard Aluli Trio played. It was big, beautiful chaotic fun—Koreans and Hawaiians and WASPs and Japanese and surfers and hippies and the Honolulu police chief—and then we spent the rest of the summer writing and surfing and barbecuing with family on Diamond Head.

But there were tensions here, too. Mindy's mother was a diminutive Korean beauty dipped in *gojujang*, hot pepper sauce, a pineapple plantation-raised former piano prodigy and serial marrier of inappropriate men. As our departure neared, she began to mutter and stalk Mindy around the house. Several times, dinner table talk centered on her or her sons laughingly describing the "lickings Mom gave"—with the most extravagant always given to Mindy. When I questioned this later, I was told "this is just the way Mom is."

Well, my mother-in-law looked like a serious case of Jekyll and Hyde to me. We started staying away all day and barricading ourselves in our room at night. On our last evening, she came at midnight, battering on the door and telling me to let her in because she needed to deal with Mindy and her "stink expression" once and for all. Her voice was icy and deeply scary. She returned with a key and got the door open, but I put my body between her and my new wife. The desire to do violence poured off her like some exotic perfume.

We flew the next day, arrived late, and slept safely and gratefully in my childhood bedroom. In the bright morning we came down too late to join the family at breakfast, due to some messing around. The long dining table had a bright new tablecloth and a floral decoration and pretty Italian plates with fresh cantaloupe. I was bringing Mindy her coffee from the kitchen, having greeted my mother with a kiss, when I caught one of the house cats licking Mindy's melon. "Hey! Get off!" I cried, and brushed the cat off the table.

Ten minutes later, we were packed and driving away, kicked out by my diminutive redheaded beauty of a mother, the piano-playing, Ivy-League-educated daughter of a Southern cotton plantation family whose aristocratic airs had always seemed as nebulous as cotton candy to me. Mom didn't give us beatings growing up, like Dolly gave Mindy, but the searing verbal blast she hit us with as we tumbled out the door that day exceeded anything I'd ever experienced, anywhere. And all over a ball of white fluff named Precious.

What had happened here that, in less than twenty-four hours, both our mothers had independently reached the same boiling point? With Dolly, there'd been inklings of resentment against her only daughter for finally running away to have the life she'd wanted, instead of staying home to support Mom. Dolly had finished her music education in Iowa, too, and even audited Writers' Workshop classes. But she never did anything with her education and lived off her parents and child support. Now, according to Dolly's crude financial calculus, our marriage was threatening her main source of future earnings, her presumably beaten-until-malleable Mindy, whom I was dead set on whisking away, once and for all.

With my mom, the cracks had also been showing for years. She wasn't a born politician, as her job demanded, nor was she a natural or comfortable person outside of our tight little family. Taking on the job of being a Civil Rights figurehead in a town and school torn by riots was no small thing, of course. But it was also a declaration of independence from her own diminutive, fiery, Southern, piano-playing mother. As most of us find out, you never can escape that maternal grip.

I think she also underestimated or never acknowledged the neurotic tension that came of being from a Southern family whose black maids helped raise her, and later, having a social life centered around a country club that admitted neither blacks nor Jews. When Mom drew her own line in the sand—the day the club asked her to remove a Jewish friend from a PTA lunch—she probably didn't realize she'd have to draw it again and again for the rest of her life. Once she backed busing, she let herself, and us, in for more than fifteen years of obscene phone calls and death threats taken seriously enough to warrant police protection.

I'm proud of my mom: she never backed down. But as her four children went away to college, I guess she transferred a little too much of her affection to her cats. With the Civil Rights movement safely in the past, she was looking forward to retirement from the school board to a life of golf and bridge. And then I'd thrown her social standing into disarray by threatening to punch an old racist *and* elbowing her beloved Precious aside.

So off we went, Mindy and I. It's good to be young and talented and running for your lives, but having a plan helps. We didn't. As a result, a couple of years after getting married, we found ourselves living in Ivy Towne, a four-hundred-unit apartment complex in a one-stoplight cowtown in California's Central Valley. While Mindy attended law school, I was living the life of a roving temp, swashbuckling among the specialty offices peculiar to an agricultural university, most memorably the Meat Science Department. It was a long two years before I landed a job as a sportswriter at the local paper, the *Woodland-Davis Daily Democrat* (circulation 12,000).

One morning, we raised our heads from our oatmeal and stared around us at another rainy winter's day.

This is not my beautiful house. This is not my beautiful life. And you ask yourself…

It has been said of Americans that we have one answer to all of life's problems, and that is to move. In our case, we decided to double down on our first lover's leap. Mindy had won a writing grant while in law school and was determined to take another shot at a literary life. As soon as she graduated and took the bar exam, we'd make a really big move and head to New York City. There we'd force-feed our novels to any agent who left his or her door ajar. And then we'd keep going, off to Paris with no return ticket.

Although we were financing the trip with wedding cash meant for china, not France, I was more than happy with the notion of renting a cozy Paris apartment and writing at adjoining marble-topped café tables on the Boulevard St. Germain. It would be good to shake off the pesticide dust of the tomato factory farms that surrounded Ivy Towne, to feel what it was like to wander and think and stroll together in a foreign place, to check our American concerns and baggage at the border. I'd just turned twenty-seven and was already in a state of premature burnout from my sixteen-hour-a-day, six-day-a-week grind as the paper's only sportswriter. I covered the gamut from eight-year-old Little Leaguers to the eighty-eight-year-old bowler who'd just thrown his first strike. ("Time to Spare" was my headline for the latter, which somehow our publisher found offensive.)

Our families, of course, had other ideas. They said we were crazy and worse—"lifelong moochers" was the phrase Dolly flung at us when we announced our departure. But we didn't have to answer to anyone: it was our money and our lives. Being in the midst of a crushing recession actually helped. Nobody was hiring newly minted lawyers or small-town sportswriters, especially ones who'd rather be writing long, lyric novels, like Mindy, or loose, baggy novels, like me. And if we did actually deposit our precious manuscripts in the hands of agents, maybe we would wake up one fine morning in Paris and find out we were glamorous expatriate successes, like Fitzgerald, like Hemingway, like Mailer.

Later we'd rationalize our bad luck by noting that we were a bit at sea psychologically after Mindy took the bar exam. We'd immediately closed down our California life, putting everything in storage or with my parents, and then holed up in a mountain cabin to finish our books. There was no real hurry, but for some reason we'd insisted on adhering to a self-imposed deadline so we could go to Europe by September.

Rushing to finish the very things upon which we had staked our future—our books—we only ensured that future was less likely to come to pass. In the meantime, instead of setting forth in summer, our delay meant we'd cross the Atlantic into the teeth of an early and nasty winter. But we went for it anyway.

The first chapter in what was supposed to be a year in Paris began in a charming rue Mouffetard flat, *pittoresque et vivant*, sandwiched upstairs-downstairs between deaf and angry senior citizens who stamped around in wooden shoes, blasted the radio all day, and hung Waffen-SS ceremonial plates on their walls. Fleeing this retirement community of Nazi collaborators—the lederhosen should've tipped us off—we'd barely settled into a second flat when its windows and skylight were covered with a tarpaulin and workmen started cutting sheet metal with electrical saws and peering into our bedroom at six o'clock every morning to see if we were having fun.

A yearlong renovation that our landlord had neglected to tell us about was commencing. Gloom, rain, snow, and the shrieking of electrical saws and rat-tat-tatting of rivet guns: this was not the Paris of our dreams. Another crushing realization—*we arrived sixty years too late to meet Gertrude Stein!*—was only made worse by running into packs of Americans with the same haunted look.

If there is one detail that stuck a pin in my little balloon of confidence—the belief that we were doing something original—it was how many expat Americans had toilet paper shipped to them from home. Believe me, nothing is more likely to bring your dreams down in a heap than to be taken aside by your host at an expatriate dinner in the 16th arrondissement and offered a good deal on a six-pack of Charmin.

One cold, dark day in December we cracked and fled Paris. Next stop, Sofia, Bulgaria, in a blizzard, then Athens, with the same epic storm on our heels, so on to Crete, and finally Santorini. By the time the hail and snow and hurricane winds caught up to us again, we'd rented a cave perched at the edge of a thousand-foot cliff overlooking a smoking volcanic caldera. The cave was chilly but nice, plastered inside and whitewashed outside, with a rooftop rain cistern for tap and shower water.

Although we didn't know it until later, the village had been abandoned after a terrible earthquake thirty years before—perfect for a couple of writers on the lam from their nosy and disapproving families, as well as our embarrassingly shattered dreams. If our shelf of housefronts fell into the sea one stormy night, taking us with it, no one would be the wiser.

No matter what we were writing in our cave, day after day, it faced serious competition from our skybox view of the smoldering volcano, which also kept our noses pressed up against Europe's worst weather in twenty years. To sit without shivering, we wrapped ourselves in every piece of clothing we owned and drank Nescafé at half-hour intervals. We lived off cabbage and feta and yogurt and tinned sardines and round loaves of bread.

We had a single book, *Ulysses*, which we cut into sections for reading. We had a manual typewriter, which we shared. A ream of paper. When we went out for long tramps along the cliff, earthquake-shattered hillsides exposed gaps and fissures from which skeletons leered out of disturbed sarcophagi. In the island's two smoke-filled cafés, we alternated between puddles of pasta from the steam table and piles of fried smelt on oil-soaked brown paper.

We recognized that this was a low point in our lives. Our dreams were a joke. Our novels had been rejected. We couldn't figure out what to do next. We hated the idea of going home. We could barely talk to each other.

I recall the worst moment, for me. Desperate to reach Mindy, to find something that might inspire her, inspire *us*, I spread tourist maps on the cold floor and called out the names of islands all over the Aegean Sea, the Ionian Sea, the Adriatic. Nothing, nothing... Mindy was mute.

"We could go back to Athens…" My voice trailed off at her look. "I hear Rhodes is nice. But it's really close to Turkey, and I guess we don't want to go there."

"Do *you?*" she flung at me.

"No."

"So what do you want?"

"I want you to be happy, for one thing."

"What's so important about me? What about you?"

"I guess I'd be happy if I knew you were."

She stared at me. "I can't believe you even said that."

We dragged ourselves back down to the same old café. Lunch had been pasta, so dinner would be little fried fish. And yet those little fish tasted so damn good. *Merides*, they were called. You ate them with your fingers, like popcorn.

In the cave upstairs were our only neighbors who spoke some English, including a daily "Good morning, America!" down our chimney. Like us, they were artists on the run: Raili, an ethereal older Finnish painter, and Michele, a Swiss sculptor and draft dodger (ironically a *very* serious crime in neutral Switzerland). We also had an overbearing young land-lord, Yanni, the kind of sharpster who snaps up earthquake-condemned caves to rent to unsuspecting tourists. He spoke some English and brought us a set of fluted, bone-white coffee cups and saucers in which we were expected to serve him and his friends their afternoon Nescafé.

Yanni also interrogated us daily on our "modern" marriage: "Do you have sex? In Greece, man has sex one time with wife, on wedding night. After, no sex." "Did you have sex today?" "How many times did you have sex today?" "German woman will have sex with man, and husband does not care. Does your husband care?"

I figured that it must be obvious that we weren't having sex. We were too cold and depressed. He must see this every winter. Yes, I decided, every winter Yanni sharpened his pitch and played on his new captive couple's nerves until they snapped. Inevitably they did, breaking down in the way that all the literary short stories and foreign films tell it, with the wife going with the hairy, lusty, garlic-smelly lout of a landlord, who in these bleak surroundings personifies life, and the husband taking his wounded pride and humiliated manhood off to the taverna to drink ouzo.

This was our society. Instead of Hemingway and Stein and Scottie Fitzgerald trading *bon mots* at Café Les Deux Magots, we got Yanni and his friends, and his father and mother, in whose parlor we were expected to pay Sunday afternoon calls—payback for loaning us what turned out to be their precious wedding coffee set. We also received midnight visits from a cracked old expatriate English couple, who slung plastic ampho-rae of *nektari* over their shoulders and spoke in alcoholic riddles. They'd come for the ruins in Akrotiri, then just being excavated, and had stayed to become ruins themselves.

But we didn't stay to become ruins. We didn't snap. We'd listened to enough Joni Mitchell songs to recognize the looming cliché. Eventually, we shook off our worries and came away with cleared heads and ragged wool sweaters that stank of lanolin. We began to amble out again, through rain and hail, poking into Minoan gravesites and Orthodox shrines of luminescent marble tucked into narrow mountain defiles. We even listened sympathetically when Yanni wept over his lost love, a German woman who'd come for a summer and never once wrote after that.

As we talked, we tried to match the places we identified with the most transcendent days of our lives to figure out where we *did* want to end up. They seemed to be either small villages or hidden corners of larger municipalities, beginning with Tonggs, the surf break Mindy grew up on in Honolulu, and Idyllwild, my family's mountain cabin in California, on up to the Cretan hamlets we passed through on our way to Santorini: Agios Nicholaos, Kritsa, Lato. At this tiny village of Imerovigli, population four, where we hit bottom, we also began to bounce back. We thought of it as a final stop on our European foray, but the month in a whitewashed cave was actually a beginning.

Crete and Santorini had taught us something: we liked islands. We liked the people drawn to islands, and we liked islanders. We liked remoteness.

We didn't mind storms and harsh conditions if we were out on the edge. It was in Paris that we'd come undone. Civilization seemed to disagree with us. Maybe, like a distracted modern couple in a B-grade disaster movie, we needed to cling to a precipice overlooking a volcano to snap out of it.

On Christmas Day, Mindy and I were walking through the town square of Thira, the island's center, when a man ran out of the post office. "You have a phone call!" he pantomimed, shouting. Amazingly, Mindy's grandfather in Honolulu, Peepaw, had been staying on the line for hours, paying the international rate, in case his favorite grandchild would walk by. He had some news, too. Mindy had passed the bar: she was a lawyer and could set up a practice.

After talking it over with me, Mindy phoned a professor in whose attic we'd stored a tent and some camping gear to set a date to pick up our stuff for the trip back. We were going home. We'd had our fling. The dream was over. And, you know, we were actually relieved to have finally woken up.

$$\maltese$$

The professor lived in Tours, where Mindy had spent her Stanford undergraduate year abroad. Like many of us who wanted to be writers, Mindy had cultivated a bit of a rough edge in college. We from the West liked our cigarettes hand-rolled or at least unfiltered and our Wild Turkey neat. We had strong opinions: hell, we'd argue over handwriting versus typewriting! Drunk on the lees of the sixties, we had also, on wilder nights, swayed raptly for hours in bare, ruined choirs like the Fillmore and Winterland, listening to the Dead and the Airplane and Quicksilver Messenger Service.

Of course we were, underneath it all, good, polite bourgeois youth from educated families, but just the same, in Tours during her year abroad, Mindy had found herself drawn into a much older and more courtly milieu, challenged to master the rules of French life and language as laid down by the formidable Madame Guedel.

Once Mindy took up that gauntlet, Madame G warmed to Mindy and, after the term ended, invited her to stay on and experience life in a real French home: the bright air of sweet civilization; the crisp routines; the measured hours; the formality of a spade-bearded husband who presided over the dinner table and his wine cave, and sang in a medieval choir on Wednesdays and Sundays; the brooding Truffaut tension of the young teenage son, Daniel, who wanted to be a writer; and Gwened herself, now on a first-name basis, transformed at the threshold from a professor into a symbol of feminine France, the keeper of the flame in terms of cuisine, manners, culture, and especially conversation.

You could say Gwened stepped into the chaos left behind by Dolly and gave Mindy a mother who acted like a mother, who had much to teach and the patience and firmness with which to do so; a mother who could call on Mindy's better self—which would be, *n'est-il pas*, a French self—and who would never, ever raise a hand to her. We've said it.

Calling from the Thira phone box, Mindy broke into tears at the sound of her teacher's voice. "You sound tired, Mindy," Gwened said after a tactful silence. "When you come back, I think you should go to my island home to rest and recover your spirits."

My island home.

And where was that? Mindy asked, sniffling. Thinking better than Hawaii, where her mom would probably throw crockery at her.

Belle Île, where Gwened's grandfather was from. Kerbordardoué, where Gwened had bought an old farmhouse and slowly, bit by bit, assembled bits of land and outbuildings to make herself a refuge.

Now it could be our refuge.

We had to look at a map to even find Brittany, then the Bay of Biscay. The island itself didn't qualify as large enough to be identified; it was perhaps one of a scatter of dots in the deep blue sea. But we examined the general area and made educated guesses. Finally, we looked at each other and asked the question: Why, after spending a month on an island as remote as Santorini, would we want to head straight out to another island, one almost as remote, to a village that sounded just as isolated as Imerovigli, in the dead of winter? Why not just pack our bags and go home?

"So what do you want?" Mindy had asked at our nadir on the island of Santorini. It seemed nothing had changed. Neither of us could answer the question. But we said yes anyway. It was as if we had to search across an entire universe for a particular island and couldn't stop looking until we found it.

Chapter Three
The Third Island

Three years later, our second winter in New York City was the worst in a decade. Too many times, Mindy and I joined the huddled masses in a bus shelter, feet sunk in a drift of slushy, dirty snow, staring at some travel poster placed there to tempt us. The photos were almost always of islands in the Caribbean or Greece—ironically, often our own Santorini. Along with the other *misérables*, we stared at the posters unabashed, drunk with longing. We wanted an island like that. Who wouldn't?

One winter's day, as I stood in the hall outside our cramped, illegal sublet apartment, tugging at my snow-soaked shoes, Mindy came to the door holding a sheet of paper folded in thirds: a letter. The moment she began reading it aloud, lightning struck. Suddenly the gods were speaking. They'd chosen a human voice so as not to frighten us off—the voice of a woman with a French accent. A familiar voice. Gwened Guedel was writing "to give a piece of news" as she quaintly put it. We heard it amid thunderclaps—unless that was my heart pounding:

"A small house, in quite poor repair, has come up for sale in the village."

Gwened Guedel wasn't really a goddess, but she *was* the first

Frenchwoman I'd ever known. And Mindy's stories had built her up grandly in my mind before I met her in person. The impressions I'd gathered over the years—we'd made a couple of visits to Belle Île since that first winter—had been of a scintillating but stern fairy godmother: love the shoes, fear the wand.

Because Mindy was always on her toes around Gwened, I was, too. Her mental energy was exhausting. Even in her kitchen she darted and jabbed, light on her feet, as if in a knife fight refereed by *Larousse Gastronomique*: "Take that, you ham! *En garde, mon tête du veau!*" Petite and fashionable, more voluptuous than any college professor I'd ever seen, Gwened seemed to invite men to flock around her while maintaining that she only cared about their minds.

Most of all, Gwened played the teacher. At every opportunity, she tweaked Mindy's accent and grammar. Similarly, lowering her aim quite a few notches, she would take pains to acquaint me with my educational and cultural shortcomings. Not intentionally, of course. Well, it probably *was* intentional. With Gwened, intention was everything. All shortcomings were to be recognized as such and dealt with summarily, without delay. Cognizance mattered. And culture. *Sans blague*, was Gwened ever cultured! But that hadn't stopped her from setting the hook on us as ruthlessly as a real estate speculator.

"...quite poor repair..." Mindy repeated, holding the letter in her hand and looking at me. She was smiling. So was I. "Poor repair" could only mean one thing: *cheap*.

Were we crazy?

Maybe enchanted was the better word. Though we joked about it, there *was* something witchy about Gwened Guedel—in the modern, chic, Updike manner. Yet Gwened hardly needed clairvoyance to guess that this particular island village lingered in our minds.

Still, her writing out of the blue like this was unprecedented. It had been three years since we'd shown up at her door—and been shown the door the next day with a brisk "Enjoy the island!"

On the island, a visit meant to last a week or two stretched into a month, then two months. Mindy and I got our mojo back, and then some, before stumbling over a new self-discovery: we couldn't bear to leave. Our families in the United States, and even Gwened herself, hinted it was time to return and face the music, but like a pair of Peter Pans, we didn't want to grow up. I'm embarrassed to say that Gwened had to kick us out.

But our reluctance to leave must've made an impression, because her letter was written as if it were yesterday. Which for us it practically was. Captives of our New York daily grind, we looked backward to "island time" as if it were a window through which we might one day stroll again into a greener, saner world.

We thought of Belle Île on dark nights when we needed to restore ourselves after some setback, such as my being invited to a *second* job interview at the *New Yorker* only to have the editor pick up the phone and arrange for "a better fit" at something called *MotorBoating & Sailing.* Or Mindy's agent calling to say he'd accidentally mislaid the manuscript of her novel for an entire *year*, calling her "Penny" the whole time. Or just a little thing like finding a drowned and boiled cockroach in the tea strainer *after* we'd finished our cups of Earl Grey.

After these New York moments, we would console ourselves with village scenes, treasures to be taken out and shaken to lifelike images in a crystal paperweight. On sunnier days, when we felt brave enough to make plans, one of us might pop the question—as in, "My dream would be a little house in a place like Kerbordardoué. What's yours?"

"The same."

So of course we were flattered to be approached, as Gwened no doubt intended. But that didn't change the fact that the notion was lunacy. When you're living on $17,000 a year, buying island cottages isn't in your Top Ten priorities.

Besides, we'd already settled on an island—that big one called Manhattan—although I must say it was doing its best to shake us off, the way a dog does fleas. Mindy and I were barely hanging on, working entry-level jobs at age thirty. And then there was Hawaii, where Mindy was born and raised. If we needed some island R & R, we could always stay with her mom in the graceful, old termite-ridden house on Diamond Head. We could squeeze in with her four brothers and fend off Mom's boyfriends, eat Korean leftovers, and surf practically off her doorstep.

And yet here came Gwened, eyes burning bright, bringing us the news that we needed another island—a *third* island—three thousand miles away. And here's what I don't understand even now, so many years later: we *listened*.

"I suppose it wouldn't hurt to ask how much," I said.

Mindy nodded, thinking the same thing: *cheap*. "I'll write her back."

"A house in Kerbordardoué. I wonder which one it is?"

"I'll call her."

Mindy put her hand on the black Bakelite wall phone, one of the apartment's 1940s relics that contributed to the musty air of a time capsule. It was, of course, a dare. Were we still crazy? Still reckless? Still unembarrassed? Did we really think there was any point or sense to pursuing this blind alley, other than to reinforce previous bad decisions and to nurture the reveries that had led to us living underground on the black housing market and in a state of constant vigilance about keeping a low profile, like fugitives from the law?

Were we, in other words, still *us?*

A month, two months, three months went by. We kept talking. Gwened's preferred mode of communication was a handwritten letter in proud English, the composing of which undoubtedly added time to the process. Each letter had to cross the Atlantic, be read and discussed, then replied to by Mindy in carefully crafted French, dictionary at her elbow. The process became attenuated like a nineteenth-century epistolary novel. But eventually Gwened obtained a key to check out the interior. She wrote back: *I regret to report that the house is in not-good shape.*

What upset her most, however, was the lack of a garden. Not to have even a terrace, where one could sit out in the afternoon, or a place to plant flowers—this was unthinkable. No wonder the house had been on the market for so long. *In good faith I cannot advise you to buy it*, Gwened wrote, *until I have looked around at property in other villages.*

We were disappointed. Already we'd grown accustomed to thinking about *our* house in *our* village on *our* island. We'd begun to save money, just in case.

For a long time Gwened didn't write. We understood. She had her teaching and her family in Tours, the pressure of being a representative of *La France Féminin*, tending to her husband and his wine cave and the teenager who threw typewriters. We knew she could only visit Belle Île during school vacations. After a couple of months, though, we wrote. Her reply came a month later, saying she would canvass the island in the summer. Months went by.

By the time she got back to us, almost a year had passed.

Dear Friends,

I am enclosing the list of the available houses in Belle Île. As you can see, the house next door is the cheapest. I went to see another one at 120,000 F but it is a ruin, damp with no sun. <u>Sun</u> is really the big advantage of the house in Kerbordardoué. Of course, I insist that it is not pleasant in July and August, since everyone is parking there.

The price is now 300,000 F. I do not think there is any possibility of having it lower. Taxes should be added (+12, 15%) and at least 200,000 F for living in the house. The roof is full of holes and should be remade. There is one tap of cold water in the house, but no sink.

…So having considered everything, I am convinced that the house is <u>not a bad bargain.</u> I went inside, and I was surprised to see that it is rather dry and healthy. Upstairs you can have two or three bedrooms, downstairs a nice, big kitchen about the size of my middle room, a bathroom, and a small room. For about 550,000 F on the

whole, you could have a nice house. Of course <u>everything</u> has to be restored from the beginning.

...I would love to have you as neighbors. I would help as much as I can for counseling the good enterprises in Belle Île. Good for you, one dollar is now worth 10 francs...

Love to you both,
Gwened

We were right back where we started. The house still didn't have any land for a garden, there seemed to be something unpleasant going on with parking in summertime, and the roof had holes. You'd think any or all of these might give us pause.

But still the idea would not die. What kept us writing letters and on the phone that second winter, listening to Gwened Guedel? We had neither the time nor the money for this, no business thinking about islands, villages, houses. Even now, I really don't understand it—or us. I only know that we both wanted out so badly. Out of this world, our lives, the jobs we held, the times we lived in.

The longer Gwened spoke, the more we opened our minds. Maybe thinking of her as a bit of a witch wasn't very polite of us, given her past generosity, proper manners, and stern professorial bearing. But it wasn't altogether wrong.

Because when Gwened spoke, we could *see*.

Because it would be *ours*.

Or so the gods whispered.

We heard. We saw. Now, when we closed our eyes at night, when we woke in the morning, when we swayed to the rhythm of the subway rocketing around a curve and grimaced at its horrific shrieking brakes, we saw the island.

When we wandered north of Hell's Kitchen in the West Fifties and found ourselves in a tiny, rundown neighborhood of French Pressing dry cleaners and grimy storefront restaurants with *Escargots à la Bourguignonne* and *Crêpes Suzette* on the menu, we saw the island. When we went to see a foreign movie at the old Thalia and it turned out to be *Local Hero*, a whimsically devastating tale of a tiny village in the north of Scotland, we saw the island. It might be said that we saw the island everywhere in everything.

In actuality, we were seeing through the prism of unreliable memory. On our first visit, we had been like castaways straggling up onto the shore and trying to make sense of a strange place whose language and habits were incomprehensible. We were dazed, awkward, and uncertain, but most of all grateful to be alive and in awe of the place that had saved us. So each thing that we encountered there—every seashell, shady lane, stone cottage, and village character—had felt like the first of its kind and the archetype for all others.

Three years later, the island we dreamed of, that Gwened conjured up for us, was mostly a shape-shifting reflection of our personal mythology. In terms of hard knowledge, all that we knew about it could just about fit on a single page of paper. But we felt we'd embarked on the next phase of our journey. It was out of our hands.

To stop now, we'd have to live with the bitterness of our stillborn dreams, knowing we'd flunked some kind of test—Gwened's test. Yes, in a way it all came down to Gwened. Who else would've had the gall to write two floundering Americans, to call us up and grab us by the figurative scruffs of our necks and state a not-so-obvious truth with the implacability of a seer:

You. Need. This. Island.

Chapter Four
At First Sight

The exterior was a blotchy gray, the white paint having long faded, with stains under the eaves and scabs of broken plaster. The cracked and gapped roof slumped like a broken-down swaybacked mare. Peeling window shutters hung aslant on their pins, missing slats. The windowpanes were cracked or absent altogether; cobwebs stretched across the gaps, dense with dust and the carcasses from repeated and massive insect attacks.

It was part of a row of houses, not one of which seemed inhabited. At the north end, a pile of stones was all that was left of what, a couple of hundred years ago, might once have been somebody's home. At the south end, at the bottom of the narrow rutted lane, was a rude, window-less stone hut. There were two candidates for the one that was ours: first, a small, squarish boxy thing, with a pair of windows and a date chiseled above a door, which had real possibilities, and then...oh dear...could this really be it?

Two years later, and a long way from home and the USA—two days' travel by plane, rental car, and boat, to be precise—at last we were standing before our house. Here it was, after nine years of rented bungalows and apartments, the first place we could truly call our own and a convenient 2,500 miles from where we actually lived. My heart was in my mouth. It was all on me, this folly. As I tried not to watch Mindy throw up, all I could think was: *Oh my God, what have I done?*

Mindy really was seeing this *thing* for the first time this very minute, because, try as we might after Gwened told us it was on the market, our memories always drew a blank as to what it actually had looked like. Despite passing within a couple feet every single day for three months during our winter visit, we couldn't have picked it out of a lineup. Our eyes must've just instinctively turned away. Which should have told us something.

We also should have hit the pause button in May, when Mindy's supervisor refused to give her any time off to fly over and inspect the place. I'd wrangled an overseas trip from my boss, but with only twenty-four hours on Belle Île in which to evaluate and then say yes or no. Mindy had insisted I go ahead, even though my spoken French was barely up to ordering *un grand café*. After consulting with a French lawyer in Manhattan, she'd filled a little notebook with phrases and questions and shoved me onto the plane. *Bon voyage!*

Now, despite all I'd seen and rued on my brave expedition, there was a heavy wrought iron key in my fist. Our key. Meanwhile, Gwened and a neighbor, Franck, were waiting politely for Mindy to finish retching. As if this was only to be expected when inspecting one's newly purchased home.

Mindy was pregnant, something we discovered weeks after I'd said *oui-oui-oui* to our brand-new ruin. Long hair flowing down, she bent over at the waist, pale, not only from morning sickness but from our visit the day before to a one-star restaurant en route to the ferryboat. Having allowed herself a drink for the first time in a month, Mindy had gone upstairs to the ladies' lounge. Ravished by the sight of a pear tree blossoming in the back garden, she'd tugged at a closed window to inhale the scent.

The window didn't open up, however, but swung out, smacking my poor girl on the back of her head. She woke up hanging halfway out of the window, arms flung out, rump in the air, without any recollection of how she got there. She didn't make it back downstairs until thirty minutes later. The waiters, having stoically returned our entrées to the kitchen, re-served them under silver cloche lids without a hint that anything was out of the ordinary. As there were only two other customers that day, maybe nothing was.

Mindy has a great poker face when it suits her. She never let on what happened at Chez Melanie until after we'd finished, paid up, and were back on the road—just as she now straightened up, wiped off her lips, and looked around, asking brightly, "Is the door unlocked? Can we go in? What're we waiting for?"

I didn't try to read Mindy's expression or her mind. I just felt an overwhelming sense of error and exhaustion. Because this wasn't a house. One hundred fifty-five years old, it looked much older. It looked like a hovel.

"See the wall and foundation stones? And the roof slates?" asked Gwened, with a cheerful professorial air. "They came from a quarry in the ravine behind my field."

We'd seen the quarry, now filled with trees and blackberry vines. Too bad the roof slates were cracked, shattered, and stained with orange lichen, destined for the dump. Not five minutes after putting my signature on a proffer, I'd been informed by the notary that if we didn't put up a new roof this winter, the house would collapse. Surely this was premature. We were waiting for a second opinion, from a real expert who was on his way to meet us, an architect and general contractor whose name was Denis LeReveur.

We'd exchanged incredulous smiles the first time we heard it: Denny the Dreamer?

At the front door, Franck and I joined shoulders and gently but steadily pushed until it creaked open. Ancient boards sagged underfoot during our initial walk across the kitchen, which ended when Franck plunged through and up to his shins. *"Oh-la-la! Quel désastre!"*

he cried, staring down at his missing feet. Our relief when he laughed verged on hysteria.

From that point on, we tightrope-walked where underlying beams supported the floor. I clutched Mindy's elbow as we both stared at the fireplace, a blasted black hole of a hearth that sent soot tendrils extending outward across the walls. They looked like octopus tentacles. Ugly gaps reminded us where the stove, sink, and counter used to be, outlined in black furry mold. The kitchen walls were stained and covered in yellow filth—old cooking grease, one hundred and fifty-five years of it.

There was a doorway to our left. "Is this the bedroom?" At the door, Mindy stopped short at the sight of the dank, peeling plaster and dangling, ripped-out electrical wires. It was like the room was reaching out for her with rotted, corpselike arms. I watched her take it all in. When her lips tightened, I suddenly realized that the dark tomblike space, with just the one window facing out on the square, matched our New York apartment's layout. Mindy was big on cross-ventilation and natural light. She hated our apartment. Why hadn't I noticed the unfortunate resemblance?

"I know, it needs work. But you said if it was…"

"I smell mold."

What a comedown. When we'd first heard about it—*a small house in the village!*—we imagined it would be like Gwened's place up the lane. We'd fallen in love with those dark, low beams, lace-trimmed windows, and white hand-plastered walls hung with copper pans and Quimper plates. Although Gwened had described the years of work she'd done to restore her farmhouse, we hadn't listened.

It's embarrassing to admit this, but we were under the impression that our house would somehow resemble hers. That it would have been left unattended, yet intact, like the gingerbread house in the Brothers Grimm fairy tale, ready for immediate occupancy once we dispatched the old crone standing by the oven door.

But no. This was a wreck, a true disaster. This was not even a house—not really. It was *once* a house, and maybe could be again. But at the moment, the best you could say would be: an extreme fixer-upper.

Gwened's trail of cake crumbs had led us to a ruin. Which I should've known, but was too blind to see before signing on the dotted line.

"The house has always had the most sun in the village," said Gwened, implacable as ever. I could hear the steel in her voice. Now was not the time for vacillation. We were here to map out our plan of attack. "It will dry out when the old plaster is removed. The walls are stone. You cannot build a house like this anymore."

"I can't breathe!" Racked by a coughing fit, Mindy clawed at her shoulder bag. Gwened frowned.

"Can't breathe!" Mindy blindly pushed past and rushed toward the door over creaking, groaning floorboards, which fortunately held up. I followed her out and supported her bag so she could dig out her inhaler. Wide-eyed, she sucked down a hit of albuterol, waited for half a minute, then hit the inhaler again.

Giving an indignant wheeze, she shook her russet mane. "Great— house makes me asthmatic." Her rapid, panicky breathing and eye-rolling were familiar to me from trips to the emergency room. Suddenly she gripped my forearm. "*The baby!* Do you think it's hurting *the baby?*"

I draped an arm around her shoulders while not quite touching them, knowing how that would only increase her claustrophobia. "Don't worry. Baby's fine. House is fine. It's gonna be good. You heard Gwened—and remember, it's been shut up for five years. Give it some sunshine and a paint job. You'll see…"

I was almost convinced. But through the open door I could see Gwened and Franck deep in discussion and looking quite serious. Franck had done much of the interior carpentry in Gwened's house to supplement the pittance he made leading charters on his sailboat. Our age, he'd been a high school teacher before moving to Belle Île with his wife, Ines. They'd been our great friends during our winter in the village and were excited to see us return. But the look on Franck's face was grave.

"Where will we get the money?" asked Mindy.

"We don't have to rush into anything," I replied. "We can wait until next year before we start any renovation. By then, I'll get a promotion and a raise..."

"But the dollar is falling *now*."

Among the many curious things Mindy had taught me about France, an obsession with currency rates had to be the most arcane, right up there with spotting the difference between a skinned rabbit and a skinned cat in a Mouffetard butcher's stall. But I caught on fast after a 3.41 franc-to-dollar ratio had translated into *No croissants for breakfast, mon amour.*

That was during my first visit to France, back when America was weak. In the past year, between Gwened's first letter about the house and my visit two months ago, the rate had gone to 10-to-1, in effect dropping the price by nearly two-thirds. Also during the year, with the goal of this place in mind—still unseen, but not unimagined—Mindy had landed a job at *Glamour* magazine and I had gotten a raise at *MotorBoating & Sailing.* We'd cut our expenses and saved every penny. We'd freelanced, applied for writing grants, entered contests.

Somewhat shockingly, our efforts had paid off. Our novels-in-progress each won a $7,500 prize from James Michener's Copernicus Society. I won a $500 award from the Secretary of Mexican Tourism for an article about Baja California and took home a set of luggage from the American Zipper Association (I'm not making this up) for a cartoon I'd drawn of a Central Park tent enclosure designed to house Donald Trump's expanding ego.

So much good stuff happened that we both came to believe that Belle Île and Kerbordardoué were affecting our luck. For instance, it seemed I couldn't attend a press lunch or conference without winning the drawing for the door prize. Steak knife sets, free stays at industrial-park Ramada Inns, hot-air balloon rides. It was hard not to feel that we were suddenly living a charmed life, albeit one weirdly overstocked with knives.

Just as our bank balance hit $15,500, the owners caved. It turned out they were five squabbling siblings, none of whom had ever lived in Kerbordardoué. Worn down by our long year and a half of hesitation, they threw up their hands and cut the price in half, to 150,000 francs— exactly $15,000 at the new rate. Taking this as an omen, I figured out how to piggyback a detour onto an overseas story for my magazine, flew over, spent a couple hours going over the house with Gwened and Franck, and... *"Oh my god, what have I done?"*

Spent every penny we had and then some—forgetting to factor in that twelve-point-five percent tax, for starters.

Gwened now strolled out the front door and smiled with all her considerable charisma. Inhaling deeply, spreading her arms wide, she said, "It's a wonderful house, Mindy. You will be very happy here. I can feel it."

Loath to show weakness in front of her old professor, Mindy straightened up and puffed out her chest like a soldier on parade. "What do we do now? Is that man coming?"

"Denis LeReveur should be here any moment." Gwened turned on her heels and gave the house another once-over. "He is a sensitive young architect, and of course, he is *Bellilois*. That is the important thing for the renovation."

But being sensitive and young and *Bellilois*, Denny the Dreamer was late. We circled the square, eyeing the house, pacing off its length, and peering behind at the adjoining shed, its exposed stone wall showing signs of collapse. "Do we own this?" asked Mindy.

"No," said Gwened.

"I'm worried it could bring down our wall. Maybe we can buy it?"

What? Here we were, flat broke and looking at an expensive renovation, and Mindy wanted to expand our little empire. I didn't know it, but this was the first indication that my wife had caught the French peasant's disease: a compulsive desire to add to one's holdings, regardless of reason or need.

"I think not." Gwened sounded brusque, wary. Was she, perhaps, feeling a bit guilty about what she'd gotten us into?

More likely I was hearing the new Gwened. On my inspect-and-commit visit a couple of months ago, I'd been taken aback to see that she'd cut her hair. Once a shoulder-length swirl, it was almost brutally short. She'd also lost a lot of weight, twenty pounds or more. And since then she'd lost more. It had sharpened her chin and cheeks, and not entirely in a good way. Now I couldn't help but wonder how much was the chemo and how much was the divorce.

So far today Gwened hadn't brought up either bombshell. It was all a guessing game. Although I'd reminded Mindy of what I'd heard and observed during my visit, I could tell that it still hadn't sunk in or else she hadn't quite believed me. Perhaps she felt my limited French was at fault. But even after we'd arrived and she'd seen that at least Gwened's physical changes were real, Mindy had scrupulously avoided bringing them up. This was her beloved professor, after all, and mentor. When Gwened was ready, she'd talk.

Not for me, such exquisite patience. I was at the end of mine, in a state of utter panic about my decision. Especially with Mindy blithely dreaming of buying new ruins, the question seemed unavoidable: *Is Gwened—our mentor and muse and sponsor in Kerbordardoué—dying?*

In May I'd sensed something different about Gwened, even when waving to her from the upper deck of the ferry. In person there were kisses, a little minuet of alternating cheeks, *un, deux, trois…quatre.* The fourth kiss among very close friends, a little late, was always a surprise to me. Then Gwened smiled and spoke in French, making the overture as if to see whether, by some miracle, Don had awakened this morning fluent at last.

Stealing sidelong glimpses as she drove, I realized she'd cut her hair. She looked modern, younger. Well, a haircut will do that. I asked in French if her husband had made the trip.

"No."

"He's well?"

"He's well."

"And your son? Daniel?" Liking that she kept her answers short to allow me to establish a rhythm.

"*Superbe!* If I could live twenty years longer, what I would give to see how he turns out."

This threw a wrench into my translation processes. Surely I'd misheard? I glanced at Gwened. She drove straight on, serene, but also awaiting my reply with a puckish smile. So she *did* say it, or something like it. Trying to construct a suitable response before too much time elapsed, I blurted out: "*Peut-être c'est nécessaire d'acheter un coeur artificiel.*" Perhaps it's necessary to buy an artificial heart. Whatever that meant.

In Kerbordardoué she had wasted no time in showing me our prospective house, joined by Franck. With the electricity shut off, it made a terrible first impression. We lingered, like guests at a party no one has attended, trying to make conversation until dusk made it impossible to see.

At her own door, Gwened asked me if I meditated. No? Well, if I would excuse her, she and Franck and his wife, Ines, would be in the dojo. Dojo? She smiled. "My old cowshed."

The mysteries continued. At dinner she served a miniature vegetarian meal that left me, ravenous from my travels, in despair afterward, lying on my bed with a hole in my stomach. What had happened to my Gwened, the toreador of home-cured ham?

My mind was also crowded with other thoughts. We'd put Gwened to so much trouble already, yet I was now certain that Mindy would not want to buy the house, once I described it. Then I'd be alone with Gwened's famous disappointed smile. The prospect almost frightened me.

The next morning, walking by Gwened's bedroom, I saw a new black-and-white photo on her wall, of a middle-aged balding Japanese man in a plain white kimono, sitting cross-legged on a straw mat. This was not at all what I would have expected from my personal symbol of France. More than disappointment, I felt bushwhacked. Was this karma, irony, God's idea of a joke? I already had a Sikh-turbaned, breath-of-fire yogi-turned-lawyer brother and a pair of lacto-ovo vegetarian sisters, plus a Christian Scientist mother who was a devotee of food faddist Adele Davis and libertarian cult goddess Ayn Rand. The last thing I expected was to have Kerbordardoué turn into a New Age commune.

There was another tour of the house that morning, just as depressing, and then, after lunch, we took a walk down our valley, through an alley of cypresses to a meadow and a marsh. We continued along the base of grassy sandhills to our wide crescent beach, Donnant, bookended by steep cliffs, each rock face pierced with a knowing, somnolent eye: a camouflaged German gun emplacement.

At the top of a tall dune, Gwened tucked herself into a hollow and gestured for me to take the one beside her. "Now you have been here long enough to remember what it is like. You have seen the house. What will you do?"

"Go home, talk to Mindy, show her the pictures."

"Would you like to call her tonight?"

The thought of Gwened's stolid black telephone, which rang so infrequently that neither Mindy nor I ever recognized the bell, had never occurred to me. "I guess that would make sense."

"Because the notary doesn't think the house will be on the market much longer at this price. He says it's getting rare for any of the old houses to come open. It's only the lack of land which has kept this one from being snapped up. Are you at all interested?"

"Oh, yes. But I must talk to Mindy, and…"

"Of course. But still, if you are interested it is almost certainly necessary for you to meet the notary. I have made an appointment for ten tomorrow morning."

Gwened stared serenely out to sea. I felt as if I had been rudely shaken out of a pleasant dream; now all I wanted to do was go back to sleep. But I couldn't, despite Donnant's opaline sands and mother-of-pearl waves. This was, I realized, my cue. Gwened intended to force a decision out of us, yes or no, before I left. She knew me, knew us, too well. If we thought that we could subsist on dreams forever, Gwened was bound and determined to put a stop to it.

As the poet once said, "In dreams begin responsibilities." We'd had our run of dreams long enough; now it was time to wise up. And just in case I didn't get the point, as soon as we returned to her house Gwened handed me the phone.

"First—where *is* it? Behind Gwened's?" Mindy breathlessly demanded.

"You won't believe it. It's right in the middle of the village, on the square, in that row facing the road. I don't know how we missed it. Gwened says it's the driest spot in the village; it's the oldest house standing."

"What condition is it in?"

"Pretty much of a mess."

"Of course it is, not being lived in for five years! Is it big?"

Hearing the excitement in her voice, I suddenly wanted to downplay the house's already modest charms. "Two rooms, that's all."

"As big as our apartment? Or smaller?"

I had paced it off. "About twice the size."

"Then it's big!"

"Actually, it felt small. Min, it's just two rooms. No bathroom, no land for a *fosse septique*."

"So we go in the fields?"

"Gwened says there's a new kind of fancy compactor-oven toilet we can get. A lady in Le Palais supposedly has one."

"God, don't you just *love* the French! How about a stove?" We'd both dreamed of inheriting a Breton woodstove, along with a *lit clos*, a sort of cupboard bed, maybe a pair of hand-carved wood sabots for our feet, along with a few lace curtains, with or without the embroidered peacocks on Gwened's.

"No stove, not even a sink. There isn't even running water. The old lady used the well in the square."

Mindy sighed. "So it's going to take a lot of work."

"Min, it's a ruin."

"So a total rehab?"

"Gwened and Franck say we'll definitely have to replace a lot of the floor and ceiling; there's dry rot."

"Termites?"

"Franck says no."

"Well…" While Mindy paused, the faint Babel of the intercontinental airwaves pulsed rhythmically in the background. "You're there— should we buy it?"

"No fair. It has to be a joint decision."

"Well, is Kerbordardoué still the same?"

"It hasn't changed."

"Then I think we should do it."

I took a deep breath. I hadn't felt so on-the-spot since I'd proposed to Mindy, back on the dance floor of a late-night party in Iowa City, the two of us slow dancing, Motown on the box, surrounded by a circle of fellow grad students. Then, I'd had the feeling that when the dance was over, I would've missed my chance. The same tingling, flushed feeling attended me now. But I didn't have Mindy's face before me, and I was panicking a little.

"Have you looked at the *cadastre*? Have you checked the zoning for the land around the village? Did you ask about the *usages ruraux*?"

"I'm seeing the notary tomorrow about all of that."

"Well." She sounded out of breath. Suddenly the heavy black phone seemed even heavier. "This will be the first real thing we've bought in our marriage. Are we nuts? We don't even have a car," she added, laughing.

"I guess it's about time. I mean, nine years."

It was getting harder to talk. We listened to each other's breathing.

"How's your French?" she asked abruptly.

I shuddered. "Your notebook saved my life."

"Listen carefully tomorrow. Write down your answers—better yet, have the notary write the answers down in the notebook."

"Okay, okay… I guess this call is costing Gwened a fortune. I love you."

"I love you, too. You did good, Young Strudel."

Young Strudel slumped back in the chair. Young Strudel—Mindy's nickname for the clumsy, beaming young blond in shorts who was always being mistaken for a German wherever we went in Europe—had a feeling that he was really in for it now.

After setting down the phone, I went looking for my hostess. Ducking under a bower of willows, I found Gwened weeding her garden. "Looks like we're going to do it."

She nodded, lips bent in a slight smile. "I am very happy to hear it. Come, help me pick some of these tiny, delicious carrots for our dinner."

After we carried the lettuce and vegetables to the kitchen, Gwened asked me if I would come with her to a special place. Leaving her house, we turned away from the village, skirting a field of immature green corn.

"For years I had heard it spoken of," said Gwened, "but the people here are very shy with strangers. Yes, I am considered a stranger," she added, "even though my grandfather was born on Belle Île. It's because I don't live here full-time. Anyway, one day when I was out in the woods collecting pinecones for the fire—they make such lovely sparks—I chanced to see an old woman walk into the underbrush where there was no path. One minute she was there. The next, she just disappeared. I had to see where she had gone."

We were in the woods ourselves, under a canopy of dense branches. Norfolk pines, planted in six rows, had grown together to make tunnel-like paths. The floor of the forest was completely covered with needles and felt springy underfoot.

"I recognized the woman," said Gwened. "A few months ago, she appeared in the village. They say she lived all her life on a farm in Ty-Néhué, as a cowherd. She lives in the house at the end of your row, without electricity or water. Perhaps you have seen her. She is a trifle, how do you say it, *touched*? She does not speak to any of us, only to Madame Morgane, with whom she takes coffee."

"I think I saw her the other day," I said. "Staring at our house, actually. She's dark-haired, wears a blue dress?"

"That's her. I have since heard more about her, but that's for another time." Gwened led the way out of the forest to a barbed wire fence at the edge of the upland. We were looking down into the next *vallon*, little valley, over from ours. Between us and a narrow road lay wild waves of blackberries and great oceanic shoals of ferns that swirled in the wind, wrapping around the trunks of gale-grayed pines.

Down by the edge of the road, silver-leaved poplars fluttered. It seemed impassable, but Gwened stepped over the barbed wire fence and down into a cut. A steep, muddy path curled under an overhang and twisted through giant ferns, skirting a brushy dome formed from several wind-beaten trees whose branches had grown entwined. We had passed this tangle when Gwened cut back, ducked down, and disappeared into its center. I followed.

We were in a natural alcove, like a nave in a church. The back was a wall of stone, some of it hand-dressed, the rest the gray-black of exposed bedrock. Stunted trees writhed along the outer rim like dancers, their moss-matted arms stylized, hairy freak-outs; and a gnarled tree trunk rose sinuously from the floor of the enclosure to form a leafy, sun-shotgunned ceiling. Rough stone blocks made seats along the wall. Water trickled out of a mossy seam and dripped into a pool scooped out of the rock floor. When I saw that stream burbling from a hidden source, I was done for.

"It is a spring," Gwened said. "She knew it was here. But it's more than that. I believe it is a Druid shrine. She has been clearing away the brush."

"The old woman?"

"*La Femme Sauvage*. That is how she is known." Gwened took a stone seat. "Nobody knows who the Druids were. All we know is they erected the menhirs, the ten thousand stones at Carnac, the alignments at Stonehenge, but we don't know why. We do know they regarded springs as sacred. The *Bellilois* pretend to be as baffled by the stones as anyone, but then you see things, and you wonder. Like the old crosses at Lanno and Herlin. They're Druid altars over five thousand years old, carved into crosses by the Christians in the fourteenth century. You will never see them without a garland of fresh flowers." Gwened touched her forehead. "You know, with my own eyes I have seen *La Femme Sauvage* speaking to your well in the village."

At Gwened's suggestion, we sat in silence in the bower. After a while, she pointed across the valley at a dark lip of stone. "That's the quarry where the slates on your house were quarried seventy years ago. The woman's name, by the way, is Suzanne," she added with a knowing smile that hinted at all the mysteries to come—if we bought the ruin.

I nodded, but actually she had me at "*It's a spring.*" I grew up in a suburb of Southern California so flat that it was below sea level in places. In fact, Long Beach was actually *sinking* from all the oil being pumped out from under it. We were told that the constantly nodding grasshopper rig in our schoolyard was pumping sea water back down to keep us all from plunging into a chasm. Far from scaring or scarring us, this lent a touch of B-movie excitement when playing in the vacant lots that were our lizard preserves and dirt-clod battlefields and Jurassic savannahs. The ground could give way at any instant!

By the time I turned twelve, though, the last vacant lot was gone. A tract house occupied its physical space. It was shocking, the mystery force sucking my old landscapes away so swiftly and with the same finality as my mother's vacuum cleaner hoovering up dust kitties. Through all my years at Sunday school, I'd never felt a grief comparable to what I felt over losing that final plot of windblown wild grasses.

Around the same time that the last vacant lot was transformed into another split-level, I came to church with my pockets bulging with toads, which I hid in the Bible basket when the congregation stood to sing. The physical realm that my mother's faith dismissed as immaterial suddenly became the focus of everyone's attention. Out of nowhere appeared a spongy carpet of living creatures, and without quite realizing it, I'd organized the end of organized religion—at least for me.

The strange thing is, though the term seems slightly ridiculous, given my nearsightedness, I was *observant* in church that day. While everyone was screaming at the ugliness of these creatures who had invaded the House of God, I only saw their amazing vitality.

Leaving our church made little or no difference in my life. Far from seeking out evil influences, at twelve I just preferred to be in nature—not easy in Long Beach. Fortunately my dad was a big Boy Scout (literally, when standing in his adult uniform) and sacrificed many a weekend so Troop 78 could go camping. It was during an expedition the last summer before middle school that I had what I believe to be my first true religious experience.

Ditching my troop in the San Bernardino Mountains, I spent an entire day lying on a log that spanned a grassy hole in a mountain meadow, my face inches above a hidden freshwater spring, watching as it boiled up to the surface. It was the source of the San Jacinto River. Watching the pale, sandy grains sift and swirl from an invisible power, I finally felt an answering tickle within, like a finger in my ribs giving me a little cootchy-coo.

Something similar came over me that day with Gwened at Suzanne's spring. It still does when I'm in Kerbordardoué. Springs are holy in every culture, and many of the springs on Belle Île are reputed to have special powers. On one of the older maps I've come across of the island, from the 1560s, the village is marked by a series of short horizontal lines (indicating a marsh was there at the time), crosshatched by a trio of vertical lines. It looks like musical notation.

The verticals leap from the cartographer's quill with exuberance and then bend slightly at the top of the stroke, their heavy black beads of ink poised as if to fall. "*Puits et Chapelle*," the legend says of these markings, in typical laconic map-speak: "Springs and Chapel."

"*Puits et Chapelle*"—it does sound restorative, even miraculous. And our waters *are* reputed to have properties, although of what kind is in dispute. In the oldest history of the island, Kerbordardoué carries the only description of its kind out of the one hundred fifty-two villages: a terse "said to be the place of the Devil." *Us?*

Devilish or not, the miraculous power of the waters of Kerbordardoué and Belle Île were definitely at work on that fateful day—and the next, when we went to see the notary of Le Palais.

It was a long and curious visit. M. Le Notaire made sure I understood that the house came with no land, that the square was communal, and the lane in front of the house a right-of-way. This was Gwened's cue to raise the subject of a septic tank. He expressed his regrets that, no, there was no place to put one. Gwened nodded and described, with mounting enthusiasm, the famous electric compactor oven-toilet installed by a most sagacious lady of Le Palais. M. Le Notaire listened, then broke into a torrent. He had heard of it himself!

It worked on the principle of certain high-technology furnaces used to create industrial ceramics for jet engine parts. The way it worked was fascinating: waste was collected in a chamber that, when a button was pressed, was subjected to immense heat, drying out the material and then compressing it into a tiny cake, which was suitable for disposal. Marvelous! What an invention! There was no odor, just a considerable electric bill. He would look forward to seeing ours in action when we had it installed. I nodded.

Since I had Mindy's go-ahead, all that was left for me to do was sign a single sheet of paper, sort of a preliminary foreclosure on every dime in our name. Then it was back to the village for another spartan lunch with Gwened. (By now my stomach had ceased growling and was making whimpering noises.) And if I was hoping for a drink in celebration, as certainly seemed earned, I was out of luck.

As I would be leaving early the next morning on the boat, Gwened suggested a farewell walk down to the beach. We retraced the familiar path, now my path, *our* path. We climbed the tall sand dune and found our respective foxholes overlooking the clamorous sea.

"As you may have noticed, I'm looking into my life," Gwened said after we were settled and had watched the sun slowly setting over foaming ranks of breakers. It was hypnotic and calming, and for the moment I'd gotten over my cold feet. "This year, I've had to make *a big change*. I just did not feel that I could go on living as a sort of idealized image of what others wanted me to be. France is a hard place to be a woman."

I said that I'd had the thought myself, on occasion—not that *I* was a woman, of course. But I'd noticed that she carried quite a load, managing her household, teaching at the college, being a mother, a wife…

"My husband has a mistress," she interrupted.

"Oh."

"When I confronted him, he wouldn't give her up. I have taken an apartment in Tours. For my settlement, I asked for the house here."

Her husband, the kindly choir-singing accountant with the neat beard and the brace of grouse he'd shot aging from the porch rafters and the wine cellar of which he was so proud—this man, to my mind a model gentleman, fully engaged in matters of the spirit, of tradition, of community, of ancient ritual—was also a typical cheating Frenchman? It was so sad. And poor Gwened. *What a jerk*, I thought.

I murmured my condolences. She nodded, staring out to sea, sitting in her purple-striped caftan, with her new short hair, which dimly reminded me of something I'd read: that women get their hair cut short when they're starting an affair. Probably in an article in one of Gwened's ageless *Elle* magazines stacked by the toilet.

"There is another thing," she said. "I have received a big diagnosis."

A *big* diagnosis? She hugged her caftan around her, face glowing in the rays of the last of the sunset, a light so strong and slant it turned the sand and the wind-flattened grasses gold. "It is cancer. In the breast. Quite serious. I do not have long to live, I'm afraid. It will be very hard on my son. Poor Daniel."

Suddenly our conversation in the car made sense. But then… *Wait a minute. What about us?* Thinking this, I was aware of how rotten it sounded, even unspoken. But at the moment I felt I must be honest—brutally honest, even if only with myself—since nobody else had been.

So they all knew: Gwened, Franck, Ines, the notary… They had to have been in on it. A little village con game. They'd just hoodwinked the American couple into taking a dog of a house off their hands.

Come on. Calm down. You know your problem: too little faith in people. It's the curse of the writer, the journalist, the person who's seen a little too much of humanity up close. It's important not to make things worse; that won't help.

Okay, okay… But it's hard, man, hard.

I sat in my foxhole and stared into the sun until spots floated across my eyelids, even when they were closed. And to give Gwened credit, she knew when to keep quiet.

Of course she had to be aware that I was wondering when and how much to tell Mindy.

"Honey? I know we've just bought this ruined house on the say-so of Gwened, sort of on the implied promise of joining our life to hers, in a way. Well, turns out there's a problem; a couple of problems, actually. First, the house is in worse shape than everyone let on, so we're going to be spending all the money we have and even more that we don't have. Second—on top of everything else—she's dying. Gwened is. Yes, dying. I know, *now* she tells me. Oh, and I know it's crazy, but I almost forgot something else. She's getting divorced, too."

Great.

Gwened stirred. "Do you believe in reincarnation?"

I shrugged but, finding myself unable to snub the possibly dying, soon-to-be divorced fairy godmother beside me, I rummaged in my New Age bag for something to say. "No. But I've had some pretty powerful moments of déjà vu."

Gwened got up, brushing the sand from her legs. "You must tell me about them someday. I'm going back up to the house to meditate." I started to rise. "No, stay. I think you should watch the sun go down over Donnant on your first night as a *propriétaire*. Enjoy."

She smiled, turned, and trudged off up the sand dune like some Bedouin sage in a purple glen-plaid caftan. Not for the first time, she had guessed right; I did want to be alone with my beach and my thoughts. *Not a few of which concern you, Gwened, you and your mysterious decision to lure us into exile.*

That night we held a celebration dinner. It was quite a contrast to my first meal in a French home, one Sunday at Gwened's years ago. Then she'd impressed me with how closely elegance was allied with austerity: a bowl of yellow squash soup silky with butterfat, a gratiné of potatoes layered in Gruyere and Parmesan, a single slice of the home-cured ham that hung in her attic, followed by a salad of bitter greens, and particularly revelatory for me, a piece of ripe fruit for dessert. That meal had been a demonstration of how the quality of ingredients could carry the day.

This meal tonight, on the other hand, seemed designed for a hunger strike. After the fresh tomato soup, Gwened served each plate with a tiny mound of rice, a slice of steamed squash, fresh grated carrots, and a half-dozen miniature Brussels sprouts. I didn't know which was more amazing to me, the fact that Franck and Ines's children tucked in without comment or that Franck and Ines kept on exclaiming with wonder over their food—for it was plain, the plainest food I have ever eaten in France: unseasoned, unbuttered, almost uncooked.

Years ago, when I had returned to California after my first visit to France, the first thing I'd done was to make a beeline for the supermarket and buy things I'd spent a lifetime avoiding, butter in particular, but cream and veal as well. To me, France was richness. Tonight wasn't France; tonight was ridiculous.

"*Tout directement du jardin!*" said Gwened triumphantly. "*Tout biologique!*"

"*S'a goût extraordinaire,*" said Ines.

"*Superbe,*" said Franck. "*Tout biologique!*"

Okay, I got it, I got it: the vegetables were out of the garden and organic. But I don't think I will ever understand how they managed to drag that meal out for twenty minutes, let alone an hour. To keep pace, I had to eat my rice a grain at a time. As for the conversation, once Gwened's forte and a demanding steeplechase of current events and literary aphorisms, it limped.

Shyly, Ines looked up at Gwened. "May I meditate with you tomorrow morning?"

"Of course."

The children grinned at their mother as if she'd scored tickets to the zoo. I glanced at Franck, expecting to see the beginnings of a wisecrack take form on his lips. But no, he was nodding, too.

Everyone's turned into vegetables, I thought. *It's like* The Stepford Wives. *You really don't have a clue about what you're getting into, do you? How much will you dare tell Mindy?*

What did Mindy know? I'd tried telling her countless times about Gwened, about the condition of the house, but it was as if she didn't want to hear it. But even now, standing in the square before an awfully decrepit ruin, I couldn't get a read on her thoughts. Which was rare for her and rough for me. I couldn't say whether she'd figured out yet the magnitude of mess we were in, whether she somehow approved of it, or whether she was just making the best of it. Maybe she was just biding her time before laying into me in private. I'd deserve it. But I needed to know. The suspense was killing me.

Just as I was about to launch into a mea culpa, Gwened turned sharply away. The grinding of gears came from down the lane, and a moment later the dull nose of a weathered Citroën truck appeared. It swung toward us, squeezing slowly between hydrangeas, rocking in the deep ruts. Behind the wheel: Denny the Dreamer. Who turned out to be tall and serious, with rimless glasses and a rumpled, handsome face.

In jeans and a thick sweater jacket open to a chambray shirt, he could've passed for a modern English country squire, the kind who drives a Land Rover in London. I could see where Gwened's description of him as a local rake and wild boy came from. But he'd married and settled down, she'd said, and was the only *Bellilois* who was certified as a *maître d'oeuvre en bâtiment*, or master builder.

As we shook hands, Denis LeReveur seemed relieved to understand Mindy's French. My mangled phrases he greeted with solemn nods. But when it came time for him to shake hands with Franck, I noticed an immediate chill. We'd heard Franck say that the locals did not take kindly to newcomers who came to seek work. As an unlicensed carpenter, even if only doing pickup jobs to feed his family, Franck posed a real threat to some *Bellilois* somewhere.

Once Franck took the hint and withdrew, gracefully, LeReveur became more relaxed. And Gwened took charge, by prearrangement. "Mindy and Don would like your opinion as to how much work the house requires this winter," she said, "and how much can be postponed. Would you care to go inside?"

LeReveur gave us both a serious and apologetic look before replying, his manner like that of a doctor in a waiting room who has come to tell the relatives the dire condition of a patient. "I've already been inside, this morning," he said in French that Mindy rapidly translated under her breath, as she usually did for me. He shrugged. "*C'est total. Le toit, le fond, le bois, les planche—tout est foutu.*" His long face lengthened as he peered over his rimless glasses to convey his deepest sympathy.

This time Mindy's sharp intake of breath was not asthma. "*Merde!*"

Gwened flinched in disapproval. LeReveur nodded.

"It *really* is not possible to postpone the work?"

LeReveur gave a slow shake of his head. Pointing to the slumping roofline, he cupped both hands to illustrate the walls, then opened them suddenly. He puffed out his cheeks and blew: *Poof!* Nodding at the jumbled stones and collapsed walls down at the end of the lane, a ruin I admired for its picturesque qualities, he said something that Mindy did not need to translate: by next spring we'd be the proud owners of a rock pile just like that one.

Mindy and I looked at each other. All I could think of was our bank balance of a few hundred dollars. This was quickly followed by wondering if there were any contests left that we hadn't entered.

But I knew it was hopeless. This was one hole no number of door prizes could fill.

❧

A small house in France. That's what we wanted.

But what did Gwened want from us?

Later—after weighing everything, years into this life-changing detour—I wondered if she'd had an atavistic calling. Maybe cutting her hair short had sparked it, reminded her of Joan of Arc rallying her army of believers. Perhaps chemotherapy woke something in the blood that told her it was her destiny to be the mystic center of a village where endless summer evenings edged into Celtic twilight and lives were performed on an ageless stage.

Was Gwened acting as a casting director for her own vanity production, Prospero of a Breton Brigadoon, without thought for how it might work out for us? In the beginning, yes. Magical thinking was involved, maybe narcissism. But there was always something hardheaded in Gwened's calculations. In an angle we didn't figure out for nearly thirty years, she seemed to have been stocking up, preparing for changes not just in her own circumstances, but for a village life after death.

One suspicion *did* actually occur to us very early on, if too late to prevent the fate that would befall us: that the whole thing turned on a misunderstanding. Gwened assumed we were rich. As a little girl in the summer of '44, she'd seen Americans riding to the rescue on their Shermans, handing out C-rations and chocolate. Maybe she hoped the cavalry would come again. Save Kerbordardoué, and then gracefully withdraw.

What Gwened couldn't know was the supreme effort it had taken us to get this far, to scratch out our meager living in Manhattan. Our housing situation at the time, for instance, was laughably precarious and illegal. If we lost it, we'd lose our toehold in the city. Everything in New York was such a struggle: finding an apartment, jobs, a place to do the laundry where it wouldn't be stolen from the dryer. We lived on pizza slices and seltzer. More to the point, when considering a house abroad: under America's neo-Calvinist office rules, I was eligible for a whole five days off a year, plus two sick days to be taken at the discretion of my employer. Assuming we still wanted to see our families on the West Coast and Honolulu at least once a year—and we certainly did—when exactly would we be able to go to France?

Maybe Gwened couldn't imagine us poor and vacationless because she'd taught at Stanford's college-abroad program for over a decade. In her eyes, "Young Americans"—cue the David Bowie song—had trivialized their legacy in France. We drank a lot, didn't learn the language, and pined for a decent hamburger while desecrating the world's finest cuisine with squiggles of ketchup. Although at times we exhibited hints of the vigor, virtue, and élan of the New World, overall we children of the liberators of '44 disappointed her.

This made her faith in us all the more touching, if a little misplaced. As a student, Mindy had *absolutely* memorized the address of the only restaurant in Tours that served a hamburger (with ketchup, too, the genuine Heinz). Gwened never knew.

And so Gwened sounded her horn, like Roland in the wilderness, in all hopefulness. Would we answer the call? Having seen Kerbordardoué, how could we say no?

No matter how cloudy her motives, Gwened's pitch was explicit in one other point: she was quite serious that we would be helping to rescue the village. We'd known Kerbordardoué when it was still a *working* village, meaning it hadn't gone over to the dark side—to tourism. But the change everyone dreaded was coming fast. The last herd of cows had been sold; the last farmer had rented out her fields.

We could help keep the village's soul intact, she explained in one of her letters. Too many outsiders were coming to the island, sniffing around for bargains. An empty house in the center of the village in the wrong hands could spell the end of Kerbordardoué. *And guess what?* she added, concluding that fateful first letter with a flourish. *The villagers took a vote on it. They want* you, *not some stranger, not another German.*

So Gwened said, and so we believed.

They want us?

In hindsight, we didn't stand a chance.

Chapter Five
At Home Abroad: Four Easy Lists

1. What a House Needs

- 4 chairs
- Table
- Bed

- Sheets (?)
- Spoons, forks, knives
  —Don, Year Two

2. Always Bring

- Louisiana Hot Sauce
- Curry powder
- Swim fins
- Swim eardrops
- Books in English

- Itty Bitty Book Light (2) & batteries
- Mosquito repellent
- Hair dryer (?)
- Scotch
  —Don, Year Five

3. Always Bring, Updated

- Surfboard
- Wet suit

- WARMER sweaters
- Books IN ENGLISH

- Mosquito netting
- Monopoly, chess set
- Wiffle ball and bat
- Frisbee
- Nerf football
- Tennis rackets

- Golf clubs
- CD player
- CDs
- Power converter (very important)
- Hair dryer (!)
  —*Don, Year Eight*

4. Bring

- Gifts for children:
  - Hawaii stickers, charms, etc.
- Gifts for surf gang:
  - Local Motion T-shirts, bumper stickers
- Gifts, adults: New York souvenir stuff

- Suzanne: Scarf
- Madame Morgane: Scarf
- Gwened: Hawaii shell necklace
- Surf booties and cold-water surf wax

—*Mindy, Year Seventeen*

Chapter Six

Summer Plans

F ollowing our on-site disaster inspection with Denis LeReveur, we sat around Gwened's patio table and had a needed drink. Gwened didn't serve the hard stuff, but even a Kir Royale at this point was a godsend. As we nibbled olives, LeReveur unveiled the process he would undertake on our behalf, as *maître d'oeuvres en bâtiment*. First, he would prepare a series of plans, architectural renderings that he would submit for approval to the Mairie du Sauzon, the mayoral office of our district.

Assuming eventual approval, he'd also start collecting bids from subcontractors and tradesmen. These would be collected in one sheaf, called the *devis*, pronounced "day-vee." We would sit down with him, go over the individual projects and their cost projections, make modifications, choose grades of materials, and okay specifications. Once a complete document was approved, we'd sign. At that point, the contract for all the work and costs would be legally binding. Did we understand?

Yes.

Did we *really* understand? We nodded.

LeReveur looked to Gwened.

"This means," Gwened said in her precise English, "that you will be responsible for payment no matter what. France has a different legal code than the United States, as Mindy knows. If you do not pay, you will be presumed guilty and may go to jail before your case is heard."

Ah, the famous *Code Napoléon*. As a law student, Mindy had always enjoyed discussions of the Emperor's reforms to centuries of feudal customs. The Code's most famous divergence from Anglo-American law was the rejection of a presumption of innocence as well as habeus corpus. As Gwened said, once arrested you could be thrown in jail until trial, without appeal. This had always sent a delicious chill down Mindy's spine. She'd just never imagined it might apply to us.

"But for now you sign nothing," Gwened continued, still in English. "Denis is happy to prepare the *devis*, but he will have to act fast to get it to you before you leave." She bestowed her gracious smile on him as he listened—attentive but helpless. Like me in the notary's office when we finalized the deal, I realized, he was basically at the mercy of Gwened's translation. However, it occurred to me that Denis didn't need the broadax of the *Code Napoléon* poised over our heads. He had something better: Gwened's disapproval would keep us in line.

"Now, Denis, I have a question for you." Speaking French, Gwened pivoted as deftly as a prosecutor grilling a surprise witness. "Don and Mindy want a *maison saine*."

Denis LeReveur nodded. "*Oui, une maison saine, c'est bonne.*"

I stared at them in confusion. Were they really saying we wanted a "sane house"? What was this, a commentary on our state of mind? Or was it a Freudian slip in translation? None of the above, Mindy explained. *Saine* meant healthy, only not quite the way we meant healthy. More like spiritual health. Or, yeah, mental health. Just not *crazy* mental health.

The conversation turned even more arcane when Gwened turned

to Denis. "Don and Mindy will want two bedrooms upstairs. Are you going to observe the Golden Mean?"

Denis nodded. "Of course, the house will be in proportion."

"So this means you will not raise their roofline higher than the neighbor's. Correct?"

Mindy shot me a surprised glance. The bedrooms were a given; we'd discussed them with Gwened, but this was the first we'd heard about the roofline or the Golden Mean. I knew what Mindy was thinking. We might have to be careful that Gwened didn't take too firm a hand on the tiller. It was our house, after all. And our money. *All* our money—that we didn't have.

Denis tried to be diplomatic: "The roofline *could* be higher, but, of course, it would not look as nice. But if it is not raised, then the chambers will not be as tall."

To me, this sounded as if Denis was signaling to us that not only could we have a taller roof, but we should. Our roof would simply jump a few feet taller. Our neighbor—who didn't live in the house, and whom we'd never met—would learn to live with it. He had to: we shared a wall.

Mindy must've had the same idea, because she leaned forward eagerly. "Well, if you *really* think the chambers would be too small…"

Gwened put down the hammer like an auctioneer: "It must be the same height as the neighbor's. Because we must preserve the proportions, and because the neighbor would never forgive Don and Mindy and might even petition the Mairie of Sauzon, who might find it better for the roof to be lowered, which would be terribly expensive. *Right*, Don and Mindy?"

Gwened's sudden vehemence made cowards of us all. We nodded, visions of crouching around and banging our noggins in a low-ceilinged bedroom running through our soon-to-be-bruised heads.

Now Denis looked relieved. Had he been hiding his misgivings about raising the roofline? Perhaps. Not an easy man to read, that Denis LeReveur.

The next subject was windows for the upstairs bedrooms, about which Gwened *also* had definite ideas. "The window cannot be too large, if it is flush to the roof."

Denis nodded yes. "A large window flush is a bad idea. It will leak. It will compromise the integrity of the roof."

"Then perhaps it's better to only have a skylight." When Gwened looked to us for assent, I realized she'd planned this, too. No windows in our bedroom, just a skylight sending down a dusty beam? At this rate, we'd be living in a crawl space with no light at all. As I took a deep shaky breath to voice my first-ever dissent to Gwened Guedel—knowing it could have untold consequences, none of them good—Mindy's voice rang out:

"We *must* have windows!"

Gwened looked at her in surprise, eyebrows arched in disapproval. "But your neighbors have no windows. You will have disturbed the look of their house by having windows."

"I am an artist," Mindy said in French. "A child of the sunny isles of Hawaii. And I have been suffering in our dark box of an apartment in New York City for too long. Sometimes I feel I'm going mad. *Mad!* When I am in Belle Île, I *must* have light. *Light!*"

We braced ourselves for the backlash, but neither Gwened nor Denis seemed shocked by this *cri de coeur*. Perhaps, in France, taste must be performed to be taken seriously. In any event, one upstairs window went into the approved column on the preliminary *devis*. Apparently the way to a sane house was through an insanity defense.

It felt good to win a round, but Gwened was already moving ahead to the next one. "The color of the tiles along the roofline should be black, don't you think, Denis?"

"The neighbor chose red tiles," Denis said, craning his neck. "She must think we live on the Côte D'Azur, not the Côte Sauvage." He laughed.

"Black is traditional. It will be black, then." Gwened folded her hands on the tabletop as if that settled it, like a poker player standing pat.

Denis eyed the roof a while longer, then gave a slight shrug. "Don't you think it might look a little odd, if the black tiles were to begin where the red tiles leave off?"

Gwened no doubt thought the traditional choice would please him, a true *Bellilois*, but she didn't betray an emotion one way or another. "That is an interesting point," she allowed. "Perhaps Don and Mindy can offer to replace her tiles with black ones."

Mindy's eyes flared, and I nearly choked on my Kir Royale, but Denis was ahead of us, pointing out that the roofline tiles on the barn across the way were also red. At this, Gwened conceded that on certain occasions a uniform look trumped tradition.

With this compromise, a rhythm was established. Gwened or Denis would deal a renovation card, then raise or see the other's bet, and ours, then call. There were many issues to discuss, many hands to play. But at least we had started to get a hang of the rules of the game.

But as the discussion continued, for some reason I began to feel slow, distracted. I had to remind myself that I should be fully engaged in creating our dream house. This was our one shot, after all; the choices we made here would please us, or haunt us, over the next fifty years. But glancing around at the surrounding houses and the square, visible in glimpses from Gwened's courtyard, I blinked at the bright afternoon and was filled with an emotional undertow that felt like dread. Yet everything was so quiet, so peaceful. And then I knew.

It's the sun.

We'd only been here in the *Sturm und Drang* of winter. We'd loved the whole Côte Sauvage thing: fast-moving storms, lingering fogs, brutal looming combers breaking on the beaches and cliffs. We'd felt positively ecstatic at glimpses of the sun: those brilliant gold jets stabbing down like searchlight beams from the blue-black clouds scudding past.

This was so different. This was a hot, naked sun. For a moment I actually contemplated grabbing Mindy by the arm and shouting, *Hey, do you notice? It's sunny! Let's go to the beach!*

But we still had pages of the *devis* to review before we could rest. Here was the dreaded flip side of becoming a homeowner in France. Looking over at Mindy, I could tell she felt the same urge to run away as we always had, to just wander out into the moor. Instead, here we were, talking about red versus black tiles, stuck in our chairs for what seemed like an eternity. It was intolerable to be nattering on when an entire island beckoned. We'd plunged into the very trap we'd tried to avoid.

I quietly panicked, letting Mindy carry on.

Gradually the village swam back into focus. As my gloom lifted, I felt a surge of pride in our best enduring value as a couple: a carefully calculated recklessness. Unlike many of our peers, or our siblings, we'd flown the coop, gotten out, made our own way. We didn't settle. And this was going to be good. Belle Île would combine permanence, which we had feared so much, with our New York City existence, where we were always living by our wits. There was logic there, a balance we'd been seeking all our lives. And maybe this time we'd get it right.

As for that constant low-grade dread... *Of course you feel strange! You've never owned or renovated a house before! Much less a ruin. Not to mention one in France. You've never even bought new furniture.* No wonder we felt dizzy and somewhat at a disadvantage. This was our first time sitting down with an architect, or even a carpenter. It was a miracle that Denis was listening to us. Didn't he know we were idiots?

Besides the newness of the experience and the fat, naked, indolent sun, what was also disorienting, I decided, was the power dynamic. We were in a triangle, but we hadn't acknowledged the fact. And so we were getting worked.

Time to apply my novelist superpowers and figure out what the hell was going on. Gwened was at the apex. As the self-appointed guardian of the village and our sponsor, she brought a lot of moral authority to bear. Given her own extensive renovations, her local roots, and her unassailable Frenchness, she'd usurped the lead, luring us here, choosing the house and even the architect. She'd come into the meeting fully expecting to control the process, her need sharpened by the ticking of mortality. For whatever reason, she was determined to allow as few changes as possible to our house.

The second point of the triangle was Denis LeReveur. As a young architect starting out, as a local competing with Parisian architects for clients, Denis was in a quandary. He needed our commission, but he needed one that would make a good impression on *les autres*, the "others" as off-islanders were called. A windowless Breton restoration might not do the trick. However much Gwened might've expected him to accede to her demands, Denis had formed his own assessment. But he'd waited for us to arrive, to sit down at the table, before revealing it.

That's how I read the dynamic. Denis was in our corner and a lot more flexible than Gwened expected. Much closer in age to us, he had a rogue's twinkle in his eye. He'd just shown both his bemusement at and underlying sympathy for our situation—and why not? We were the clients, not Gwened.

Of course, we couldn't just hand over the reins to Denis. No doubt he was eager to exploit his commission with these deep-pocketed Americans, children of the Yanks of yore. We'd have to expect a certain amount of give-and-take, with an emphasis on take. But at least Denis had agreed to observe the Golden Mean and to give us a sane house. It could all work out. Right?

When I looked over at Mindy, she was smiling back at me. I could swear that she knew exactly what I was thinking. We'd withstood the first wave; now it was our turn to really think about what we wanted in this place we would call our own, and what our role would be in the village, this community. It was an exciting prospect. We didn't have to be idiots forever. For the first time in our headstrong lives, we'd found something that could make the idea of responsibility inspiring.

Chapter Seven
Seeing and Believing

Y ou have done well," Gwened said after Denis departed and we had eaten lunch. The portions were no less austere than those a couple months before and there was no bread, almost unthinkable in a French home. Perhaps Gwened read my expression, because with furrowed brow, she asked if there was any way that I might *somehow* possibly *still* be hungry.

"Oh, no!" My competitive spirit, aroused by the *devis* dealings, refused to allow me to admit any weakness.

"I'm so glad to hear it," she replied. "The last time Daniel came home, he had a fit! One forgets how much boys need to eat—especially Americans."

A bit put out at being compared to a boy, I gave a private cheer for Daniel, last seen throwing a typewriter five years ago. With a mother as controlling as Gwened, a little rebellion could be healthy.

Gwened clapped her hands. "Why don't we take the bikes and ride to the beach?" she asked, which brought forth sighs of relief. This is what we'd come for, after all. At last the details of house renovation could wait. We hauled three-speeds out of Gwened's shed and hopped aboard, weaving downhill between deep ruts, skidding around a turn, then standing on the pedals to get up the first hill.

We were passing the old farmhouse behind our house when we saw its owner, Madame Morgane, wearing her familiar light blue apron over her darker blue shirtdress. At our squeal of brakes to say hello, Madame Morgane reared back, retreating into the dark tunnel of overarching elms. Muttering and shaking her head, she vanished through her door.

"She didn't recognize you. She thinks you are tourists," said Gwened. "She hates the summer, with all the strangers. We will drop by this evening to remind her of who you are." With a shrug, we kept going.

But I wished we'd stopped. Madame Morgane was not just our back neighbor; she was the heart and soul of Kerbordardoué. It was her door we'd first come to, late that January night, in search of the key to Gwened's house. We'd tiptoed up, inhaled, knocked. *Quelle consternation!* A crashing in the dark, a shout from within, Mindy shouting back. Then a bolt thrown, the door opened a crack, and a wild-haired, wall-eyed, outraged face glaring out.

Pleased to meet you, too, Madame.

The next morning, our first on Belle Île, had found us lying abed, shivering, peering through cracked eyelids and lace curtains at Madame Morgane, who was calling and whistling outside our window. At first I thought this was payback. But slowly a line of cows filed past, trudging toward a twenty-foot haystack. She raised a pitchfork against the rising sun and began hurling clumps of hay over her shoulder to the herd.

At one point she turned and stared directly into our window. The way her blue-black eyes pierced the flimsy lace curtains, as if seeking our faces, was too much this early. We rolled over and went back to sleep, only to wake up later to find Madame standing by the haystack, pitchfork in hand, staring through the window at us again. Though her face was in darkness, a bold slash of morning sunlight crossed her chest like a sash.

"She looks like Death dressed as a Girl Scout," I muttered.

"This is getting creepy." Mindy groaned. "Can't you do something?"

I got up and walked to the window and tried to pull the stiff velvet drapes closed.

"Don't!" Mindy cried. "Put some clothes on!"

But Madame Morgane didn't move. She didn't betray a bit of awareness that a naked American man was standing on the other side of the glass. Puzzled, I snapped the drapes shut.

Later that day, Mindy came back breathless from a chat in the lane with Franck's wife. "It took a while, but I finally wormed it out of her. Madame has cataracts."

"So?"

"That's why she stares at our house—not because she can see us, but because she can't."

During the rest of that first winter's stay on Belle Île, we'd occasionally sense something, turn, and see her standing there, way across a raw, furrowed potato field, a tiny figure barely perceptible against a windbreak of dark, soggy cypresses, fixing her blind eyes upon us.

We got used to it. But we couldn't bring ourselves to drop by her farmhouse, per Gwened's instructions, to buy our butter and eggs. Madame Morgane's expression was so severe, her alarm and shock the night we arrived so violent, that we'd actually become a little afraid of her. It seemed less of a hassle to cycle the five miles to Le Palais to do our grocery shopping. One day, though, just as one of the proprietresses rang up our eggs, who should happen to walk in under the tinkling bell but Madame M.

Funny how sharp her eyes could get when she really needed them. "What, are my eggs not good enough?" she grunted.

After stammering excuses and apologies, we fled the shop, but not before hearing Madame Morgane turn to one of the shopkeepers and proclaim, with a snort, that Mindy spoke French like an immigrant. It was a long, sweaty hour's ride back, up and down hill and dale, our humiliation compounded by being buzzed by a gray-haired hell-raiser on a moped, baguettes extended at half-mast from both of her saddlebags. Madame M again!

Back at the village as night fell, we unpacked hungrily, only to discover that my rough pedaling had broken the eggs. They'd oozed deep into my knapsack. Without them, dinner would be thin soup.

The sensible thing to do was to buy more eggs from Madame Morgane. But this was also a worst-case scenario, so, of course, Mindy made me go. Would the legendary charm of Young Strudel, especially his mangled pronunciation and gender-bending pronouns, arouse pity instead of scorn?

When I returned, ducking under our low kitchen doorway and handing Mindy just one egg, the inevitable conversation ensued. "*One* egg? What? Didn't you say anything?"

I reminded her of Madame's pointed glance at the dozen eggs we'd bought in Le Palais. Mindy considered. Sighing, she rose and got her jacket off a hook. "Come on, we're going over."

"Why? I was just there."

"Because we insulted her." Mindy took a wicker market basket off the wall, paused, then picked up the lonely egg and handed it to me. "Gwened warned me. The *Bellilois* are very prickly. They take offense and they hold grudges. We don't want Gwened to get a bad report of us from Madame Morgane, the way she did for the Neil Young guy"—who, having arrived with a couple of other American students, had played his guitar and organized sing-alongs that lasted deep into the night.

The villagers had never heard Neil Young before and were traumatized. To hear Gwened tell it, the incessant refrain of "Don't let it bring you down. It's only castles burning" had turned cows' milk sour and stopped hens from laying for weeks.

"But if you knew all this beforehand?" I asked.

"I don't want to eat dirty farm eggs! That's how you get salmonella."

I shook my head at her. It was risk salmonella or starve. Our stomachs finally won out and Mindy knocked next door. A chair scraped, and the door opened. Summoning her most docile expression and dulcet Tours accent, Mindy charmed Madame Morgane with protestations of apology and mortification, going all the way back to our late arrival the first night and failure to pay a call. Madame's fixed scowl softened—until the subject of eggs came up.

Treading carefully, Mindy thanked her for the one egg and asked if giving it had caused a hardship, perhaps preventing Madame Morgane from baking a cake or making *crêpes*? Because, if so, we could always return it. At Mindy's nod, I produced the egg from my shirt pocket and held it aloft.

Non, non, non, said Madame. The hens would lay again tomorrow. Well, exhaled Mindy, then perhaps it *was* true, as Madame Guedel had seemed to say, that one could find eggs here? Perhaps even enough to feed this large, dim-witted American man who was always hanging around and spoke less French than a duck? I frowned at Mindy, who looked pleadingly at Madame M.

"*Beurre aussi.*" And butter, added Madame Morgane. "*Entrez.*"

She stepped aside and we ducked our heads under the wooden lintel, entering a stuffy, crowded room. It was narrow, its once-yellow walls impastoed with a sticky brown sludge of age, smoke, butter, cigarettes, cat hair, fish scales, and who knows what else. A plain tabletop was against one wall, a large dark armoire against the other.

The hearth was small, a blackened hole set with smoke-bleared tiles. The two-burner stove was hooked to a propane tank. A smell of ammonia pricked my nostrils. At the table sat a man: very old, gaunt, narrow of head, mustached, unshaven for days, a dense patch of hair swirling straight up, eyes deeply set, filmed over, fixed straight ahead on nothing.

Madame Morgane beckoned us to the chairs on our side of the table. "*Café?*" she asked. This I could understand, *café* being the first word out of my mouth on so many mornings in freezing Paris. Her offer at seven at night touched me. It seemed we were to have a proper visit.

And Mindy had brought her proper manners, honed in conversation with Gwened and her family, but also instilled by her Grammy Nez, an unyielding and, it has to be said, intimidating presence who lived alone in the Connecticut woods, pounding animal skins with giant mallets (for bookbinding purposes) as if in some fairy tale.

While the man and I stared away from each other at right angles, Mindy and Madame Morgane spoke in a measured cadence: unrushed, choreographed by the time it took water to boil and coffee to brew, each remark punctuated by the stirring of spoons and dipping of sugar cubes, nothing topical to be discussed beyond the weather and its effect on the plants and animals.

"*Le temps, n'est pas trop beau, oui?*"

"*Non, mais c'est très beau pour les fleurs, il n'est pas?*"

"*Oui, pour les fleurs, il n'est pas trop mauvaise.*"

For me, this maddening waltz of the double negatives suddenly found a counterpart: the childhood tea parties beloved by my Southern grandmother Gigi. All those hours of boredom after Sunday school now paid off. As I'd previously experienced in Imerovigli, in the sitting room of Yanni the Greek's parents, the crucial difference between city and village psychology may best be explained by something called "the manners of time."

The conversation crawled to Madame's satisfaction. Only after twenty minutes did the old man speak: a muttered interrogative. Madame Morgane replied: "*Lui? Américain.*"

"*Américain?*" At last his eyes moved, fastened on me.

"*Oui.*" I nodded for good measure. He nodded.

"*Américain,*" he repeated. "*Pas Allemand.*" Suddenly the armoire began to rattle and shake. There was a sound, high and cackling—like a chicken. What was in there? Was *this* where Madame got her eggs?

The doors of the armoire flew open, and out popped the head of a little lady, mouth wide open like a baby bird's, skin white and wrinkled, with tiny red dots on each cheek. She was talking, or trying to, as Madame Morgane got up and deliberately made her way to a shelf where she removed a tiny pair of dentures from a glass of water.

Teeth in, the little lady chirped excitedly, eyes bright. She was the oldest person I had ever seen by a wide margin; also, probably the smallest. The bedding inside the armoire was fluffed around her like cotton wool in a cardboard box. We stood to pay our respects; when the chirping bird held out her hands, Mindy took them and then gently covered them with hers to warm them. The smell of ammonia returned, stronger.

Another quarter hour passed before Madame Morgane made a suggestion that perhaps it was time for bed. After all, the cows were already asleep. To the tiny bird in her box, she suggested that perhaps we would come by earlier tomorrow.

Bien sûr, Mindy said in a tone of pure affection, as if addressing a porcelain angel whom the slightest off-note might crack.

Only at the end, after Mère Morgane was tucked back into her *lit clos*, closed bed, did Mindy allude to the reason we'd come: to get more eggs. An offhand gesture toward me provoked Madame's first laugh, a gruff bite of air. I knew the crushed eggs in my backpack would be the talk of the village tomorrow. Thus is fame distributed by the gods.

Madame went to a shelf and returned with a stub of butter, and discussed price with an unembarrassed air. We said our good nights. Walking back to the house in darkness unbroken except by stars and the periodic sweep of lighthouse beams, Mindy filled me in: Madame had no more eggs today but would check tomorrow. Some of the hens were playing games with her, hiding their output. Well, she'd show them! And butter, we could have a bit now and then. But no milk—it all went into the steel cans and was taken away by the cooperative.

"Thank god," Mindy added. "I don't think I could drink unpasteurized."

One other thing: "The old man? The reason he didn't speak for so long is because he thought you were a German."

"I guess they have bad memories here, too." In the country we'd found the war still fresh in the minds of the French.

"Actually? I think he thought the Germans were *back*."

I paused to consider what that must've felt like. Was this how the war years had gone, a rap on the door, soldiers dropping in unannounced to buy—or, more probably, to confiscate—eggs and butter? Had they stayed, chatting up the women? What else had they done? Was that why the little bird lady had stayed so quiet in her nest in the armoire?

"Well, that explains his expression," I said, shivering a bit. It was cold tonight. But not as cold as that first few minutes with the old man.

Two minutes later, we'd arrived at Gwened's house. Taking a last look at the night sky and its fast-moving clouds, we rattled the door latch, ducked our heads, and stepped inside. Without a word, Mindy took a black cast-iron frying pan off its hook on the wall. I opened the small refrigerator. Then we set about making dinner: an omelet for two, made with one egg.

※

Not a terribly auspicious beginning to our first stay in the village. Yet, during the next three months, our across-the-lane salutations and across-the-field waves morphed into longer chats. Soon, hardly a day would go by without a visit to Madame Morgane's home. It was from her that we learned the truth about villages: that they are about multiple encounters with the same people every day.

Everything else is of secondary importance to running into each other here, there, here again, there again—a dozen times a day—and that doesn't count the peering, the glancing, the double-taking, and even the spying out of windows, doorways, barn doors, cattle stalls, hedgerows, and lanes.

All of which is to say that it felt a bit wrong to bike on with Gwened and Mindy, leaving Madame Morgane in the dust of our clunky three-speeds. We should've dropped everything, even a trip to the beach, to pay our respects. But Gwened undoubtedly knew best.

Any regrets about Madame Morgane evaporated once our bikes crested the slight hill outside Kerbordardoué and we saw the island's tabletop plateau glowing golden in the full blaze of late summer. Paradise! We'd never seen Belle Île like this. We'd never even *imagined* it like this.

Where the road diverged north-south, Gwened surprised us by turning away from the beach route. "Aren't we going to Donnant?" Mindy called.

"Too many tourists! It's terrible, the crowds! All noise and smells!" She picked up the pace. "Donnant is horrible! You must never go there, except in winter!"

Pedaling on behind her, Mindy and I exchanged a sorrowing glance. Ever since our first visit, we'd dreamed of Donnant's long, empty curving beach. For years we'd talked about going for a swim there, but because it was always winter or early spring on our ensuing visits, the notion remained strictly theoretical. We were water people and we had high hopes, stoked five years ago by Mindy's exclamation at watching wave after glassy wave come crashing down with the zippering finality of a North Shore tube: "Man, these are *intense!* They remind me of Pupukea. You know, I think they're *surfable!*"

The island had a hundred other beaches, including a nice, small cove half a mile from Donnant. But Gwened took us along the central plateau, then down a valley, up the other side, and into a net of continually branching lanes. Passing by fields and stands of trees, we found it beautiful and tranquil except at one place, a crossroads, where we were rudely introduced to the concept of tourist traffic by a pack of speeding Peugeots and Renaults and Citroëns swaying as they zoomed around us, beeping their tinny horns. Back into the lanes we dodged, threading the stone-walled alleys of several small villages with names like Goelan, Bangor, Kervilahouen, Calastren, Herlin… Where were we going?

Finally Gwened stopped. Propping our bikes in a ditch where a newly threshed field ended at one of Belle Île's jagged cliffs, we scrambled down a gully and along thin terraces of blue-green schist until we could drop onto the sand. After spreading out our towels in a rocky nook, Mindy and I walked down to the sea and, for the first time ever on our island, wet our feet.

A surge of foam sluiced around our ankles. We jumped back. *Brrrr…* It wasn't warm, that's for sure, even in the summer heat. We expected that mentally—the island was on a latitude with Labrador, after all—but the reality was tough to swallow. A second surge of icy water slithered up. I stood my ground as Mindy, the Hawaiian, retreated.

"It's the same temp as California," I coaxed.

"Southern?"

"Northern. Like Santa Cruz," where I'd gone to college. Which was an acknowledgment that it was damn cold, in the very low sixties Fahrenheit. But, by taking a deep breath and gritting our teeth, it was within our capability to withstand and maybe even enjoy.

Like astronauts testing the atmosphere on a new planet, we waded in, shuddering, yelping. At last we were in up to our necks, finning. Gasping at the cold. The icy fire of the sea contrasted with the blazing sun overhead, sending conflicting alarms to my nervous system. The mirror-bright glints of sun on the surface already had me squinting when, rotating around to get a 360-degree view, I saw a backlit female form walking sinuously down the sand toward the water's edge. Voluptuous as a goddess, she carried herself with the unself-conscious pride of naked Aphrodite popping out of her scallop shell and traipsing through pink sea foam.

"Um…Mindy?"

"I'm seeing it."

Parting the waves and breaststroking toward us was her old professor, our mentor, muse, and now inspiration in her altogether, Gwened Guedel. What a different Belle Île this was turning out to be. We'd never seen a summer on Belle Île, never felt its heat; we'd never even seen a swimmer, certainly not a nude one. And now: Gwened Godiva.

Of course, *we* weren't that shocked. Not us. Nudism was fine by us, only bothersome because there was an obligation to participate or else be thought bad-mannered or, worse, prudish. But the contrast between this nymph and Gwened—the formerly buttoned-up defender of culture, taste, and grammar—was jarring.

Back on the sand after a frigid ten minutes, we retained our swimsuits, though Mindy set aside her top in sisterly solidarity. Slowly the sun warmed us, a different sun than ours back home, a northern sun. It actually made me want to take my clothes off a little, like a Swede, maybe.

"Don? Mindy?" asked Gwened.

Something about her tone suddenly put me on guard. With nudists in California, particularly those of the hot tub variety, there occasionally comes a delicate moment when someone asks The Question, usually after you've been dodging their foot caresses under cover of dark water. I prayed this wasn't about to be our moment with Gwened. But she *was* a college professor, and life among the professors of California and Iowa had acquainted me with much that, in retrospect, had little to do with book learning.

"Hrrruummm....aoooo..." Mindy was pretending to be asleep, the coward.

"*Oui*, Gwened?" Cringing inwardly at what was to come, I reminded myself not to be flip. Whatever she found comforting, given her cancer, I'd try to understand.

"Have you given any thought to your *fosse septique*?"

Our septic tank? God bless the French! From what I'd learned in May, when I'd come out to inspect the house and make the big decision, few things come closer to the heart in France than a discussion of one's plumbing.

As proof of this hypothesis, Mindy suddenly opened one eye and inquired, in a sepulchral tone: "What about it?" With that, the two topless *demoiselles* launched a discussion that would doubtless have deflated the erotic aspirations of any eavesdropping nudist or voyeur.

❧

While Denis LeReveur was off drawing plans and canvassing contractors for bids, we adopted Gwened's schedule. After her early morning meditation, we'd go off on a cycle or walk; picnic at a beach or cove or valley; stop off in the nearest town, Sauzon, to see what kind of fish the boat had brought in; do a little gardening or some household chores; take an afternoon siesta, pick vegetables from the garden, eat a light supper, and then head back out into the endless evening.

We respected her new regimen: no coffee, few fats, no beef, lots of organic produce. Though it made me light-headed, we even followed her calorie-restricted diet (long before that term was popularized). She explained—the only time she dwelt on her illness—that she'd rejected a radical mastectomy. She just couldn't do it. *En France, les seins sont sacrés.* And so, instead, she was trying to starve the cancer.

After the excitement of the first couple of days of our visit, however, Gwened became melancholy. Her eyelids seemed heavy, her smile *triste*. But she held it in or else talked about her son, Daniel—his talent, his potential. He wasn't a good fit in the rigid French education system; his college studies weren't going well. Perhaps she would send him to a school in the States. She spoke wistfully of our mentoring him. Could we do that? Did we find the life of a writer satisfying? It was so hard to break through in France. It must be so much easier to be a writer in America.

We answered as best we could, conscious that our goal was to give hope to Gwened, not actionable suggestions. It was a bit of a joke, having to pretend to be successful. Mostly, the talk about Daniel only made his absence all the more glaring. Where was he? His college in Paris wasn't more than four hours away. Not that we minded being here for Gwened, but it was a heavy burden to bear, and we weren't family, exactly. If either of our mothers had been diagnosed and gone through treatment and then refused surgery, preferring to self-medicate and thus raise the odds against making it, wouldn't we have come home for the summer?

Finally we slipped away to have coffee and discuss this and other matters with our neighbors, Franck and Ines, who were renovating their own shambling collection of sheds and huts across the lane from us. They exchanged glances. With exquisite silences between arduously chosen words, they hinted that there had been a kind of *rupture*.

The breakup between Gwened and her husband had hit Daniel hard. He'd chosen to take his father's side, perhaps because he feared he'd be losing his mother, anyway. Anger for teenagers is often the only accessible emotion, Ines said. But here, anger was inflicting a deep wound on top of Gwened's cancer.

Accepting the difficult situation for what it was, we sighed and agreed that the best thing we could do for Gwened was to simply follow her lead and support her wherever we could. Teaching was her profession; lecturing came naturally. So we started asking questions. We had a beginner's grasp of island culture and history. But, we asked, could she tell us more? Gwened had a theatrical streak, and once she got started quilting together bits and pieces of *Bellilois* history, she always seemed to grow happier, especially when unveiling like a stage magician some secret island grotto or describing an obscure island custom.

She also revealed her evolving spiritual life. She'd become a Buddhist, she explained, but had not left the Church, even with the divorce. (God and the French having long had an understanding that the soul is too precious to be wasted on dogma.) Naturally, she couldn't resist instructing us, minute by minute, on the intentionality of our every act. We listened respectfully. After all, we were certifiably crazy, too—and had a deed to a ruin to prove it.

We could feel the spiritual and physical halves of Belle Île converging in many places—at a crossroads marked by a fourteenth-century stone cross, at a turning where two massive standing stones kept watch like Celtic sentinels, down inside any of the grottos of the Côte Sauvage. But Gwened helped us see something closer to home when she walked us through her house and pointed out the basics of a Breton *maison saine*: a front door that opened directly into a combined kitchen and common area, centered between stove and fireplace; a long rectangular table with bench seats perpendicular to the door; and a couple of armoires at opposite ends, one for dishes and the other for linens. You drank water or cider from brown clay bowls and ate galettes and *crêpes* off brown plates. The delicate white-and-yellow-trimmed Quimper platters stayed in the armoire, on display, except for rare occasions.

It was a pared-down life, organized around working the family farm, but one that always set a place for beauty. Whether breakfast, lunch, tea, or supper, once everything was washed up and put away, a piece of hand-knit lace was placed on the table and, upon it, a pitcher or bowl with a flower arrangement, inevitably incorporating a large, pale lavender blossom snipped from one's own hydrangea by the front door.

A *maison saine* made sense. If you were going to live in two or three rooms, as many Breton families did, you'd need a house that facilitated cooking and cleaning and chores. You'd also want it to make an orderly and attractive first impression, one not overcluttered or fussily decorated or unduly idiosyncratic. So, no tchotchkes or geegaws. As a point of pride, a *maison saine* had to look welcoming from the get-go—to reflect its occupant's readiness to offer a seat, a cup of coffee, and a slice of buttery *kouign amann* to anyone who happened to drop by.

Disregarding any guilty thoughts about our messy, slightly desperate life back in New York City, we assured Gwened that this was our goal, too. We, too, wanted sanity and promised to create it in our house. But if we thought that would placate her, we were mistaken. Because she was intent on giving us a sentimental education of another order: the basics of a *moral* house.

For a house to be moral it had to belong; it had to be right. And for a house to be right, it had to know its place, which by Gwened's lights meant putting the character and beauty of the village and island above any and all personal claims and architectural pretensions. This was what underlay her anxieties about our roofline, our upstairs windows, our red tiles…and our *fosse septique*. This was the real and true Way of the Island, one we had yet to show that we understood.

Chapter Eight
French Regulatory Style

To a couple of kids raised on the melodramatic landscapes of Hawaii and California, Belle Île was as subtle as an exhalation of wild rosemary after a summer rain, a tone poem of open fields, cypress windbreaks, and neatly clustered villages, all encircled by a fractal fringe of coves, cliffs, and beaches. In place of a grand operatic showstopper, a Mauna Kea or a Yosemite or a Golden Gate Bridge, it offered a little melody that you couldn't get out of your head.

Another thing the island didn't offer was big-city action or Côte D'Azur glitz. Maybe the two-thousand-plus year-round residents of Le Palais thought they were the cat's pajamas, living in the shadow of the looming ramparts of its seventeenth-century fortress, the Citadelle Vauban. But the most impressive, pervasive, and surprising thing about Belle Île was an absence, one that we noticed and reregistered every single day: there were no tourist villas jammed up to the edge of the coast and no cookie-cutter developments, unlike everywhere else we'd been in the developed world, whether in Crete, Santorini, Hawaii, Long Island, or California.

Right up to the moment we'd initiated the buying process, we'd assumed this was a magical accident, that people just loved Belle Île too much to despoil it. But first Sylvie, our Breton lawyer, and then Gwened, our one-stop mentor and architectural muse, had set us straight. There was no invisible hand to preserve the island. But there was an iron one: government regulations enforced by local zoning.

The coast was off-limits; building was kept within village borders; and since 1765, almost every new house in the one hundred fifty-two villages had turned out white-walled, slate-roofed, and designed to the same floor plan. The rare exceptions predated the regulations—such as the elegantly skinny, early-eigthteenth-century townhouses crammed in along the quays of Le Palais and Sauzon—or else were one of the island's three large hotels. Brazen yet low-rise, these were tucked away and out of sight, unlike those in Mindy's flashy Waikiki.

A process of preservation that could survive two centuries fascinated us. The old Waikiki had vanished in the ten years of Mindy's childhood: hotel building had destroyed the shoreline, the reef, and its sea life. The Greece we'd seen was a disaster of unregulated development: cheap cinder block additions, concrete mixers in every yard, and sewers discharging directly into the sea. And I'd grown up during the great tract house explosion in Los Angeles, with shag-carpeted beachfront and high desert right before my eyes in hundred-mile swathes.

Later, working in Central California, I'd seen how it was done: houses stapled together in a week, then given a spray coat of paint and a filigree of prefab embellishments punched out of a sheet of plywood. One day, while painting false-front dovecotes that would go under the eaves of tract homes, I had the revelation that the children in this house would grow up waiting for the birds, and they'd never, ever come. It seemed like a nasty trick to play, and I wondered about the minds behind it. Surely someone had come up empty in the soul department. But was I any better, making my $11.25 an hour, going back to my trailer, and eating pizza from a box with a six-pack of Bud?

Once that job was done, I never worked construction again. But I kept seeing those birdhouses everywhere, along with giant billboards: "Welcome to Highland Castle Park, Regency Uptown Estates, Alta Huntington Arms…"

So how did Belle Île save itself from a similar fate, from the overdevelopment, the overpopulation, the craziness with cars that engulfed Saint-Tropez and Cannes in the south or the isles of Jersey and Guernsey to the north? Where did all these *moral* houses come from? Or, more to the point, how and why and when did the people here decide to take a different path than the obvious one of bigger, cheaper, uglier?

The answer, once we skip over the first 30,000 undocumented years, emerged from an irreproducible mix of war, sardines, valor rewarded and ruinous folly, literary and artistic fame, and location, location, location—in particular, happening to be the place where some of the earliest icons of celebrity culture frolicked for the news media.

From the start, Belle Île was one of those Helen of Troy islands, always seemingly desired by somebody, always starting wars. Populated by toolmaking Mesolithic and then Neolithic peoples since 7000 BC—when it may have been connected to the mainland at low tide—the island was always a stopover between the Mediterranean and Northern Europe. Phoenicians paused to water and provision while picking up loads of tin from Cornwall's mines; they were probably the first *étrangers*.

Basque whalers, pirates, monks in rowboats: every navigator knew Belle Île as the safe place to put in, away from the mainland's sweeping tides and rocky coasts. But it first entered recorded history around 56 AD as the site of a Roman naval battle won by Brutus, with his superior, Julius Caesar, looking on. After the Roman Empire collapsed in the fifth century, the island proved hospitable to mainland Bretons and monks from Redon but, unfortunately, all too handy for foreign navies, Viking raiders, and more pirates.

Around 1000 AD, the Benedictines took over and turned the land to cultivation. The King horse-traded the Benedictines off the island in the sixteenth century because of their inability to stem piracy and as a reward for a battle-tested Medici partner, Albert de Gondi, who also received Provence on the same day in 1573. (A *good* day to be a Gondi.) After a hundred years of the Gondi family, Nicolas Fouquet, the flamboyant, Trump-esque finance minister of France, made the Italians an offer they couldn't refuse.

The Benedictine order had run Belle Île like a forced labor camp, yoking together men to pull plows and making them sleep in barracks. The Gondis developed trade and fishing. Fouquet had a different notion: turn the place into a Fantasy Island, complete with strolling musicians strumming mandolins. In three years his vision rivaled Versailles. But Louis XIV, the Sun King, was jealous and suspicious of the expense. Fouquet was arrested and returned to Paris, it is said, by none other than d'Artagnan of the Three Musketeers. It does not do to rival the Sun.

One hundred years passed. The most important event for the *Bellilois* was now at hand: the island's 1761 capture by the English. France would lose that war with England, and when the redcoats sailed from Le Palais two years later, the farmers and villagers were given title to their land and homes. Imagine that: a monarchy giving the means of production to the people. Or this: a democratic redistribution of wealth before the American Revolution started a decade later or the French one after that.

Losing the war also meant France lost North America, and in 1765 the Minister of Defense got the idea of sending some of the Acadians expelled from Maine, Cape Breton, and Prince Edward Island to reinforce Belle Île. *Le Grand Dérangement*, as it was called, settled seventy-eight families on the island. Many were separated from their relatives, some of whom ended up in Louisiana, where they became known as Cajuns. The Acadians of Belle Île were given a house, a horse, a cow, and thirty measures of land—the amount a farmer could plow in one day. None settled in our village, Kerbordardoué.

Some say the *Bellilois*, who then numbered about five thousand in population, didn't take kindly to having strangers placed among them and given a starter farm complete with animals. But, ironically, the French government wasn't trying to do the Acadians any favors. Far from it. The new arrivals were expected to serve as frontline fodder in the event of invasion and were placed in stone houses of special design, in rows facing outward with no rear doors or windows. It must have been like living in a shooting gallery, knowing that, if the redcoats were coming, the commandant at the Citadelle would pass out muskets and force you to stay and fight until slaughtered.

Fortunately, neither the Acadians nor the *Bellilois* had the leisure to sit around waiting for the next war. And while they may have held a grudge for the next two hundred years, they mixed, danced the two-step at the *fest-noz*, and married. They also applied the Acadian custom of exterior decoration to the new Breton style of house. This usually took the form of a thin band of color stenciled around the windows—pink or pale blue, more rarely yellow. The color of the wooden window shutters was pale green for farmers or blue marine for sailors.

By the time the next invasion rolled around—the German one in 1940—the idea of the house as pillbox was moot. It would be nice to think that the houses were just too pretty to be used for fighting, but in truth the mass devastation visited on the mainland passed Belle Île by. It was no longer of strategic importance.

What it *had* become was a fishing center, way back in the 1850s. After a brief boom in sending lobster to Paris on the new railway, the island became one of the first places to export tinned sardines. The perfecting of a safe method of canning food—by a Frenchman, Nicolas Appert—created a Gold Rush in the little fish, heretofore rare and a favorite of gourmands.

The island served as a home base to a thousand *chaloupes*, sloops slung with nets, their cantilevered masts making a forest out of every estuary and creek. When this fleet came in after netting one of the enormous sardine schools that swarmed the Bay of Biscay, the entire island population gathered at the Le Palais cannery and worked straight through until the last can was sealed.

The wealth of sardines stabilized the fortunes of Belle Île during a time of upheaval and industrialization elsewhere. Many *Bellilois* owned *chaloupes* or took shares of the catch; the rest made cash from canning. This money went into the pockets of the naturally frugal *Bellilois*, raising their standard of living and allowing them to hang on to their farmlands and houses. Even after the sardines mysteriously vanished in 1911—the same year they disappeared from the Monterey commemorated in John Steinbeck's *Cannery Row*—the island retained a proud identification with the noble pilchard. And, fortunately, by 1900 the island had found a new fish to fry: tourists.

Tourism elsewhere has been synonymous with development and the death of a regional culture. Belle Île was lucky to be separated from the mainland by twenty miles of water, and lucky that the first tourists followed on the heels of poets and painters, particularly Claude Monet and John Peter Russell. Visited by the most famous person in the world in 1900—Sarah Bernhardt, who was the Muhammad Ali *and* Lady Gaga of her time—Belle Île famously won her heart and hand.

Bernhardt bought a retired fortress on the most forbidding piece of coastline, made the island her home between world tours, and ensured that Belle Île would be the center of many a news story by doing such well-publicized stunts as shooting seabirds while lying in bed taking her morning coffee and receiving the Prince of Wales for a farewell-to-all-that night of love while en route to his coronation as king.

By the time the national railroad service began flogging the masses into motion with the notion of tourism, Belle Île was perfectly positioned in a number of ways to thrive without losing its soul. First, most tourists chose to stay on the mainland, convenient to the railroad terminus, which had the effect of turning Belle Île into a day trip. The closest mainland towns, Quiberon and Carnac, got the Edwardian-era hotels, the arcades and dance halls, the promenades along the beach with their endless cafés, and the bustle-skirted ladies with parasols and yapping poodles.

Belle Île became the place to go for a breather from all the froth and excitement, a place to take a deep breath and enjoy nature like a celebrity, as sublime spectacle. You came, you swooned, you sunburned, you went home. Plenty of trinkets, saltwater taffy, and postcards got sold in

Le Palais, but the island's beautiful vistas and vertiginous coastal crags were left alone—and still are.

But how did the *Bellilois* manage to control their fate during all this, or at least keep their dignity and their land? Why didn't they pander, succumb to temptation, take the money, and run? Perhaps the money wasn't good enough. Perhaps they were just stubborn, preferring to live on their farms the way their forebears had. In *The Old Regime and the Revolution*, Alexis de Tocqueville (famous for *Democracy in America*, but equally on point about his native country) speaks of the intensity of the peasant's attachment to the land. Alternatively, perhaps the *Bellilois* were never taxed to the point of surrender by developer-controlled city councils, which is California's story.

As part of the refurbishing of France's architectural patrimony that went on after World War II, someone in the national government must've realized natural beauty deserved protection—probably someone with a second home on Belle Île, who after a trip to Saint-Tropez appreciated its harmony anew, saw how easily it could be lost, and in 1975 managed to push through zoning that would protect the coastlines from development. Other laws soon forbade deviation from the stripped-down style of Breton *maison*.

Not everyone was happy to have their options restricted; every family with land has a member who'd gladly bulldoze for dollars. Every decade there has been a fight over expanding village limits to allow development. But today anyone with eyes can see the regulatory experiment validated: just drive or take the train out on the Quiberon peninsula to the ferryboat landing at Port Maria and you'll see a crazy quilt of houses and neighborhoods and villages jammed together, every structure bloated, Hobbity, touristy, and grotesquely corrupted by the freedom reinforced concrete affords to tiny, kitschy minds.

This was French regulatory style on Belle Île, and this was why we were hiring Denis LeReveur. Because if we were to ask for a non-functioning birdhouse under the eaves, he'd tell us *no* straight off. He had to live here. Whereas a Parisian, or any other mercenary from the

Continent, would rub his hands together and ask, "How many chambers for ze bird?"

❧

Our stay was drawing to a close, but we couldn't seem to summon any sense of urgency. The sun stayed up so late at this northern latitude— setting at ten o'clock when we'd arrived in August, now sinking into the mirror-bright Atlantic at eight thirty—that it had confused our internal clocks.

Often we'd find ourselves wandering the moors like Lapland reindeer herders, hours after dinner in the long-extended twilight. In our hearts, we knew this was the summer before the storm of renovation, a last soap bubble of innocence soon to burst. Gwened encouraged us, knowing what was to come. She'd had a baby. She'd restored a house. She knew.

Only nobody knew. What really was about to happen, not even a seer of Gwened's abilities could divine.

For the two weeks that Gwened had been gently but insistently imparting all her knowledge, giving her utmost, staging our days, Mindy and I had conspired to ignore any suggestion that these were "last instructions," her way of passing the torch—just in case. But we could do nothing about the seasonal turning toward fall, and Belle Île's elegiac landscape of dry threshed fields and rolled-up balls of hay, the flocks of sheep moving to new pasture.

Try as we might to ignore it, the metaphor was everywhere. Having our poor ruined house as a focal point allowed us to talk about what otherwise was unspeakable: we would bring it back from the dead. And if we kept faith with the house, perhaps this would be a way of saving Gwened, of staving off the inevitable, of diverting that scythe-toting shade from his appointed rounds.

❧

On our last day, we had another noon drink with Denis LeReveur on Gwened's graveled patio, from which, if we craned our necks, we could just glimpse the slumped roof of our sad little ruin. Denny the Dreamer looked like he hadn't gotten much sleep, but he'd pulled together a sheaf of estimates and sketches, apologizing for their unfinished appearance. They looked fine to us, crisp and professional. More than fine: magical, a house resurrected, better than ever.

"Oh, look!" exclaimed Mindy. "There's a dormer window!"

Denis beamed. One bedroom had a neat A-frame thrusting out like a balcony, overlooking the square. After peering at the drawing, Gwened pulled back with a polite smile that did nothing to hide her disappointment.

"Do we sign now?" asked Mindy.

"No, no," Denis said. He still had to get a few more estimates; some of these weren't nailed down. But there was one thing we could do. He rose from his chair, smiling. "Now we make the handshake." He laughed at our expressions, proud of his one English phrase, and extended his hand.

Mindy and I looked at each other. She nodded. We rose at the same time. Our three hands collided in the center of the table. Laughter, then an exchange of firm handshakes.

"*Bon*," we said over and over.

"Excellent," said Denis. "Very good."

More laughter. Then kisses, including a trio from him for me, our two sandpapery cheeks a prelude to the job itself.

Farewells brought forth more handshakes. And then we said good-bye.

"*Non, pas au revoir*," scolded Denis. "*À bientôt.*"

Not good-bye—see you later.

Once we were alone, Gwened turned up her radiance. "Next year you will have a beautiful house. I guarantee it."

Mindy and I exchanged a coded glance. *Not if we can't pay for it.*

"Maybe we can just get the roof done," Mindy said.

"Hold off on the other stuff," I added.

"I think not," said Gwened.

Suddenly the three of us were back to playing our game of poker: House Hold 'Em. I checked my cards. Mindy laid hers on the table: "We can wait for the *devis* and then just sign for the minimum amount of work to be done."

Gwened shook her head. "Mindy, there is only one opportunity to convert the attic space into chambers, and that is when the roof is replaced. You will need to get as much work done as you can right away. Workmen here have plenty of jobs. They won't wait for you. Everything must be done at once, scheduled so that as soon as one thing is done, the next is ready. Once it begins, it all goes quite quickly. You will see."

"Gwened, we're worried about money," Mindy said. "We didn't think I'd get pregnant."

This was not quite true. While I was in Belle Île inspecting the house and shaking hands on a deal, Mindy had been researching an article on childbirth statistics for *Glamour*. By the time I'd come home, she had a number in her head. That night we went off birth control. The pregnancy made itself known in July, just as our bank balance hit zero.

"I think the *devis* will be quite reasonable," Gwened replied, confidence unshakable. "He will be fair, and he will pick only the best and most honest contractors. They will not gouge you the way they might if you'd hired one of these Parisian architects who come in and think they can have their way, not use local people, and show no respect for the local architecture."

We'd heard this speech before.

"It was a surprise to see the dormer," she added. "He must have spoken with the owner of the neighboring house—he'd have to grant his approval. I'm sure he also spoke with Madame Morgane. The *Bellilois* don't take change lightly. That is why it was so important that you chose a *Bellilois*."

She looked at the drawing of the dormer window again. The roof over the other bedroom had a tiny square in the center: a skylight. She looked at it so wistfully that I almost felt sorry.

Not long after we were back in New York, we had a drink with our Breton lawyer, Sylvie, to tell her our stories and show her the *devis*. She looked at the front-view sketch of the house. Nodded. Spoke:

"Two dormers. No discussion. Each bedroom must have a window for light and for air, and a dormer to extend the square footage. Understand?"

We sent back the change order, our only one.

It would be two years before we set foot on the island again, and eight years before we spent the night in our completed house.

Chapter Nine
The Black Book

Before we'd gone to Belle Île, the owners of our building in Manhattan had sent a letter to say they might turn it into a cooperative to sell the apartments on the open market. If so, state law mandated that renters would get a special insider's deal, half the estimated price, once they signed the initial offering. In New York, these kinds of apartment conversions had been building to a frenzy.

A real estate Gold Rush was going on. All over the city, people prayed for the arrival of the Black Book, as the prospectus was called. For many older renters, going co-op was like hitting the lottery. They could buy their apartments, flip them immediately, pocket a few hundred grand, and buy a cheap condo in Florida.

Straight from the airport and France, we'd dragged our suitcases out of the stairwell and stopped, staring. A thick book lay on our frayed doormat. Not a new phone book, it was the Black Book. What every New Yorker hoped for, we dreaded. For us—subletters, and illegal ones at that—it meant the jig was up. We had no insider's rights. We'd have to move.

Losing our place was bad enough, but then the delayed reaction hit. The cheap rent that had allowed us to save for Belle Île was going away, too. We'd banked on it when signing the *devis* with Denis LeReveur. Where would we get the money now?

At least, if we could hang on for a year or so, we could sock away our savings—although a significant portion would have to go toward forming a war chest for finding a new place. Moving in New York often sucks up half or all of your savings, regardless of how much you have socked away. But even that hope vanished when our neighbors, the only residents of the London Terrace to whom we'd confided our illegal status, invited us over.

"They're going to push everyone out or make them buy in," said Bob. "They've hired a management company that specializes in clearing people out. You won't be able to escape these guys. I've just met with them. Sorry."

But we hadn't gotten this far just to give up, especially with a baby coming. Mindy called the elderly legal tenant, a crusty former gal-about-town who'd once dated Mindy's grandfather. Irene had made it clear that she wanted nothing to do with the apartment; it was ours as long as we could fool the doormen and the management. We'd lasted almost three years, thanks to bribing our doormen lavishly and keeping a low profile—never being seen together, never even taking the elevator to our floor.

Mindy pleaded with Irene to sign the initial agreement, which would take the heat off us by giving management what it wanted, a buyer. "Look," Mindy said, "you can always back out, but down the line they may even make you an offer to take it off your hands. You could make a lot of money."

Irene wasn't impressed. In the end, she agreed to meet and discuss it. But she wanted Mindy's grandfather there. Could we bring him to lunch near her little house in rural Connecticut? We guessed she wanted to get one last look at him, the one who got away.

In a cold slant rain of November that brought down all the faded grandeur of the fall foliage, the two cranky Yankees, former lovers now in their eighties, ate their toasted tuna-fish sandwiches in a diner in

Darien. Then we followed Irene back to her plain, white-painted saltbox cottage, which Mindy's grandfather circled, checking the rain gutters and inspecting for dry rot. Inside, at a rolltop desk, Irene signed the papers. "Okay, kids, I hope you're happy."

She looked at Mindy's grandfather. "Are you happy?"

He snorted. "Don't be silly."

Later, Mindy told me that was when she had her wild surmise, which, as we drove off in the rain, Mindy's grandfather indirectly confirmed. "I bought that house for her," he said. "After I remarried."

All the pieces came together with a brisk click. On our train ride back to the city, Mindy described fuzzy memories of visits to Hawaii from Grandpa and "Aunt Irene" when Mindy was very small and Grandpa was still married to Grandma.

"Irene must've been his mistress." A little later, out of nowhere, she added, "That was when he promised me a pony."

We amused ourselves, as novelists do, with the notion that this plot twist worthy of a French *film noir* might buy us time. If the management didn't kick us out in the next year, maybe we'd even save enough to carry out the renovations of Belle Île. As things stood now, however, we lacked the money for the demolition of the old floor and for pouring the new one and building the staircase. Any downstairs renovation would have to wait.

Mindy wrote Denis and told him to only complete the roof, the twin upstairs chambers with their dormer windows, and the bathroom.

We were doing the thing that Gwened had warned us against: not getting the work done all at once. The agreements and schedules of the workmen would now unravel, with no guarantee or obligation to ever return and finish the job. But we had no choice: all our money was gone.

❧

"Push."

"It hurts."

"Push."

"Oh god!"

"Look at the wave!"

As I'd noticed when we first toured New York Presbyterian Hospital, the plain, white birthing room had a large blank wall opposite the foot of the bed. Thinking of how it would feel to be undergoing the greatest pain short of dying, as our Lamaze teacher had described childbirth—helpfully, I'm sure—I'd packed a poster from Hawaii in our go bag and tacked it up the moment we arrived.

The nurses and doctor were taken aback, but I knew Mindy would be inspired. The poster showed a perfect fifteen-foot Pipeline barrel throwing out a 360-degree lip with a spiraling tube that seemed to go on forever the longer you looked into it. This, I figured, would remind Mindy of the birth canal and give her encouragement.

"Just look at the wave."

"I don't want to look at the wave! *Ow! Ow! Ow!*"

Mindy's brown toes spasmed open and closed. So far everyone in the hospital had noticed and commented on her feet. This nurse, the one who was monitoring her cervix, was no exception. She did a double take: "Good heavens, your toes, they're as wide as fingers!" Luau feet, I explained. Children in Hawaii grow up going barefoot on the sand.

"Shut up! It hurts! *Fuck!*"

The nurse looked shocked.

"*Ow!* It hurts! Oh my God, it hurts! Do something! I can't stand it!"

The nurse leaned forward. "Do you want an epidural?"

"No. No shots."

"Okay, then. I'll leave you two together…" Out the door she went.

"*Ow! Ow! Oh my God!*"

I pointed to the Pipeline. "Okay, look at the wave. Look at the wave on the wall. Look at the tube. You're inside the tube…"

"Oh god, oh god, oh god… I don't *want* to be in the tube! *Fuck the tube.* Oh, oh, oh… It's not helping. The-tube-is-not-helping!"

"Okay, we're going for a walk…"

"A WALK? I'm dying! How can I go for a walk?"

"Shhh… It's an imaginary walk. You have to take your mind off the pain. Here we go."

"I-don't-want-to-go-for-a-walk, GODDAMMIT!"

"We're on Belle Île. Summer. Everything is golden. We're at the top of the road that leads into the valley. The road that runs below Kerbordardoué. We've just left the village square, and you remember how it starts, the walk, with those tall elms and the high hedgerows with flowers making it feel like a deep cool tunnel, and there's Queen's Anne lace growing in the water ditches and…"

"It always stinks, the water in the ditches. It's that damn *fosse* smell."

"Yes, you're right. It really does smell."

"Why does it smell? Whose *fosse* is responsible? I hate that smell."

"It's okay. We're past the water ditches. The smell is gone. Let's keep walking."

"When we get to Belle Île this year, we have to find out and put a stop to it."

"That's right, that's right. And now we're past the water ditches, and we're passing the slope filled with blackberry brambles, and all the berries are ripe and we can stop and pick some on our way back. Look, there are spiderwebs everywhere! Look at that, will you? They're shining with dew and those huge, yellow-bellied spiders are bouncing in the breeze…"

"The valley's so pretty."

"Yes, and look: above us a hawk is hovering. Looking for rabbits."

"There are always rabbits in the pasture."

"Yes!" I felt our imaginations merging. "And just a little farther down, now, look, we're passing the tall cypress windbreak on our right. See how the tips of the cypresses bend in the wind, like the tips of paintbrushes swaying over the sky like a canvas…"

Three hours later, after two or three trips up and down the valley and a long walk along the beach at Donnant, a baby boy was born.

❧

As life got more complicated, options narrowed. Buy a ruin, have a child, sign a paper, bribe a doorman to ignore the stroller in the hall. Now the wife couldn't bear to leave the baby to go back to work, perfectly understandable in light of the ten days he spent in critical care. But that meant it was time for the husband to find a real job, not one like at the boating magazine, with its casual travel itineraries and adventurous, even loopy subject matter.

As for Belle Île, a curious transformation took place after baby Rory's arrival. Suddenly we wanted to see more of our families. Suddenly we understood why our parents had kept stressing how far away France was, thousands of miles in the wrong direction. It was as if our relationships with our parents had reached a turning point, or halfway point, and the rubber band of attachment had snapped us back home.

We also woke up to the fact that they needed us, our support. A couple of years earlier, my parents had skirted bankruptcy in a real estate deal. *Père* Wallace had also suffered a mild heart attack, though nobody would talk about it. Time was no longer on our side. But we had a solution, we thought: like new parents everywhere, we believed our baby could restore animal spirits and morale. And Rory didn't let us down.

Funny how time flies when you're living *La Baby Loca*: May, June, July, August, and September passed before we even noticed that we weren't going to Belle Île that year. Instead, I spent a lot of time on one of the strangest beats in journalism: simultaneously covering the preparations for the upcoming America's Cup in Australia and the antics of the speedboat-racing, cocaine-smuggling kings of the Colombian cartels. It was amusing how blue bloods in tasseled loafers and *jefes* in white jumpsuits could want the same thing: a cover photo on a boating magazine. What was frightening was the lengths both would go to get it.

I spent the first part of 1987 covering the America's Cup in Perth, while Mindy and Rory stayed with her mother and grandfather in

Honolulu. We'd just settled back into life in New York City when a new blow fell: my sister Anne was given a terminal cancer diagnosis.

For anyone, a terrible shock. In the case of someone as vital and generous as Anne, the diagnosis had the effect of a moral crisis: Where had I been? We rushed back the moment we heard. Disliking the fatalistic attitude and ameliorative treatment plan of her doctors, we persuaded her to visit UCLA's top cancer center for a second opinion. Risky and experimental neck and jaw surgery followed. She lived. But her husband sued for divorce. From that moment on, I had to be a better brother and to be as present in Anne's life as I could.

No sooner were we back in New York than the next phase in the co-op transfer arrived, in the form of a request for a nonrefundable thousand-dollar deposit. This would formalize a future purchase agreement. No deposit, no apartment: thirty days to sign or vacate.

So that was it. We'd gained a year; now we had a month. It didn't give us a lot of time to look for a new place, or me for a new job. Any chance of going to Belle Île in 1987 went out the window. We dove into the newspaper listings on both fronts. Rent for a one-bedroom apartment ran about $1,750 a month, and I only made $30,000 a year. So far nobody had given my résumé a second look. Things began to feel more than a little desperate.

Then inspiration struck. Perhaps we'd been living in the same city with Donald Trump for too long. But the implications of Irene turning down the chance to buy finally sank in. There was nothing to prevent us from following the deal to its conclusion, if we had the nerve. There was something dark and a little shady about it that appealed to the New Yorker in us. We'd scuffed about the city, living on pennies. Now we were going to do what investment bankers, Wall Street traders, and other go-getters had been doing for the past ten years of the real estate boom: leverage ourselves and make a killing. With the proceeds we could buy a bigger apartment with a bedroom for the baby. Maybe there'd even be something left over for the Belle Île renovations.

We paid the thousand dollars down by cashier's check, after drawing up a side agreement with Irene, who signed to buy the apartment in exchange for $10,000 of our future gains (and one more supervised visit from Grandpa). Now all we had to do was find me a new job, scrounge up the down payment, get a mortgage, arrange to complete the sale to Irene, and have her flip to us on the same day. Easy.

Then we had to turn around, find a buyer, and flip it again fast. Even if we were on the hook for more than we could ever pay, we figured it was all worth it. For little Rory's sake, of course. In the week or two or three until we flipped and made our killing, we would experience life like financiers, flying high and living dangerously in a leveraged world. *What the heck. We're already on a treadmill. We'll just run a little faster, that's all.*

Not without effort, a key piece of the puzzle fell into place when I got a job at a perpetually struggling small-business magazine. My salary would jump over a third, and we would qualify, barely, for a mortgage if our subterfuge worked. I was sorry to leave *MotorBoating & Sailing*. There I'd worked under my first real boss, Peter Janssen, who'd taught me magazine editing and, with a wry smile, enabled our trips to Belle Île by allowing me to do stories in Brittany and Europe.

I'd made my first friends in the city through the magazine, and many friends in the field. I'd stalked cocaine smugglers and Nicaraguan *contras* in Key West, America's Cup skippers in Perth, Richard Branson in his attempts to break the transatlantic power-boat record, solo ocean racers in Trinité-sur-Mer—the latter *so* conveniently across the bay from Belle Île.

A chapter in my life was closing with real regret. Only as I was leaving *MB&S* did I pause to reflect on how I'd gotten the job in the first place. Or at least cinched it—because when challenged by a snippy New York Yacht Club member during my interview to provide some evidence of nautical ability or experience, I'd broken out the tale of a mad winter's night sail with our neighbor and sometime skipper, Franck, at the helm of his twenty-two-foot sloop. Yes, it had certainly been a near thing during that stormy Bay of Biscay crossing. Why, at midnight the winds reached Force 6 and laid us on our side in crazily foaming seas… We came about and dove into the lee of a rocky islet to spend the night.

Soon after we dropped anchor, a splendid sailing yacht arrived to do the same. A gorgeous woman in a party dress and high heels stepped down into the inflatable dinghy. We watched, soaked and clammy in our foul-weather gear, as her men in formal evening wear handed down a bottle of Champagne and glasses. And then a terrific gust of wind hit and blew her out to sea, into the night, standing up all alone on the dinghy with her arms outstretched, bottle in hand. The men scrambled to raise anchor and give chase, aiming a spotlight on the rapidly disappearing inflatable until…well…

"The woman, what happened to her?" demanded the New York Yacht Club member.

"Never saw her or the yacht again."

"What island was this?" he asked, like a policeman demanding to see my license.

"Houat."

"What?"

"Yes, Houat," I replied. "Slept like a baby."

When the New York Yacht Club member shuddered, I knew I had the job.

Thank you, Belle Île.

My new job came with a different tale. Two weeks before I started at *Success!* and one month before the apartment sale was to be completed, the stock market crashed. It was the largest-ever up to that date: October 19, Black Monday. Mindy and I stood before our ancient black-and-white television, staring at the streaming numbers. What would it mean? The answer came over the next few months. With forty thousand jobs lost on Wall Street, the real estate bubble popped.

But before that was made eminently clear, we'd gone through with the sale, like robots, because we had to. Naturally, it went off like a charm. Only afterward, no buyers queued up at the door. Just like that, we were locked into a dingy apartment at a precrash price in a building full of newly renovated model units going begging for buyers.

Meanwhile, I'd traded a job following the lordly sea for one following the almighty shrinking dollar. The morning I started my new job at *Success!* workmen on stepladders were taking off the exclamation point. People were shouting at each other when I stuck my head in. The receptionist, I was informed, had just been laid off. The publisher was swapping ad space for bartered goods, including a pallet of soft drinks. *Have a Coke, Don?*

Time stands still when you're on a slow treadmill. At home, we were crammed into two dark rooms with a foldaway kitchen in the foyer. Every night the three of us ate at a table sandwiched between our two writing desks, Rory gleefully hurling his dinner and yowling like a banshee. (A happy banshee, I must add.) Every night we folded out our futon-style sofa bed on the floor, while Rory got the crib in the bedroom.

We hung a map of Belle Île in the hallway beside the bathroom door. We put a cracked Quimper vase, found in a Greenwich Village antique shop, on a shelf to hold flowers and remind us of our village's blooming hydrangeas, our *maison saine*.

Sometimes, to console ourselves, we brought out our dreams and gently blew on the embers until they sprang to life. Sometimes we brought out memories of our first winter in Kerbordardoué, shaking them into motion like snowflakes trapped under a dome of glass.

Chapter Ten
The French Position

A second year passed without our seeing Belle Île, except in dreams. At this point in our plan, we were supposed to have sold our apartment and moved to a two-bedroom. Now, prisoners of our mortgage and the recession, we couldn't move up, down, anywhere. A lot of people in New York City were in our position. Nobody was in our French position. As my father took pains to point out, at last we'd succeeded in becoming utterly pretentious: "What's the use of owning a French house if you don't go there?"

Our mothers were worse than exasperated. Watchful already over who would get more time with the baby, they regarded Belle Île as an interloper of flesh and blood. *La jalousie!* Our more sardonic friends picked up on this theme: how *interesting* that we'd picked a spot as far away as possible from our mothers—in Mindy's case, halfway around the world from Hawaii.

The truth of my father's remark became clear when we were contacted by a friend who was the assistant to Adam Smith, famous for his borrowed moniker and as a money columnist who'd blithely promoted the very market madness to which we'd fallen prey. Would we like to be featured in his next column? Sort of a cautionary tale, *heh-heh*, but the exposure could be good for our careers.

Though I was tempted, Mindy saw right through it. "No way we're going to make ourselves into a laughingstock for all the world to see." We didn't need that kind of publicity. What we needed was to pinch ourselves every day and then give thanks that we had such a wonderful baby boy to take our minds off our idiocy.

Rory was certainly bright and curious, a shining little being. He wasn't large, but more than held his own against the other milk-fed monsters in our Chelsea neighborhood. His will was truly something to behold. Two early babysitters quit, each demoralized after Rory went on a Baby Hercules exhibition, shoving and pushing all the furniture into the center of the living room, then climbing atop the pile in triumph.

Meanwhile, the recession reverse-gentrified our neighborhood. Crack vials crunched underfoot, used condoms bloomed like flowers on the withered shrubbery, and transvestite hookers with multicolored Afros nodded off on bar stools at the Empire Diner. They adored Rory. But while we had a beautiful boy, this was not a beautiful life. This was not our *maison saine*. We owned a ruin in a village we couldn't visit and a cave in the city we couldn't leave. We owed every cent we had, and then some, for as far into the future as the eye could see.

As far as we were concerned, all that remained of Belle Île and Kerbordardoué were memories.

※

"Hey, do you remember…?" one of us would ask. Lying flat on our backs in the dark, we'd whisper, careful not to wake the baby. *Sure, sure…* And off we'd go.

One morning that first winter, we woke to the thump of surf echoing in our village square. After admiring the acoustics, funneled up from miles below, we set forth down the valley lane to check out the source. It was another gray winter's day, but windless.

At a low point, where the rutted road dips down to cross a shallow stream, a dozen cows stand around, munching weeds and nettles. We almost miss the man off to one side, in dusty overalls and a long-sleeved undershirt. He's stout and large, with a cylindrical head topped by an oversized newsboy's cap.

"*Bonjour,*" says Mindy. He nods and lifts his cap an inch off his bare skull, his skin the same tawny yellow as his cows.

When Mindy tries a little conversation, he squints at her, mouth open, as if taken aback, so she slows down. The cows flow between us, ruminating. Mindy steps back to let one pass. "He thinks I'm a Parisian," she says in an aside. "His name is Dede"—*day-day*—and when he overhears his name, he ducks his head and shyly looks away. When we say good-bye, though, his face splits into a huge smile.

We hop across the stream, then follow it down a lush meadow of wild grasses and cattails. One side is a hill so overgrown with gorse and vetch and blackberry brambles that it takes a minute to notice that it's actually a huge sand dune. To our right, the valley's opposite slope hangs over the meadow like a dark wave, broken in places by white limestone crags poking through the gorse. Beneath each crag is a cave, like a blind eye socket, turned toward the sea. Immediately I am possessed by a desire to climb the crags, explore the caves—and Mindy has to grab my sleeve. "Down, boy."

We follow the stream as it wends around the dunes, and we hear the roaring of the ocean before we see it. But when we do top the last dune, the sea is in a mad fury, rank after rank of white-water walls exploding and racing forward like cavalry. The odd arena effect that we've noticed before is even more pronounced: the harsh winter light on the sea and spindrift and white sand hurts the eyes. Mindy whirls around to shout: "*It's like 'The Charge of the Light Brigade'!*"

After a long walk above the high-tide line, we reverse our steps and head back up the valley. It's actually a relief when the sound of crashing surf is muffled and we can talk again without shouting. But the effect of the ocean on our spirits is measurable. We're floating along when here they come again, a little farther along the stream, the herd of cows.

This time Dede, the cowherd in overalls and newsboy cap, is more sociable. He hails us first: "*Bonjour!*" He tips his cap, smiling. It seems as if, having had forty minutes to think it over, he's decided this makes us old friends.

What a great, big sweetheart of a guy! With that shy smile, he comes out way ahead of his American Gothic counterparts in all those places where I've lived for most of the last decade: California's Central Valley, Sonoma County, Nipomo, Long Beach, even Iowa City, where Grant Wood painted *American Gothic*. A snap judgment? Sure. Maybe I'm getting sentimental. This valley is so beautiful and the light so pure that it has an exhilarating effect. He's just a cowherd, after all. But at least he's a *friendly* one, and in all my jobs so far—in agriculture, construction, the oil fields, teaching, and most recently, as a sportswriter—I've encountered enough woofing, chest-bumping, and territory-marking to last a lifetime.

While I'm having these rather uncharitable thoughts about the state of my country's yeomanry, Mindy and Dede are chatting away like neighbors over a backyard fence—only it's over the backs of cattle walking slowly to and fro between them. Mindy goes from looking askance to a little alarmed, then more alarmed, because it does seem that Dede is somehow making the cattle parade back and forth, to judge from the glottal clicks, whinnies, whistles, and snickers that issue from the side of his mouth, even as he is making small talk with my wife.

Gradually Mindy backs away, despite Dede's increasing flow of chat. She steps close to me. "Time to go," she says brightly, our old signal that something, or someone, is getting out of hand. Since Dede is smiling, shyly but proudly, I figure it's just the cows.

In the spirit of Franco-American amity, I step forward, daring to slip between a pair of slo-mo Bossies—though not without eyeing their docked horns—to extend a hand to Dede. He's diffident, shy, looking away as he shakes it. "*Bonsoir*," I said. He nods, mumbles.

"Don." Mindy gives me the look that goes with the old signal. "He just asked me to *marry* him."

"Ah."

"He says he is the owner of twenty cows and a house and barn. He says the cows do not sleep in the house with him, but in the barn with his sister."

"Okaaaay…"

"So can we please go now?"

"Sure. You bet. Time to go." I turn, wave to Dede. *"Au'voir."*

As I reach Mindy's side and we turn to go, Dede raises his fingers to his lips. We're edging around the cattle, trying to get on the path, but in the mud and cow pies and trampled cattails, the going is slow, slippery, *fragrant.* Dede gives a long, sharp whistle, loud and commanding. The herd of cattle pause in their chewing and raise their heads. Dede whistles again, piercing. There is a moment of gathering tension. Then, as one, the cows empty their bladders. There is a thunder-in-the-mud sound, like that of a heavy rain in a land of monsoons. Steam rises around us. We are surrounded by a low-lying cloud bank of piss.

And then we're running, if not quite for our lives, then at least to put as much ground between us and Dede as we can in one breath.

Once we are safely up the steep valley lane and out of sight, we break into gasps, then giggles. "Quite a trick!" Mindy shudders. "Do you think I'm supposed to be flattered?"

"Totally. He's got magic. Like Merlin. The old spells, that kind."

"How come you've never done anything like that for me?"

"Don't get me started…" I fake a grab for my pants zipper. She lets out a little shriek. "Well, look at it this way," I continue, trying to sound like someone who's taking the long view, a man of the world's view—a *French*man's tolerant view of this attempted dalliance under my nose. "At least your accent must be good, if he thought you were from Paris. And he did offer to do the honorable thing by marrying you."

"I think he says that to all the girls."

"Uh-huh."

"No, I mean, really. I do feel sorry for him. He was so proud when he told me about his cows and his house. I think he really is very lonely."

Once sympathy enters the picture, all appetite for even the gentlest kind of teasing fades. We continue in silence, enjoying the chatter of the nesting birds, the soughing of the wind in the treetops. The road up to the village turns into an alley of windbent cypresses, their tops dense and green, their trunks reddish-gray and weathered, marked by old and new scars where branches have been twisted and broken off by the storms of the Côte Sauvage. The sun at our backs lights the center stripe of grass, leaving a trail of red-gold for us to follow. Somewhere behind and far below a cow gives vent to a lonely moo.

※

At times memories were not enough, and we succumbed to doubt and despair. Did we make a mistake? Would we ever get back there?

Perhaps most alarming was how sometimes, when we shook the imaginary paperweight to reawake our memories, nothing happened. To fail to summon the spirit of Belle Île was desolating. Here's a question for philosophers: Has something you can't remember ever happened? What we thought we had on Belle Île, who we were there, was vanishing.

In our different ways, Mindy and I both struggled with how badly we'd managed things. The apartment was sucking us dry. My job at *Success* was purgatory, punishment for a literary dreamer. Several of my coworkers were in the same straits, chained to mortgages and babies like galley slaves on a ship of fools. We consoled each other and conspired on plans for escape. But two coworkers were noxious, scheming, feral. Fans of an Anglophile club that called itself "Vile Bodies" after the Evelyn Waugh novel, they did everything they could to live up to the name in hopes of being asked to join.

The editor in chief was a puffed-up tyrant, a brilliant suspender-snapping orator given to venting lava flows of rage upon his underlings.

He loved to make the girls cry. For us boys, he'd provoke quarrels by picking favorites and then inviting us to "take it outdoors" and settle our differences "like men." Reality TV was still twenty years in the future, but this was the pilot.

There were days when I felt myself becoming just another faceless cheap-suiter wearing out his shoes on the Gotham sidewalks, but each night after putting Rory to bed, I emigrated upstairs to a vacant apartment and wrote. I wasn't going to let that dream get snuffed out. Belle Île had worked like a charm before when we needed a change in the weather, a lucky break. Time to conjure up the luck of the island.

What we got was a call from a friend who'd scored a film deal with her first novel, saying she wanted to help with our house. It was a sincere and tactful offer, but at bottom the underlying question hurt: "Want to sell?" Of course we could always come for a visit.

Next we got a letter from Gwened saying she was embarrassed for us but, more seriously, embarrassed *personally*, that we had not paid Denis LeReveur so he could pay the contractors.

What? Had there been a bill that we'd missed? We went through our folders, ransacked drawers. Nothing from Denny the Dreamer in over two years, which *was* a little strange. And we were a bit remiss for not noticing. Perhaps he'd gotten the address wrong?

Mindy wrote Denis and Gwened, separately, saying the same thing to each:

"This summer we are coming back to Belle Île."

Easy to promise, but could I really hope to reason with my boss, a man who bragged of getting by on four hours of sleep? He once boasted he'd never taken a vacation in thirty years—not once. ("My wife thinks I'm an asshole," he'd added with disarming modesty.) Until tonight I'd always avoided him whenever possible.

Tomorrow, however, I'd track the dragon to his lair.

Chapter Eleven
Wards of the Village

W hat a bewitching land it is! What a garden! Surely the leagues of bright green lawns are swept and brushed and watered every day and their grasses trimmed by the barber... Surely the long, straight rows of stately poplars that divide the beautiful landscape like the squares of a checkerboard are set with line and plummet... It is wonderful. There are no unsightly stone walls, and never a fence of any kind. There is no dirt, no decay, no rubbish anywhere—nothing that even hints at untidiness—nothing that ever suggests neglect. All is orderly and beautiful—everything is chastening to the eye."

Or so Mark Twain said of France, writing in his first book, *The Innocents Abroad*. For us, on the other hand...

❦

Dust, dirt, mold—everywhere. Shutters so battered, so rotted, so delicious in their deliquescence that someone has taken their photo and turned them into a popular poster: *fenêtres paysannes rustiques*.

Just off the ferry, we stop dead in the street of Le Palais to stare into an art boutique.

"Isn't that our window?"

"What!"

"Rustic peasant windows?"

Laughing, we hurry on to see the real thing.

The downstairs is dank and dusty and exhausted. But the new roof's black slates shine in the sun. Inside, the two dormer windows inhale the light, breathing it into the upstairs bedrooms where it blazes in the panels of pale yellow northern pine. Too bad we can only see this by standing on the rough dirt floor: there's no staircase. No way we can stay up there, even if we climb up using the ancient, termite-holed ladder we find in the weeds behind the house. Rory is at the fearless stage and there are no railings.

But we've lucked out. We can rent Madame Morgane's green *cabane*, a wooden hut nestled out in a cypress windbreak. It's snug and well-made, if tiny as a doll's house. Apparently it was once used to shelter family from the mainland who came to help with the harvest. It makes no concessions to modernity: no toilet, no shower, no electricity, no heat. Plenty of mosquitoes, though. During the daylight hours we go to our house to use the bathroom, climbing up the fifty-year-old ladder. (Rory is still in diapers and sometimes I envy him.) At night we go in the fields behind the windbreak.

Once, up in the night to answer nature's call, I march out into the field. Standing in the rain wearing a poncho, Wellingtons, and nothing else, I spot a large shape moving toward me in the dark. Sure I am being charged by a bull, I lift my poncho above my knees, prepared to run…

"Don?" calls Mindy, for it is she, in her poncho, obeying a similar call.

Another, more cheery ritual involves bathing Rory in a great tin tub out in the yard among Madame Morgane's chickens. We heat the water on the stove, then let Rory steam in the sunshine, while scandalized roosters cluck and cluck.

We've come in early September, the time of great, sweeping tides. At the beach at Donnant, *la grande marée* exposes half a mile of undulating golden sand that ripples like the waves that so recently departed. Each day while the tide is receding, Rory and I build scores of interconnected canals and dikes, channeling the draining water into lagoons, shoring up levees as they bulge and breach. Searching for weak spots, Rory scampers over this maze of ours, shouting, "Stop the water! Stop the water!"

On the second or third day of the *grande marée*, a team of French sand engineers—well, a father and son, the latter about nine years old, both in Speedos—spend the entire afternoon building an over-the-top château below us, closer to the waves. I think I recognize it from our long-ago visit to the Loire Valley: Blois? Chenonceaux? No, it's my favorite, Azay-le-Rideau. To give them credit, they're really getting it right.

But Rory looks a little dispirited, and understandably so. Our levees and berms aren't anything special to look at, though they do hold back the water admirably. Meanwhile, our rivals are boasting and exclaiming as they construct ramparts, dig moats, dribble witches'-hat towers. They're even using tools, and argue spiritedly over details as they work. They'll probably produce a sheaf of regulations before the day is done.

I try, but their loud self-congratulation and preening is hard to ignore and finally gets to me. *Just do the castle, all right? Don't march around blowing your horn. Don't think I don't see you sneaking looks at us, too.* As his father, I can't help but get a bit defensive on Rory's behalf, even if our fortress is Neolithic in comparison.

Late afternoon, long shadows like wraiths are bending across the rippled sand. The sea has retreated a half a mile, at least. The flow of water is reduced to a trickle. But in our construction zone far above the water's edge, we've created a network of dams and impoundments. We're holding back a good thirty or forty gallons of seawater, by my estimate.

I'm wondering if my engineer grandfather, Charlie Wailes, would be pleased with me. Funny to think he was invited by the French government after World War II to come and help guide the reconstruction of Paris...and here I am having to watch this mini DeGaulle frown and stare and frown again at our massive pool and finally point down at his château's dry moat and look directly at me with a prissy *fonctionnaire* look.

"I guess we've taken all the water," I tell Rory. "See, we're good for something."

He has a fierce look. Uh-oh.

"Shall we give them a little? To fill their moat?"

"No!"

Well, he is only two and a half years old.

"*S'il vous plaît!*" The father gestures impatiently. "*L'eau! L'eau!*" He makes digging motions, and I can see the thought forming behind his thick eyeglasses: Hey, American moron, can't you see what's at stake here? The national patrimony of France!

"We should share the water, Rory," I say gently.

Rory pouts.

"But I'll tell you what. We've got to get up to the village for dinner, anyway. So let's share all of it."

His eyes darken at first, but a smile lights up his face as my suggestion sinks in. We take up our positions, legs wide, bent at the waist, hands prepared to scoop. "Ready? Set? Go!" We make a breach directly above a natural spillway that leads straight to the sand castle thirty feet below us.

With cries of anguish, the man and his son dance about, throwing handfuls of sand in the path of the flood. But all is in vain. In a matter of minutes, Azay-le-Rideau is no more.

A crowd, drawn by the shrieks of the boy, heaves a huge communal sigh: "Ah!" Heads turn accusatively toward us, then swing back to the father, to see what he will do. There's no doubt where the sympathy lies.

Wearily, a bit sore in the back, the father straightens up. He lays a hand on his son's shoulder to comfort him. Then he turns, draws himself erect, and wags a finger at me. His eyebrows make a black V in his forehead. He is doing his best to act out his outrage at our villainy when I think I detect a histrionic note and a wee glint in one eye.

Drawing myself up, I place my hands on my hips and glower back at him.

He squares his stance. "*À demain.*" Tomorrow. He stretches out a hand to his ruined castle. "*Içi. Pour la satisfaction d'honneur.*"

I nod. *"Avec plaisir, Monsieur. À demain!"*

The crowd gives a thrilled titter and someone claps as we walk down to greet our new friends.

※

It's easy for Rory to make friends at the beach, and life in the *cabane* grows on us. We cook on a camp stove. Rory follows roosters and hens around, narrating their inner lives. To fool the mosquitoes as night falls, we learn to close the doors and windows and tell stories in the dark; after an hour, it's safe to turn on our battery-powered Itty Bitty Book Lights and read.

The village feels quietly preoccupied and insular, as before. We see few people, although we sense them—hanging laundry behind their hedges, clattering away in their kitchens. Who are they? Relatives from the mainland, come for off-season holidays. Houses dark in winter show a light at night. A stick figure with a dog walks in silhouette at the edge of a threshed field. Blue-black smoke drifts at treetop level, bringing a subtle mist of charred sardines.

We're glad these villagers make no particular fuss over us, the careworn gypsies in their midst. After all, we're preoccupied ourselves, what with the daily business of shopping and preparing meals on our camp stove, carving our *steak au poivre* with matching Swiss Army knives. True, we feel a bit abandoned, left to our own devices, because Gwened has rented out her house to bring in money for needed repairs. This is quite a change from our summer of moral and cultural instruction three years ago.

Our other village friends, Franck and Ines, are scarcely to be seen. He's sold his sloop and invested in these new things, *planches à voile*—windsurfers. Requiring calm water for the tourist trade, they operate from a large tent on Grand Sables on the other side of the island. Too exhausted to return to Kerbordardoué on the weekends, our friends sleep on beds of damp wet suits. The children love it, naturally. The parents walk with a rubbery gait familiar to us, fellow members of the fraternity of exhaustion.

Her cataracts cured by surgery, Madame Morgane still occasionally squints at us as if we are poachers who've snuck onto her back forty. She dotes on Rory, however, and her somber formality—that of the lifelong country dweller—seems to gratify his own childlike sense of self-importance. She enjoys our after-dinner visits, which always begin with cups of instant coffee and conclude with a purchase of eggs for the morning, but her days are reserved for her chickens and garden. And, lately, a new old friend, who has made an appearance in the village.

A better word than "appearance" might be "apparition," since we've hardly caught a glimpse of her. Considering that she is our neighbor, occupying the ruined hut at the end of our row of attached houses, this is quite a feat.

The first time we'd come up late from the beach and surprised her picking green plants out of the water ditches. In an instant she was off, darting up the lane, cutting through the hedges, weaving through the tall corn, off into the fields. She resembled a large hare wearing a faded blue denim shirtdress—with a complementary apron in a blue floral print.

Mindy and I looked at each other: "What was *that?*"

At first we didn't connect her to the ruin at the end of the row, which continued to present an unlived-in appearance. It hardly seemed habitable; you could easily miss the door behind all the ivy, hydrangeas, and a growing pile of dank compost, which gradually became a mountain of decaying vegetal matter sprouting pale green shoots. It was the compost that gave her away, of course. But we couldn't be sure it was *our* female apparition until the kittens appeared, romping through the overgrowth, pausing to sip from a saucer filled with milk. Putting two and two together, we realized this had to be our neighbor. But who? Why?

We didn't get a satisfactory answer until the universal and mandatory French vacation ended and Gwened herself arrived.

Gwened looked surprisingly good, tanned and rested and *spiritual,* her lips bent in a slight but constant smile as she looked us over. "I am very happy to see you here, at last. Come, help me pick some beautiful garden vegetables for our dinner."

Classic Gwened: not even here for ten minutes and already taking charge.

We went for a walk, following her lead. Each villager has his or her private routes. Each family has an itinerary on the first day back, stations of the pilgrimage of return. To be invited on Gwened's was an honor. And somehow, by the time we got back to her house for dinner, the place had changed. We could see the other villagers, standing in their yards, strolling the lanes, waving casually. It was as if the village had woken up now that the witch was back.

Now the long island September was truly upon us: the peace and quiet, the endless days, the weather hot and dry and crisp, the nights clear and starry. We walked amid a myriad of seasonal reminders: lizards and pheasants made bold by the departure of the tourist crowds, a thresher moving across a burnt gold horizon, a flock of sheep herded by barking collies across Donnant's beach at low tide, a dozen white flowers blossoming in the sky. The latter slowly floated earthward onto Madame Morgane's fields, where they turned into parachutists on a military exercise and walked toward us gathering their silks around their waists, like Victorian ladies on promenade.

When we dined late at Les Embruns, the quayside *crêperie* in Sauzon, we often had the place to ourselves. In the town to the south, Bangor, we attended a *fest-noz* that would go until morning, *Bellilois* dancing the two-step I'd seen Cajuns do. Mindy swayed with sleepy Rory in her arms as the accordion wheezed and the *bombarde* and the *binioù*, Breton horn and bagpipe, squealed and droned. A bonfire blazed against the white wall of the Bangor church. We ate grilled sausages and drank *cidre brut*, the alcoholic kind.

With the tourists gone, the windsurfer business fell off sharply. Franck and Ines and their children, now up to three with a new baby, filled the gaps in our social calendar. If we didn't eat with Gwened, we ate with them. And if by chance neither invited us, somebody always seemed to leave a bowl of fresh sardines on our stoop, or a wicker basket of tomatoes and yellow runner beans.

After meals, we walked around, usually crossing paths with Madame Morgane on her own stroll, trailed by a tabby cat, and once in a while her son, a brooding figure who lived in Nantes and, we were told, only liked to come when pheasant season opened. I soon learned to carry a flashlight; also, a spare bag in my hip pocket to fill with the bursting-ripe blackberries that overwhelmed nodding vines.

Gwened didn't join us on the longer walks, saying she preferred to meditate. Of course this worried us, but given her steely composure, we didn't dare ask about her health. In a sense, one look at her told us all we needed to know. She was brown (and probably brown all over) and she was strong, something we realized the day we accepted her invitation to dig up the potatoes in her garden. How she made the dirt fly! The former archetype of French womanhood now had muscles.

One morning Rory got us up very early and insisted on a ramble into the village. We'd passed Gwened's house and were on a narrow lane to nowhere when suddenly something flashed past. A bird? No, an arrow. We could hardly believe it, but there it was, quivering in a bale of hay. Peering over a scraggly hedge, we beheld a figure wearing a white karate *gi* with a black sash and a white headband: Gwened, standing stock-still and holding an enormous bow. As we watched, she reached behind her back and pulled an arrow out of a quiver.

We retreated.

We got the story later in the day. In the years since her diagnosis, Gwened had dedicated herself to mastering the ancient art of Japanese Zen archery: *kyudo*. The money she'd saved from renting her house would go toward converting her old cowshed, what she'd laughingly called her dojo, into a real dojo, with students, she hoped.

Gwened the guru? Nothing, it seemed, was beyond our mentor's powers.

Chapter Twelve
The Game of No

By the last week of September, Kerbordardoué had come all the way back, as if from the dead, resurrected for us out of the mists of memory like the mythical Brigadoon, the Scottish village in the Lerner and Loewe musical that only comes to life every hundred years.

All that was missing was our architect, Denis LeReveur. We'd paid a call at his office soon after we arrived, and he'd greeted us warmly. He looked exactly the same: the same rumpled handsome face, the same glinting rimless glasses, the same thick sweater and open-collared shirt. In fact, we actually joked that he hadn't changed clothes since we'd last seen him three years before.

As was proper on Belle Île, the small talk stretched on…and on, except we never got to the important part: getting down to business. Instead, we made dinner arrangements. Denis wanted us to get to know his wife. Right now, he was in the midst of the busy construction season, so we'd set a date later.

Mindy and I had been exchanging glances as he edged us toward the door. "But," she protested, in her finest florid French, "we are absolutely chagrined not to have received a bill from you in such a long time. It is deeply embarrassing not to know what to pay you."

"Pay me?" Denis looked astonished. He glanced down at the piles of paper on his desk and pretended to search among them. "I'm sure you have already paid me…"

"No, really, Denis, we haven't even received a bill. In fact, we were thinking perhaps it was sent to the wrong address."

"But here is your address: see?" Denis pointed to a 3x5 card tacked to the wall, where, in Mindy's hand, our address was written. "Is it not correct?"

"Yes, but we never got a bill for the roof, the construction of the bedrooms and the bathroom…"

"Oh, well, then, I'm sure it will soon come." With an encouraging nod, he put a hand on each of our shoulders. "Do not worry. The French post office is very good." He twinkled. "One of the *only* things the government does well."

Gently but firmly he guided us out the door. Stood there waving as we walked off.

Once we'd turned a corner, we compared notes on what we thought had just taken place. Did he honestly think we'd paid him? Was he actually saying he hadn't sent the bill yet? Or that the bill was in the mail? Or was he stalling for another reason? Perhaps he was gauging how much to gouge us?

To give even a moment's consideration to such a disloyal thought was depressing. But as New Yorkers, weren't we compelled to at least acknowledge the possibility? My experience in the American construction industry had already told me to brace myself for chicanery. And there *had* been a moment in the beginning of the renovation, funny in retrospect, that had taken us aback.

Gwened had written us a year or so after we'd signed the *devis*. Her usual circumspect self, she took a few paragraphs to get to the point. But then:

"My dear friends, I have heard something from the people of the village about your renovation. I did not quite believe it, even though Franck and Ines both assured me it was true. But in the off chance that this is not what you wish for the house, after all our discussions of what is appropriate for Kerbordardoué, I hope you do not think it forward of me to inquire whether you did, in fact, order a rather enormous bathtub, of pink enamel, with gold faucets and gold taps for your chambre du bain? *Because upon my arrival here today, that is what I see on the ground floor, awaiting installation."*

By the time Mindy and I had gotten over our fit of hysterical laughter, the implications were sinking in. What else might Denis be dreaming of? Mirrored ceilings? A disco ball?

It required phone calls (expensive and rare in those days) and letters and Gwened's stern visit to Denis in his office to effect the removal of "the solid gold bathtub," as the offending object would henceforth be known. We also took pains to establish our taste in fixtures generally—which could be summed up in two words: simple and cheap. But we forgave Denis. The roots of the whole misunderstanding probably lay in Gwened's suggestion that we order an extra-large hot water heater. In her visits to America, she'd become addicted to the long, languorous bubble bath.

Here was the basis for our twinge of paranoia. Even before this incident, though, we'd been at the receiving end of a nonstop stream of suspicions directed at us by friends, acquaintances, and parents. They never let up: *Who's minding the store? A Frenchman? Well, that was smart. And you're using local contractors? God, they'll take you to the cleaners. They'll pad the bills, and you won't be able to do anything about it. Boy, I wouldn't want to be in your shoes. You're screwed. Doesn't it make you mad to know they're taking advantage of you because you're American? Here we saved their butts in the war and they do this to you. Don't you just hate the French? I don't know what possessed you to buy a house over there...*

However reluctantly I floated the idea, Mindy flat-out refused to play along. She shook her head and said: no, not, never. Not Denny the

Dreamer. We looked at each other. We believed in our Denis, in our Belle Île, in our sense of people. Call us fools, call us idiots, but that's who we were. Even if the skeptics were proved right, we wouldn't trade places with them in a hundred years.

So then the question was, now what? It all felt impossibly tangled. There was only one thing to do. We turned around and marched back to his office.

Denis glanced up over his spectacles and did a double take, followed by a greeting that was note for note as effusive as the first one. "What! You're back so soon? This is wonderful. You honor me. Please, come in."

"Denis," said Mindy, as firmly as she could between involuntary smiles, "I think you did *not* send us the bill. And even if you did, it has not arrived. Can you therefore *please* make us a copy of the bill, so that we may be assured of receiving it?"

"But of course! Why, I can do it today!"

"Now? Perhaps? Please?"

His expression fell into melancholy. "Ah, no, not now. I am terribly sorry." He indicated the piles of paper. "There is a client who demands a plan and I am late. Can you give me until tomorrow?"

"Of course… Can we come by to pick it up?"

"Of course, of course. We can have a coffee around the corner."

The next day we made a swing through Le Palais in the afternoon. The sign on Denis's door said: *Fermé.* We'd lost him. Afterward, our shopping trips to Le Palais never coincided with Denis being in his untidy office off the Place du Général Bigarré.

Suddenly, with about a week to go, we awoke to the realization that we still hadn't seen the bill and probably wouldn't, at this rate. Neither of us liked the idea of leaving without paying. We knew that bill would never make its way to America.

We decided that we'd somehow confused Denis in our first meeting. Perhaps he'd had trouble with our accents—well, my accent. Yes, perhaps it would be better for Young Strudel to *just shut up* next time there was serious business to be conducted, and stop trying to make *those stupid bilingual puns.* Young Strudel, however, seemed to remember not having any problem going alone to the notary's to *buy the house.* It was only in the *renovation* that we seemed to be having problems. Perhaps, Madame, the fault lay somewhere else?

Once that little tiff was over, we vowed to somehow trap Denis, even if it meant going to his home at night. We would not return to America without paying our bills!

It was then that Mindy remembered the Game of No. She'd come up with it during our rambles across the hinterlands of France and Greece. In social situations, particularly among the older generations of country people, we'd come to realize that nothing good happens until you say no three times. If you sit in a parlor, you will be offered tea or coffee three times, offered lump sugar three times, offered sweets three times. Also, the deeper into the country you travel, the more likely you'll be offered some absurdly generous favor or invitation three times. The trick, we'd learned, was to say no. Not once. Not twice. But three times—with a sort of last second caving in to the host's supplication. It was a kind of passive-aggressive dance that honored both parties in the transaction.

Both parties understood you would eventually accept the offer of coffee. Both knew you wouldn't mind a sweet. But you didn't want to seem too eager, in case your host was in tight circumstances. Perhaps she didn't really have any lump sugar! Truly, it would be a terrible person who would take her host's last lump of sugar, or worse, reveal that she had none. The only thing worse would be to embarrass or insult your host by acting as if you thought she didn't have any coffee or lump sugar to offer. Of course there were limits, and certain offers had to be declined: a string bag of live escargot still in their slimy shells, for example.

Formulating the Game of No was Mindy's shining hour, really, because when we remembered it in time, and if we had the patience and steel nerves to go the distance to that third no, which became "*no— well—perhaps—if you insist,*" it always worked like a charm. The parlor would become suffused with a warm glow. The conversation would flow.

Soothing, diplomatic, always stressing the other's person's welfare over your own, the Game of No had become our basis for finding friendship among villagers from Imerovigli to Kerbordardoué.

🌱

Visits to Le Palais in search of Denis increased in frequency, cutting into our dreamy days, but we felt these visits were a matter of honor. Once on the way into town we caught sight of him, driving down the central road in the opposite direction; he flashed his high beams in the universal salutation. Once we saw him sauntering down the street in the company of a couple of local men. We rolled down our window and begged for an audience. "Of course! Just come on by the office."

"But we've come by…"

"Oh, I'm there all the time now. Really. Come now. We'll have a coffee."

"We're just going to park. We'll be right there."

He was only out of our sight for five minutes, but he was gone by the time we got to his door. He was avoiding us, clearly. But why? We owed him a lot of money; our best guesstimate came in at close to ten thousand dollars! He had to need the money. More to the point, as Gwened had pointed out, his subcontractors definitely would be expecting to be paid, and here it was, already a year late, more likely two years.

With pheasant season upon us, strangers began showing up in Kerbordardoué, men with dogs, often pairs of Brittany spaniels. The men wore Wellingtons and carried long sticks in the crooks of their elbows, like shotguns. Which is the impression they intended to give to the wary pheasants: pay no attention to that man with the stick. He means you no harm. You can safely ignore him.

But in a week, when the season began, things would be a little different.

Mindy hated seeing the hunters in our valley and feared for the pheasants. But she also understood that this was the way of the island. Still, when she burst into the *cabane* one morning, breathless, and started babbling about a hunter in the valley, I thought she must've gotten into an argument. But no—she'd run into a fierce older man with a bristling mustache who'd given her a piercing stare. Somehow she found the courage to introduce herself and, when he merely grunted, to ask his name in return. At first he'd actually seemed disinclined to reply. But he'd probably guessed that, from the look of her, you snub Mindy at your own peril.

"Monsieur Borlagadec!" Mindy looked at me expectantly. The name meant nothing; I shook my head. "He's the main subcontractor! Once Denis got him on board, we got all the best on the island: the plumber, the electrician, the carpenter, and the roofers…"

"Did he know who you were?"

"He…" Mindy paused to take stock. "He knew. He got this look when I said my name and said I lived up the valley."

"Well, did he look like a man who hadn't been paid?"

"That's the thing." She went over to our suitcases and pulled out the brown legal envelope that held our *devis*, our title, our dream house on paper. "Right, right, right." She leafed through the sheets. "He's the specialist in foundations and floors and staircases. The best stair man on the island. The only one who can do an old house like ours the right way, Denis said."

"And we've stiffed him? Great."

"No, we haven't. He's not done a thing yet."

"So…what's it mean?"

"Nothing. But it's important that we met." Mindy's brow was furrowed with intense concentration. "Yes, it's important that he *saw* me. That I'm not just some abstract American woman who doesn't know what she's doing. I just feel it."

❧

When Denis called Gwened to invite us to dinner at his house on one of our last days on the island, we made a difficult decision: to simply write him a check for 31,750 francs—about five thousand dollars—and leave it on the table, telling him to send us a bill for the remainder. Everything about this felt wrong, un-*Bellilois*, crudely American. It felt worse when we met his wife, a tall and beautiful brunette, a little shy at first, then warm and funny. The two children were bright Celtic elves, a tawny blond girl and a dark curly-haired boy with enormous eyes.

There was a pause. Mindy hesitated, then reached into her purse for our checkbook. Just then Denis gave a huge smile and asked if we'd like to see the bathroom. This seemed a little odd and at first we declined, once, twice, three times. But he insisted, and since everyone was laughing harder and harder, we realized something was up and gave in.

Indeed it was a large and impressive bathroom with a skylight over the tub. Which was pink. With gold faucets and taps. "*Le bain Américain!*" they cried, applauding.

As the night wore on, it became obvious that we would be friends. And friends, in this part of the world, don't spend social evenings settling bills. They especially don't leave checks under their dinner plates, as if in a hurry to get to the theater. So we chickened out.

Gwened made disapproving noises when she found out we'd missed the opportunity. But her expression was wry. "These are strong people," she said. "They will do things their way. I guess Denis has decided that, for whatever reason, he can afford to carry you. Perhaps he has paid the subcontractors out of his own pocket. Perhaps he has explained your situation to them and they have agreed to hold off." She shrugged and rolled her eyes, a distinctly American affectation she must've picked up from her students.

Then it was time to go. We had a ferry to catch.

"Please," Gwened said with a farewell kiss—four of them, on alternating cheeks—for both of us. Rory briefly suffered to be held, then broke away with a wild-eyed look: another conquest for Gwened Guedel.

"Don't let this go on any longer. *Finish the house*. For yourselves… and for the *village*."

On the way to the port in our rental car, we swung past Denis's office. The sign on the door said: *Ouvert*.

"Pull over!" shouted Mindy, digging in her purse. I squeezed into an illegal space and yanked on the parking brake. She jumped out and darted into the office. Telling Rory to stay put and read his book, I followed Mindy.

Inside, Denis was sitting at his paper-piled desk with a bewildered expression on his face as Mindy counted out giant, colorful banknotes like fall leaves—we'd visited the bank twice for this eventuality. "Please, Denis. We *must* pay something."

"No."

"Denis, too much work has been done. You cannot carry us another year."

"No, no. I am not carrying you." He held his hands up. "Please, stop it. Take your money. This is not proper."

"Denis." Mindy took a deep breath and visibly composed herself. "We can't wait any longer for the bill. Here is thirty-five thousand francs. That isn't enough, I know, but it's a start and you can pay the subcontractors something…"

"Stop it! Stop it, please." By force of will and a deep Celtic glower, Denis silenced Mindy and scared me a little. He looked on the verge of an explosion. And, indeed, when he spoke, he sounded like a sputtering fuse. "You, you are too"—a hand flung at the sky seemed to help him find the right words—"too *American!* It must always be your way. Always money, money, money."

"That is not true," Mindy said. "You are unfair. We deeply appreciate what you are doing for us. The work is magnificent. But you must allow us to pay our bill. To do otherwise is to place us in an impossible position. We are personally embarrassed. Why, the other day when I met Monsieur Borlagadec in the valley, I could not be sure that he wasn't looking at me like a, a, a…"

Mindy never did find the word for "deadbeat" in French. But Denis understood. He also seemed intrigued about something else. "You met Monsieur Borlagadec?"

"Yes. He was walking his dog, I think getting him ready for the pheasant season."

"It opens this weekend. So that's where old Borlagadec is planning to shoot?" Denis got a crafty look on his face. "Tell me, are there a lot of pheasant in your valley?"

Mindy stiffened. "I'm not going to tell you if you're just going to shoot them."

"I think you answered the question, thank you. It's good you met Monsieur Borlagadec."

"Do we owe him money?"

"No, no money. It's just that, well, he knew Jeannie, who lived there in your house all her life. He was very fond of her. He knows the house well. So it's good he met you."

By this time Denis's expression had completely softened. He smiled, then began to laugh to himself, quietly shuffling and arranging the banknotes according to denomination. "Monsieur Borlagadec, when he heard about your *bathtub*, made a special trip over to see it himself. The whole village turned out. Some of the ladies took turns lying in the tub." He snapped a rubber band around each of the piles, stacked them neatly. "With their clothes on, of course." He laughed, pleased with the joke, and caught my eye to see if I, his fellow kidder, was impressed. My slow head shake of bemused disappointment seemed just what he was looking for.

"Now. This is not the way to pay," he said gently, shoving the stack over to our side of his desk. "Please, put this away somewhere safe. When you are home in New York City, which I someday hope to see with my wife and children, you will receive a bill. You may have questions. If so, please do not hesitate to write or to telephone. Okay?

"Have a safe trip." He turned and offered me his hand. "Be careful in the train station at Montparnasse. There are so many pickpockets in Paris."

It was the proverbial third no, but this time we wouldn't prevail.

Chapter Thirteen
Belle Île-en-Hudson

It's like a scene from a nineteenth-century novel as the little family from Brittany arrives in the Big City, wide-eyed and gawking. The husband isn't afraid of these Parisians and their sophisticated ways. Watch how with cunning and élan the cash mule Wallaces evade those slinking pickpockets of Gare Montparnasse!

As we take to the streets of Paris, Don brazenly wears a leather dress belt stuffed like a sausage with five thousand dollars in enormous, gaudy French banknotes. Thirty-five thousand, two hundred twenty-five francs! It feels like I'm holding my pants up with a rope of money. But better to be embarrassed and safe than blasé and robbed.

Yet, somehow, when we reach New York City, a half-inch of the circumference of the sausage is mysteriously gone. Missing in action. Main suspect: Paris.

It began innocently enough. We'd set out to enjoy the city we'd once tried to live in. We visited our old neighborhoods: Mouffetard, Les Halles-Beaubourg. Rory was still strollerable, though the cobblestone streets of the Latin Quarter made him bounce around like a bobblehead doll. We went to all our old haunts: Jardin des Plantes, Arènes de Lutèce, Jardin du Luxembourg, and that *pâtisserie* with the perfect *tarte au citron* on rue de Fleurus. Yes, there was a visit to a couple of dress shops on rue Jacob. (Nothing happened, officer, I swear. We were just looking.)

And after an evening meal at an outdoor café on a side street, we started walking back to the hotel. The night was warm and bewitched by warm breezes. Most stores were closed or closing up, but one bright, modern, all-glass storefront glowed: Agnès B. Homme. Mindy tugged on my arm. "Let's go in." I knew what was up. Maybe something *had* happened on rue Jacob. My memory, officer, it's not so good anymore.

Up until entering Agnès B, I'd resisted any clothes shopping. Although I'm a cheerful mule for carrying cash and Mindy's purchases, shopping for myself reminds me too much of those annual trips to outfit me for middle school, my mother picking out shirts with too-bold stripes and button-up sweaters over my moans of dismay. Even in New York she sent me bright pastel golf shirts for every special occasion. It's so hard to feel hip in the West Village when you're sporting alligator and whale logos.

But a half hour later I walked out with a coal-black, stovepipe-legged, narrow-lapeled suit of flat, tightly woven cotton. "I'll never wear this!" I halfheartedly complained, knowing that it didn't matter if I ever wore it. The main thing was that it was from Paris and it was cool and it was *mine*.

We don't mention the losses. We take them in stride. In our account books, they come under the heading "Blame It on Paris," chalked up as an occupational hazard to owning a house, or even just half a house, in France.

❧

After we return, fall floats past like a dream. By December, though, life reverts to dreary, a darkness without end. What's changed? It was too early to count the days before we could return to Kerbordardoué.

But we did, and it feels like a fatal mistake. Now we're haunted by the prospect of not being there for another ten months.

My editor in chief also rues letting me go to Belle Île. (How did I ever put that one over on him? What was in those french fries?) I inherit every crummy assignment he can think of—which I have no choice but to accept with a big smile on my face. Ultimately he's doing me a favor, as I begin to understand that I've been sending mixed messages.

I know I've got the chops to rise in the business, but I'm always hesitating, my head full of dreams of what I'd rather be doing: reading novels and trying to write them, staying on Belle Île, tramping and traveling with Mindy. A nice life if you can pay for it, but we're not independently wealthy. And so far it hasn't been happening. What's the plan here?

Mindy is in a similar fix. She wants to write, too. So day after long, dark winter's day, she pushes Rory to a park where a circle of strollers, lined up end to end like Conestoga wagons in a Western movie, provides protection from the bums. She stamps her feet and blows on her hands for as long as she can stand the cold before retreating to that notoriously dingy, transvestite-hooker, heroin-addict haunt: McDonald's on Eighth Avenue and Twenty-Sixth Street.

There she drinks watery coffee and Rory slides down the tongue of Ronald McDonald over and over with a score of screaming, snotty kids, some of whose parents are barely off the nod. Like several others, Mindy carries sanitizing wipes to dab handrails and Ronald's tongue before Rory's ascent and descent. Perhaps as a result, he's robust and never sick. But she gets every cold in town, as do I, and then we give them back to each other. After a couple of months, Mindy can hardly remember what it feels like to sit down alone and enjoy some peace and quiet, let alone try to write.

Hard to believe that only a couple of months before we were building sand castles on the beach at Donnant.

By spring of 1989, it's time to ponder Rory's education. We're late out of the starting gate; the maneuvering for September has already begun. The postcrash recession is biting down hard, too. But as gloomy friends assure us, picking a pre-K program is really picking a college. Of course this spells p-r-i-v-a-t-e s-c-h-o-o-l. As in ex-pen-sive. A public-school product, I balk. But P.S. 44 in our ZIP code is already oversubscribed before we even hear there was a list. God, I love New York.

So there goes the rest of what we owe Denis LeReveur. At least for the moment we've dodged the question of what comes first, Belle Île or Rory. Even to us, our priorities seem a little suspect.

❧

Naturally, at this point Denis LeReveur sends along the *devis*. Ah, dear me, where did the money go? All those banknotes we flourished in Denis's office? Mindy sends a paltry check, less than a third of what we owe, makes excuses, and promises the rest *tout de suite*. A promise we can't honor, realistically.

Once again we've got no money—but, a voice whispers, we sure did go to France, didn't we? The apartment is darker and smaller than ever, and escape farther away—but surely not because we went to France, right?

How much is this obsession going to cost us?

We wonder. And ask ourselves: Are we the brave cultural adventurers we think we are? Maybe Belle Île would've been better off left as a memory.

If only there was something at stake in our village life, something noble like removing land mines from the beach at Donnant, bringing sliced bread to the *boulangerie* or the Word of God to the heathen Suzanne, or at least ending silly fights over parking in the square, something defensible, so that when we go home at Christmas and Uncle Frank cracks jokes at our expense, we can retain our dignity.

But all we have to show for it are a pair of bedrooms and a bathroom twenty-two feet up in the air without a staircase.

❧

Belle Île and the *devis* ever on our mind, we take on more work, free-lance articles. Most of mine are about business: "10 Ways to Improve Your Cold Calling," "How to Close the Sale," "Join the Entrepreneurial Revolution," "How to Pick a Power Suit." I kid myself by thinking that 2.5 articles equal a one-way plane ticket to Paris. Counting a return ticket, trains and boats and taxis, I figure I'll need to sell a baker's dozen. And if all goes well, once I have this summer's trip in the bank, then I'll write for Denis LeReveur. Articles are my new currency.

I'm also reviewing novels for *Kirkus Reviews* at thirty-five dollars a pop, so I up my pace to one a week, reading them on the subway and at lunch, lying on the floor of my tiny office. Reading so many novels quickly and critically sharpens my eye, but unfortunately this only shows me the weaknesses in my own novel. A tome years in the making, it suffers from every disease known to writing. Eventually I deep-six it after composing a savage *Kirkus Reviews* epitaph: "…ponderous, pontificating prosody, poorly plotted…"

One day at work I come across a file from my old job: twenty pages of an article I'd started a couple of years before about a Coca-Cola bottling manager who wanted to be a professional bass fisherman. At some point the story switches gears into fiction. The fisherman's wife, a sort of proto-Sarah Palin, wants to be a soldier of fortune. The writing feels fresher than anything I've been working on, and so, breaking all the rules of publishing, I send the pages off to an editor whose name I've read in the newspaper.

When Anton calls back and asks to see the rest of the novel I am almost, but not quite, speechless. I say I'll finish "typing it up."

My new schedule is this: At night after dinner I put Rory to bed with a story, pour myself a strong cup of Earl Grey, put a chocolate chip cookie in my pocket, and head up a couple of flights of stairs to an empty apartment. There I drink the tea, eat the cookie, and put a cassette tape on the boom box—a mixtape of Dvorak's *New World Symphony*, followed by three minutes of James Brown screaming "I Feel Good!" Thus fortified, I write until my forehead bangs the keyboard.

I'm staggering in exhaustion through my days. But every week I send a new chapter to the forbearing editor, who accepts my increasingly dubious claim of "typing it up." At work I take to closing the door to my office at noon, lying down with my head against it, and going to sleep, risking a broken neck if someone should open the door too quickly.

A couple of my fellow editors cover for me. The phone rings: "They're coming!" warns a hushed voice. When our snooping Tweedledum and Tweedledee come knocking, our editor in chief in tow, I'm upright and very professionally marking up a manuscript with a red pencil.

I can laugh about it. It's ludicrous. Because it's working. Here at last I have a secret hope: a novel. Soon I'm typing "The End" and printing out a copy, popping it in an envelope, and sending it all of twenty blocks away. Now it's sitting at the elbow of an editor named Anton. An escape hatch. A redemption of my soul. A Hail Mary in every sense.

Mindy writes Gwened about the house and arranges to rent it. What about Denis LeReveur's bills? The novel, I tell Mindy, will pay for everything. Just you watch.

❦

When Anton called to invite me to lunch, we met at a venerable Gramercy Park watering hole (as the book trade gossip columns so suavely called it). I walked in trembling with the conviction that we were going to get that staircase and floor this year. And, oh, yes, I'd also be publishing a novel before I was forty, which was my new private default setting (adjusted upward from thirty exactly seven years ago).

An hour and a half later, I reeled out the door of the pub like someone under the influence. Which I was: Anton had wanted to drink a couple of pints before getting down to business. Then, in an alcoholic haze, I began to realize that I'd succeeded as a writer of fiction, beyond my wildest dreams. My book had so affected Anton that he'd determined I really was a Coca-Cola bottling manager from the South who'd written a story about his favorite hobby, bass fishing. I probably shouldn't have interrupted him to set him straight.

So the lunch didn't go well and I didn't sell the book. I left unsure that I'd even convinced Anton that I wasn't Garfield Foote, bass pro extraordinaire and leader of the Bass Commandos, the world's first "paramilitary fishing team." He did register my mild protest, however, and gave me the name of an agent whose name sounded like a type of fish.

🌿

In June we do the numbers and realize that we have a choice: pay Denis or go to France. We can't do both, and as we still have some scrap of honor left, we cancel our stay at Gwened's. We will stay home. With solemn ceremony we take the money we've made freelancing for France and write Denis a check for the rest of what we owe him. Then we drink most of a bottle of Sancerre. It's funny, but we feel good doing it, as if we're parents sending money to a child who's far away and badly needs it. And that's our Belle Île for this year.

At Christmas we accept a family offer of a plane ticket to California. They want to see their grandson. Maybe us, too. Sooner or later we hear it from both families: We're so glad *that's* over. Are you going to sell it now?

🌿

In the new year, to save pennies and slough off the sour smell of *Success*, I walk home at night instead of taking the bus or subway. Who needs a gym? As far as I'm concerned Manhattan is just one long treadmill anyway.

I usually pick up takeout. We sit down at a little table overlooking Rory's playpen and eat our greasy grub—cheap Italian, Greek, Hunan, Peruvian (try the chicken, not the guinea pig), Southern, Afghan, or simply diner—all of which, Mindy often points out, are unhealthy and which, I retort, are keeping us from saving any money *so why don't you cook?* to which she retorts, *Because I've spent all day with the baby and we don't have a kitchen!*

This last isn't strictly true, but I concede the point. We have a strangely flattened galley in the foyer that hides behind folding accordion-style panels. When we fling them open at night it looks like an ant farm, there are so many scuttling roaches.

Two visits from the pesticide guy later, with visions of string-bag shopping in Le Palais and Sauzon and on the rue de Buci in Paris, I am emboldened to go farther afield in search of true food. Under the rusted iron train-track trestles and piss-yellowed concrete underpasses of the Port Authority I find a small cluster of open markets in the French style.

Well, maybe "French style" is overdoing it, but I am excited. There's a bread shop! A pork store (that is actually what the sign outside says: Pork Store). A West African market full of exotic vegetables and rudely carved icons that turn out to be roots you can eat.

What really grabs me is the block's bookend fish markets: long, white fingers of crushed ice, be-ringed with shimmering vermillion *poissons du jour*, stretching out to claim the sidewalk and snatch me inside. Wherein all is clamorous and chaotic and grungy, the fishmongers scornful of any attempt to please the customer—especially timid, bespectacled Young *Sophisticate* Strudel in his thin poly-cotton Oxford shirt, half-knotted necktie, cheap chinos, and scuffed black Rockports. The clientele around me is mostly thick-bodied, half-shaven men in wool duffel coats. I watch them grunt and point and peel twenties off fat rolls, buying by the case. The fishmongers look right through me.

At last I spot an elderly black lady going right up to the head Italian fishmonger standing in his rubber boots on his wooden box. No nonsense, she grills him about his porgies. He gives monosyllabic answers, no allowance made for her age and maybe some subtracted for her race. But she gets her porgies, and when she asks to have them cleaned, they do it.

Before the lady's arrival I'd been staring, transfixed, at a great, wet, whiskery head resting on the ice like the head of John the Baptist. I've seen that face before. On the *quai* of Le Palais after the fishing boats came in. *La Lotte.* The first time I ever tasted *lotte*, during our winter of 1980, we'd hiked in our *cagoules* in the rain across beaches and moors to Belle Île's only one-star restaurant, La Forge. Mindy had made reservations. We were the only customers all night. The chef and his wife were the only staff. In the end, after our repeated urging, they joined us at the table for coffee and a discussion of what we'd eaten.

It was that dinner that made me want to try to recapture some of the magic of the tastes I'd experienced in France with Mindy—me, the guy who learned to cook in the Boy Scouts.

So I bought the fish (not the head). When I asked for *lotte*, though, the fishmonger shrugged. I pointed. "Goosefish," he said.

That night *La Lotte* was not a success. Every time we tried to cut into the triangle-shaped wedge of taut muscle, which I'd baked in one piece like a pork roast, our knives rebounded as if there was a force field protecting it.

Finally Mindy laid down her fork and knife. "You didn't ask them to clean it."

"It didn't need cleaning. Look"—flipping it over in the dish—"no guts."

"It's the *capuchin*," she said, poking at a nearly invisible membrane encasing the *lotte*. "On Belle Île they remove it without asking."

"Capuchin? As in monk?"

"As in a monk's robe. That's what they called it at La Forge."

Eventually we sawed our monk in half and pried out chunks, but it was not an encouraging start to my culinary ambitions. The evening's end was worse. When she woke up in the predawn to feed Rory, Mindy flipped on the light and let out a scream. The roaches were back. By the time I got to the tiny foyer-kitchen they were almost all gone, the little devils, but the dozen I saw doing a six-legged can-can under the *cabanet* were enough to chill the blood.

On the upside, at least they loved my French cooking.

※

Of course, glutton for punishment that I am, I do send the book to the agent, with Anton's recommendation.

Eventually "Ron Pickerel" responds and, in our meeting in a boarded-up storefront in the West Village, tentatively accepts the burden of representing me. Can I make four copies?

Months go by without a word. Occasionally I stop by the boarded-up storefront and pound on the door. Once in a while Ron Pickerel answers and invites me in, shuffles through files and hands me one with a couple of form rejection letters in it. Gradually his office fills up with boxes of typescripts, loose pages everywhere. Ron's mumbles grow indistinct, as do my hopes.

※

Despite the ecstasy of *les cafards*, the cockroaches, whenever I cook in *le style Bellilois* and the lack of encouragement from the fishmongers, I persist in my quest. Striped bass, halibut, mullet, shad, sardines, squid, clams and cockles, tiny rock shrimp from Maine: nothing is safe from my smoking skillet. When I take a wide sailor's stance over the stove at night, I forget myself and New York. I'm back in Kerbordardoué.

Mindy says the apartment smells of fish. Of course. I need to vary my offerings.

Fortuitously, a couple of gay pioneers in Chelsea have just opened a tiny store: Epicure Cheese. It's the first "gourmet" thing to dare show its face here. We're a dark and struggling no-man's-land; seven out of ten brownstones across the street are burnt-out ruins crawling with all kinds of strange shadows after dark. But at Epicure Cheese I can get little paper-wrapped slices of *pâté de campagne*. Dried mushroom tortellini. Cheese, of course. A good baguette, praise God. And—what are those sausages dangling from the ceiling at the back of the shop? Why, I know those dark-red, hard-gnarled fellows from the market in Le Palais!

"Is that chorizo?"

"Of course it's chorizo."

"Is that the Don Moroni brand?"

The sardonic chubby gay shouts over his shoulder to his partner, the skinny, tall gay with the beard: "Hey, we got a wise guy here. What'd you say your name is—Don Moron?"

"I'll take all you got."

"No, you won't." He sniffs. "You think I don't have other customers?"

I've only actually seen a couple of people ever come into the shop. "Not for chorizo."

In the end we compromise. He needs a few to dangle from the ceiling so the place looks like a real Old World *fromagerie et charcuterie*. The rest I take home. On Belle Île this particular chorizo is my miracle ingredient. Just add a half-dozen slices to a mess of sautéed zucchini and tomatoes and onions and peppers, to *lotte*, to a potato-kale soup, to an omelet, to the sweet clams called *palourdes*…

❧

No word on the book. Itching for action, I decide to go downtown, fire Ron Pickerel, and rustle up another agent.

But, it seems, the Pickerel has bought the farm. A trout farm. Or so his landlord tells me when I come knocking. He's gone off to raise rainbows in Vermont. Authors keep showing up, looking for their books, his landlord says. But he threw everything in the Dumpster.

When you have a story like that to tell, every writer you meet will have one that tops it. You'll end up feeling better, too. But after you get home, the nights will still seem endless.

❧

Okay, world, you win. I've had the stuffing knocked out of me. Let the roaches take back the kitchen, because I give up cooking. We sit blankly before our cardboard cartons of gluey Hunan Pan takeout. Fatigue is our friend, our enemy; we sleep instantly, deeply, but this just brings the next day closer. A busy city orbits outside our dark little cave.

We keep on going through the motions, getting exercise, reading books to Rory. He's the energy source now that our dreams seem dashed. A wonderful glowing spirit. We give ourselves a shake and admit how lucky we are. At least I can go to my job wondering how to apply my latest skill: building castles and galleons and space stations out of Legos.

Hey, don't laugh. I'm serious. When I was a kid, I was all thumbs, the only one who couldn't make an identifiable object out of Popsicle sticks in art class. Now look at me. I have reconstructed the Middle Ages with Legos, taking up every available inch of our living-dining room floor, and my three-year-old admires me for it. He's the first person in my life who doesn't know I'm all thumbs.

And you should hear me do the voices of the Lego action figures. I do a Chaucerian monk, a Monty Python Silly Knight, a poor, wee old woman crouched by the fire who has a cracked voice and reads omens at the bottom of Hunan Pan takeout cartons. I do Sir Gawain the Grouch, Good King Arthur, snippy Queen Guinevere (who bears a strong resemblance to Gwened, no matter how hard I try), and vultures.

Why Lego put vultures in a kid's puzzle kit I'll never know, but boy are Rory and I surprised when they begin to talk! "Excuse me, sir Knight, are you dead?" "Pardon the interruption, my King, but are you dead yet?" "Sire, may I enquire if you'll soon be dead?"

Rory shrieks with hilarity and demands more variations. Mindy comes in from the bedroom looking alarmed. Now I can't have a minute to myself without Rory coming at me with a black plastic vulture and the imperious demand: "Dad, make him say *die!*" What have I taught my child?

The Vulture Variations dominate my home life. Trying to change the subject, feeling haunted by what I've unleashed, I tear down part of the Middle Ages and, to Rory's intense interest, begin to build a humble village out of the ruins. We can't live with it; we can't live without it. There's no avoiding it, Kerbordardoué.

One late spring day Mindy comes back from a warm Saturday outing with Rory. As we're moving about the kitchen, preparing his snack and our cups of tea, she remarks that she met a rather odd person at the swing sets at the General Theological Seminary, the only bit of green grass in Chelsea.

"Boy was she pushy!" says Mindy. "But in that native New Yorker way, kind of nice. Very nosy. Wanted to know everything. But she raved over Rory, kept saying how beautiful he was, so I think she's all right."

"Of course. That's all that matters."

"Her name's Laurie, I think Colwin."

"The *New Yorker* writer?"

"Well, I thought that, of course, but I wasn't going to ask. I mean, there were other mothers around and we were pushing our kids on the swings."

Very carefully, neither of us said anything more about it.

"Tell me about your novel. Mindy says it's funny."

"Well, it's about a Coca-Cola bottling manager who wants to be a professional bass fisherman and his…"

"Okay, so it's funny. I've been telling Juris," nodding ahead to her tall husband, walking with Mindy toward the bright lights of the Empire Diner, where Rory and Rosa are already choosing an outdoor table. "Juris hasn't been doing anything funny. It's just so damn serious over there."

"There" is her husband's publishing house.

The deal with Juris and his partner, Laura, is that I throw out the second half of the book and set the final showdown between the Bass Commandos and the wife's soldier of fortune squad in Las Vegas. Makes perfect sense to me, especially as it comes with a contract and a check with some very slot-machine-like zeros on it.

And look: Is that summer on the horizon? Approaching in slow, agonizing, penurious motion? Yes. Are we really going to go back to France? Yes, it seems so. We write Madame Morgane, but the *cabane* is booked for relations who used to stay there and help with the harvest. Mindy writes Gwened, who replies that her house will be rented through September 15. Gwened herself is teaching summer courses in Tours to pay for an upstairs addition to her barn, a sleeping loft for her fellow kyudo novitiates. Once that is done, a guru may visit. The dojo is nearly complete.

The tone of her letter is brisk, a bit reproving. Between the lines we hear: *Why are you asking to use my house when you have one of your own?*

Because (we don't say) you got us in this pickle, dear Queen Guinevere.

Midsummer, I turn in the final of *Hot Water*—Laura having rejected my title, *The Bass Commandos*, and my backup, *A Rod and Gun Marriage*, and me having rejected her suggestion, *See How It Wiggles*. It's done. Will you look at me? I'm actually ahead of schedule, having just turned thirty-eight.

We're still uncertain about going to Belle Île when the August renters cancel at the last second. And that means Gwened is soon offering us her house at a reduced rate. Our Breton Brigadoon is pulling every string, working its magic, to reel us in. We scramble to buy tickets. We're coming home.

Chapter Fourteen
Who Steals a Road?

Straight off the red eye from New York to Paris, we board the eight thirty a.m. train departing Gare Montparnasse for Rennes, where we will switch trains for one to Auray on the coast, where we will switch again to the Corkscrew to Quiberon, where we will catch the ferry *Guerveur* to Le Palais and then, at last, a taxi to our door.

We take turns nodding off while Rory gazes out the window at the slow-changing, eternal landscape of France, narrating the journey in a voice of bemused delight. "There's a cow in a yard with his friend the dog. They live there with an old lady. There's a bus. It's not a big, fast bus like the ones on Belle Île, but a slow country bus…"

An elbow bites into my ribs and my eyelids roll up. Mindy nods at some people a few rows ahead. Sitting with his back to us is a man my age whose thick sweep of hair pulls back into a stubby ponytail. Mindy tugs my own stubby playfully. "Look…" she whispers. Bobbing above the seat, between the man and a pretty brunette, is the crown of a little blond head. "Our doubles," says Mindy.

Three hours later, the train pulls into Rennes Gare. We have three minutes to pull down our bags and descend from the train, struggle down the *quai*, stumble down a long, slippery set of stairs into a tunnel under the tracks, then climb up another set of stairs to the *quai's* other side, where the Auray train is waiting, chuffing impatiently. We vent curses and exhortations to each other and to Rory—"Move it!" "You move it!" Then we hear and see our doubles barking and stumbling ahead of us. Even in extremis it's enough to make us smile.

On the Rennes–Auray leg we don't see our doppelgängers. Napping hard, we awake in a couple of hours to find the red-tiled roof and pink stone walls of the cozy Gare D'Auray before us like a gateway to summer. Gone are the dark tunnels of Paris, the dank, wet black hills of Rennes. Sunlight blazes forth, Southern California strong. Heat washes over us as we sluggishly descend, slothlike mammals emerging from millennial hibernation.

On the swaying, creaking, stifling hot train we shed sweaters and jackets. So does everyone else. The seaside soon heaves into view and, boy, are we ready for it.

By the time the train is passing the beach, I'm down to my last layer of clothing, a classic French sailor's blouse, horizontal blue-marine stripes on white, no collar. Rory is wearing an identical shirt. We must look cute, the way people are smiling at us. But maybe we're too cute? Because now people are turning their heads, looking and laughing. Finally, on the off chance that it isn't us they're chortling over, we turn around and look behind, into the faces of our doubles, who are already giggling— because my ponytailed opposite is wearing an identical French sailor's blouse and so is his son, Rory's age. Mindy and her French counterpart break into laughter at what they've wrought, because, of course, they've *dressed their men.* The guy and I roll our eyes at having been had, again.

His name is Bruno, hers Valerie. The boy is Leo. And yes, they are going to Belle Île. It's pointless to resist, and why would we want to try? We've doubled our summer family.

The first hours back in the village are spent in a jet-lagged daze under the long Nordic twilight, which goes on and on. We go for a walk, slipping past our house—we've agreed not to make a formal inspection until morning—but there's no ignoring the drab exterior, unpainted walls, and rotted shutters charmlessly set off by foot-high weeds running the length of the front. We hurry on.

Still, New York falls away. Respiration and pulse slow; eyes widen, feeding on the dense, subtle tones. When a silhouetted figure across the close-cropped plateau appears, our first *voisin* of the summer, the light picks him and his three spaniels out like an engraving tool. Even at a half mile, he registers our gaze and lifts an arm. We do the same.

Rory narrates: "This is the ditch. It has water in it, very good for birds. A dog can drink it, too. Farther down there are sometimes cows." At a bend in the road he stops and inhales and exhales rapidly, staring. It's a landscape of stubble field and hay in round ricks called *buttes*, stretching away a couple of miles to the old *moulin blanc* on a hill. The mill's vanes don't turn anymore but it could be straight out of Cervantes.

Gwened's house is nowhere near as airy as ours, if we could but live in it. It has that feeling you get in premodern houses, that the people who lived there were much smaller. We duck our heads to enter, duck the pots hanging from the beams, duck to take the stairs up to the bedrooms. I have to contract, bring my arms close to my ribs, to navigate the hallway. It's appropriate that up here was where I read Gwened's well-thumbed copies of *The Hobbit* and *Lord of the Rings* during that first winter. By the time I'd finished those two thousand pages, I felt that I might very well be a hobbit.

Moving in slow motion, we make the beds and tuck Rory in and then ourselves. The room is dark and enclosed. We've forgotten that Gwened has no dormers, only skylights. It occurs to us that this is where her obsession with our windows comes from, not from some need for control. She only wanted us to live in a dark hobbit burrow like her own.

That first night's sleep lasts, as always, well into the next afternoon. When we tumble downstairs we go straight outdoors to sit on the slate-topped stoop, joining the lizards basking there. Seeing them, Rory rises and with kung-fu stealth begins his annual stalk, the start of a twenty-one-day hunt; although who's hunting whom is a good question as he falls headfirst into the bushes after an unsuccessful lunge.

Twenty-one days this year. Twenty-one days of light—versus three hundred forty-four of dark. That's what it feels like.

Bowls of *café au lait* and *chocolat chaud* resting in our cupped hands, we begin to discuss what a perfect day might be like, today, and the day after that, and the one after that…

🌿

After coffee we're ready to do our duty and inspect the house. The door groans open like a cliché. Inside all is dirt, windows obscured by huge spiderwebs clotted with hundreds of desiccated midges. We stand in a patch of dusty half-light, fighting the impulse to flee.

"Well…" says Mindy shakily.

"Yeah." There's no denying it. We made a mistake, buying this place. We're poor. We live in a dark, two-room apartment in Manhattan, and for our one vacation we come—here?—to a dismal hovel in the mud and gloom? Nice change of pace.

I'm unable to meet Mindy's eyes, afraid she'll echo my thoughts out loud. Once spoken, the unraveling will begin. She sighs. "Looks like we got here just in time."

We open doors and windows cautiously, letting in air, coughing, and wiping cobwebs on our hair, our pants. Upstairs we go, via our rude cowshed ladder, to a sense of relief, then quiet astonishment at how light, golden, and clean the rooms are. The workmanship matches the exquisite design: two large pyramid-shaped chambers completely paneled with *sapin du nord*, Swedish pine; the dormer windows two spacious coves in the ceiling; the windows large and commanding a roofline view of the square and our little *allée*, the lane, bursting with hydrangeas. We have gone up the beanstalk.

170

"*Bonjour?*" calls a voice below. We chorus back excitedly, expecting Suzanne, Franck and Ines, perhaps even Madame Morgane, but when we peer over the unguarded edge of the second floor we see two strangers, a man and a woman, dressed in crisp Parisian leisure wear, dark glasses in hand, standing on our ground floor without so much as a knock.

An echoing, overlapping, overloud conversation takes place, us up high, they below. It seems they have been waiting for us, driving by each day. But why? We don't recall ever meeting them.

"But you're not French," she suddenly says.

"No, we're not," says Mindy.

"We thought you were workmen," the man says, speaking slowly. "We will fix it up."

"Fix it up? Are *you* workmen?" asks a bewildered Mindy. They rear back at the affront. The purpose of their visit becomes clear: they want to buy the house.

"But it's not for sale," I hear Mindy saying.

Their faces turn down with a prissy exasperation. Her voice is pure sneer: "This house is wasted on you."

"It really isn't for sale," Mindy says firmly. "Now I must ask you to leave."

"Ah!" Throwing her hands up, the woman cocks her head around her at the downstairs mess. "Enjoy your vacation!"

They go, taking with them our short-lived euphoria at how nice the second story looks. Now we are only aware of how far we have to go.

❧

Riding on waves of jet lag, we crash into a second disappointment: Franck and Ines and their three children are nowhere to be seen, and what's worse, there's a new name daubed in white paint on their mailbox. They've moved? Can it really be true?

Suzanne confirms it. She doesn't know the new people yet, news she conveys by blowing air out of her nostrils like a horse when we ask. *As if,* she's saying, *I have time to keep up with all the changes in this busy crossroads of the world!* She doesn't even know where Franck and Ines have gone. We hope their windsurfing school, always precarious because weather-dependent, hasn't failed, forcing them off the island.

The next house over from Franck and Ines's has new faces, too, but hasn't changed hands. As sometimes happens on Belle Île, an island family has redistributed the real estate. This is how *Bellilois* hang on to their land. This is how Suzanne came to us after decades as a cowherd a few villages over; her little hovel had been waiting fifty years for her. After a succession of cousins or aunts or uncles (it was a granary for over a century) passed away, it came her way. Title doesn't seem to change, and neither do the faces, bearing the same distinctive nose, the blue-black eye, the angular jaw, and other telltale signs of near-consanguineous island ties.

The new people don't give us a second glance. That's typical of first interactions (and second, and third) with villagers, we tell ourselves. Time is the only leveler. But it's also true, of course, that these new people are the old people, the true *îliens,* islanders. After all, to them we are the new people, and always will be. Party crashers.

Mindy stands in the square, puzzled. She can't quite put her finger on it, which bothers her.

But errands beckon. We've got Gwened's old Renault 405, a luxury. It beats years past when we had to cycle into Sauzon for even the merest scrap of bread. Sauzon may be a picture-perfect little port with a perfect waterfront *crêperie,* Les Embruns, but for supply shopping it's a hard slog by bike: twenty-five minutes to get there and more like forty minutes on the return, thanks to a long steep hill, hell when you're wearing a backpack full of groceries.

Anyway, with the exception of the fish lady of Sauzon, who is not only charming and chatty but refuses to let pushy old ladies cut in line in front of foreigners, we won't miss the vendors. What a crusty lot they are: the twin *boulangerie* ladies, grouches, sour from being shunned as collaborators after the war; the black-bearded butcher who talks of suicides he has known, whose final flights he commemorates in his scary oil paintings of vertiginous cliffs and the tourist-eating grotto; the frosty ladies at the small grocery, who aren't so bad but have simply seen too many mosquito-bitten, hungover campers. Ah, but with a car…

Now we can go into Le Palais for the open market, which an hour-long bike ride each way put out of reach before. Roaming the stalls we select fresh fish, clams, vegetables, lettuces, local goat cheese, every purchase accompanied by a proper conversation.

On the way back we hit *le supermarché* on the hill. Okay, it's a super-market, but listen, they're different in France. This one is the only place to get the freshest shrimp and sole, plus handmade buckwheat *crêpes*.

We can also buy sacks of potatoes and onions, grated Gruyère, sliced ham, yogurt, tubes of tomato sauce and merguez sausages from Algeria and the Moroccan hot sauce called *harissa*, rolls of paper towels, boxes of toilet paper, cases of Kronenbourg 1664 beer and *cidre brut* and bricks of UHT milk, not to mention good cheap coffee and chocolate and wine, including four-buck Muscadet and three-buck Gros Plant. With Gwened's car, for the first time we can buy all this in one shopping trip instead of strung out over two weeks. It's something we can't do even in Manhattan, being carless. And so we go a little overboard.

The pleasure of having Gwened's house to ourselves for the first time since 1980 is doubled when we catch sight of her vegetable patch: rows of runner beans, zucchini with bright yellow blossoms, tomatoes sagging from green vines, parsley, cabbages, carrots, frisée, and peppers. We have Gwened's blessing to take all we want and give it away, too.

Finally there's Gwened's *jardin*. Her tree-shaded grassy lawn has a hammock and a pair of old wicker chairs, perfect for whiling away an afternoon reading. We're set.

❦

After our over-the-top shopping trips to town, we won't need another for weeks. We can still zip into Le Palais or Sauzon to buy fresh fish,

Brittany's famous salt lamb, and baguettes, but to top off our staples there's a Thursday panel truck that beeps its horn and opens its side to reveal a mini mobile grocery. The truck is where Suzanne and Madame Morgane shop, avoiding town as much as possible. Suzanne doesn't even go to church, unlike Madame Morgane. She's got her religion right here, growing and flowering all about her. We've all got it right here. There's no greater glory than a day spent in Kerbordardoué.

But one day when the jet lag has fully worn off, Mindy again stops in the village square, frowning and looking around. "Something's changed," she says. Just then the sound of a car makes us look down our *allée*, our one-lane road. The car turns up the tilted track and trundles toward us, wobbling from side to side in the ruts and potholes. We step aside to let it head off to the left, to the last cluster of houses. But it doesn't turn and we have to step aside again, backs against our wall. As it passes the occupants stare straight ahead with that eyes-front expression particular to Bretons from the Continent.

The car goes past our house, headed for a dead end. Suddenly it cuts around our north wall and rumbles away into Madame Morgane's barnyard. We follow. And watch as the passengers get out—elderly, tiny, the two women in proper woolen jackets—and go in the front door of a blinding white, brand-new, prefab-looking version of a classic Belle Île house.

"Oh my god," says Mindy. "A tourist villa! Where did that come from?"

We study it for several minutes, commenting to ourselves, the no-peeking village rule suspended by disbelief. The front door opens and the people, two couples, come out again and get into the car. The engine starts. There's a gravel driveway in front of them leading to the main road, but they slowly reverse in the barnyard, turn around, and head out. We pull back and stand in our doorway as they drive by, only inches from our doorstep, with that same impassive—or is it gloating?—look.

"Why are they using our lane?" Mindy's expression is granitic. "They came much too close to the house. They could hit Rory. They should take the road…" She looks around. Her eyes narrow. "Wait a minute—where is the road?"

The main road into the upper village and our square, the old threshing ground, is wider than our *allée* and doesn't squeeze between stone walls. Or was wider, because it's gone. In its place a thick, tall hedge blocks our view and indeed makes even the idea of a road a spurious fabrication by foreigners. We walk over and feel stupid. How can you not notice a missing road for three days? Well, we have been gone two years.

And this is a professional job: a landscaped berm, then a row of large terra-cotta pots holding flowers and tomato vines, then the wall of shrubs.

"How could they let this happen?" says Mindy, running down the names of neighbors in her head while I do the same out loud: "Gwened? Franck and Ines? Suzanne? Madame Morgane?"

We descend our lane to the road and follow that around the corner and up to the houses that formerly bordered the now-not road. On the other side of those heavy shrubs is a picnic table, a homemade brick barbecue, and a white wrought iron patio table with matching chairs. Both sets of new neighbors seem to have collaborated, as a second row of shrubs, these immature, set off a similar patio at the house opposite. They've divided the road down the middle.

That evening we go to talk to our new neighbors. They come from the suburbs of Paris. Their friendliness seems sincere. Mindy drops a few hints. Oh, I see you have a nice patio. Yes, isn't it. We'll have to have you over.

Back at the house we agree that the neighbors obviously thought we were angling for an *apéritif*, not a lawsuit. They seem agreeable and innocent; if not, they're such good dissemblers that we'll never get anything out of them.

"Their kids are nice, too," Mindy says sourly. We know what we're up against. It's the affair of the well all over again.

❧

```

# DON WALLACE

One of the few charms of our house when we bought it was that it came with a well. Or, I should say, it once came with a well, a beehive of drystone, situated on the opposite side of our dirt lane. But somehow we lost it.

How? We were careless, I suppose. Village usage and ownership of common space is a tricky thing. A grove of trees, a trickling spring, a parking space, a crumbling wall—all can be sources of intense obsession over who actually owns it and what they can do with it. Alexis de Tocqueville writes in *The Old Regime and the Revolution* that even for open space there may be a proprietary connection going back two hundred or more years. *(Move your shadow!)* And that was certainly the case in Kerbordardoué. Lean your bicycle against the wrong barn for more than a couple of hours and you may hear about it, not from the owner, but from your neighbor who heard from someone else. You have incurred a village demerit. Take care or your children may inherit it.

In the case of our well, the link was broken somewhere in the buying process between the verbal representation of the notary and the formal plat, or *cadastre*, filed with the Mairie, or mayor's office, and we didn't even know it. We only found out years later, when someone said something about one neighbor refusing to let another neighbor run a hose from the well during a drought, because it was his. We were appalled at our neighbor's uncharitableness. But then it struck us: *"His? Oh, really?"* we replied. *"That's odd. Because it's actually ours."*

The villager we were talking to looked at us. *"You know that it's yours?"*
*"But of course. Why wouldn't we know?"*
*"Oh. I see. It's just that we thought… But how did you know?"*
*"Why wouldn't we know?"*
*"I see. But how long have you known?"*
*"Forever. Since we came here."*
*"Oh. But if you've always known, why didn't you say something?"*
*"Why should we say something? We know it's our well. That's enough for us."*
And so forth.

Once in a while that summer we looked at our neighbor's house and

176
```

thought: *But we're friends! When did you decide to take our well? Did you do it because we were Americans? Did you think we were thick? Too wimpish to fight?*

We thought about visiting the Mairie to reassert our ownership of the well. We thought about starting a whispering campaign to spread the news that we were aware it was ours and would lay full claim to it. But to stake our rightful claim to the well carried dangers, some we could see, others we couldn't. A visit to the Mairie might open up a discussion of other cans of worms we didn't want opened.

Also, we *liked* our neighbor and his wife and their children. To quarrel over the use of a well seemed petty, particularly as we could quite possibly be living next door to each other for another thirty years, and our respective children might be after that. At last a village truth dawned on us. We had no use for the well. Why pretend we cared who owned it? The well wasn't going anywhere. We could still look at it all we wanted. The day we agreed to make no more noise about it, we felt a load taken off our backs.

❦

There's a rumble and the glass in our front door vibrates as a car passes, too close. The renters, *locataires*, again.

Hour by hour, day by day, Mindy grows more furious, and not just at having our peaceful sanctuary violated. The communal spirit has been desecrated in a premeditated act, Franck and Ines and the new island neighbors collaborating to steal the road during the dark of winter. Then Franck and Ines must've used the garden, and lack of a road, as a selling point as they quickly unloaded their house.

But other than a complaining, muttering Suzanne, we can find no one who will admit to what has happened. Late every night Mindy threatens to go to the Mairie de Sauzon and demand to look at the village *cadastre*, but every morning an instinct for self-preservation kicks in—or else the day is so fresh and beautiful she just can't bear to gird her loins and go into battle with the French bureaucracy. Best to wait until the last week of August when Gwened arrives. Then we can strategize.

We cook a lavish welcoming dinner on Gwened's first night, *coquilles St. Jacques*, cold langoustines with mayonnaise, barbecued baby lamb chops with springs of fresh rosemary, garden potatoes and carrots and salad. A portrait of composure, Gwened honors our efforts with a great show of concentration and over each dish pronounces a mandarin approval, although, being Gwened, she barely eats. Still, we have passed a test, and in a Frenchwoman's own kitchen. That's a big deal.

The whole time we're bursting to tell but holding our tongues. At last Mindy can no longer stand it. She tries to sound calm: "We noticed that the road is gone."

"Yes, it is quite a change. I'm afraid our poor little village is losing its character."

"Then we should go to the Mairie. Surely someone can't just steal a road?"

Gwened readily agrees that this is how it must look to us, but, she adds, we must understand that there is a Belle Île way of looking at things, too. Her manner is resigned and her point of view Olympian.

Naturally the story is more complicated than we might guess. First Madame Morgane's son sweet-talked her into allowing him to build a summer house in the barnyard, so that he could bring his family and her grandchildren to visit more often. House done, he turned it into a holiday rental. The renters driving back and forth in front of Madame Morgane's also passed her daughter's house, at all hours of the day and night, which led the daughter to bar the gravel driveway. Whereupon the son told the renters to drive down the road, hang a right at the corner of Franck and Ines and, when they reached the square, to continue on through the rough terrain behind our house. Their tire tracks became the basis of a new road.

But all the traffic disturbed Franck and Ines. Actually it terrified them. Their youngest was a toddler given to wandering out the door, which opened directly onto the road, like ours. Anytime Ines's back was turned, he'd make a run for it.

A kitten was run over, squashed flat, on their doorstep. That's when the idea of blocking the road came to them, Gwened says. It was a coincidence that the neighboring *Bellilois* house happened to shift occupants, but also a blessing because the new faces were parents and sympathetic. (Also calculating; as anyone who is familiar with *Manon of the Spring* would know, the French country mind is always thinking about new ways to add more land.) And so, Gwened shrugs, one day the backhoe arrived, followed by the truck from the nursery. Deed done, all parties could sleep easier—literally.

"Except for us and Suzanne! Since all the traffic is now funneled past our doors!" In exasperation and anger, Mindy has raised her voice to her old teacher.

Gwened is silent for a long time. Then she explains that the deed of sale is signed and registered. We know all the parties involved except the buyers, and they are such delightful people, are they not? Her tone is clear, as is her inference: maybe we are not delightful people, as she once thought. Maybe this is what you get for not finishing the house all those years. All those years, the village looked the worse for your neglect and you didn't care.

She shrugs. Anyway, when the time came to change the road it was just accepted, because nobody lived on your lane. So that was where the traffic belonged.

"But we have no garden, no land, between us and the road," says Mindy, close to tears. "There will be dust, noise. And Rory. He could get run over, you know."

"Yes," says Gwened, "I'm afraid you will suffer, especially in the summer. You might want to consider selling the house. Or, if you do finish it, to come only in the winter."

Mindy is shocked. "I just can't believe that everyone could stand by and let this happen."

Gwened nods. "I very much disapprove of how it was done. But it is done."

"What about Suzanne?" asks Mindy. "She's old. Someone could run her down. She has kittens, too. Didn't anyone think about what this does to her?"

Gwened's silence is devastating. Could it be that Suzanne is a nobody even to sensitive Gwened, who sings the praises of her flowers all summer long? Really?

Somehow, Mindy finds the strength to stay silent, bottle her anger.

There are moments when the force and rigidity of class culture is revealed in all its cruelty, like substrate rock underlying sandy soil. It takes a big storm to reveal it. We're having our big storm. Now, with the new title registered, remediation will be much more difficult. *Usages ruraux*, our Breton lawyer Sylvie had said, can change over time if it is not contested. We know where we stand. We won't contest it.

On one of our last few days, Mindy goes into Gwened's shed and comes out carrying a pickax and a shovel. "Come on," she says, heading out into the square. I follow, alarmed. She can't really be thinking of tearing out the neighbor's hedge and leveling the berm, can she? We'll probably end up in jail.

She stops in front of our house, though. Staring hard, she walks along our wall, dragging the pickax behind her. It makes a line in the powdery white dirt about four feet away from our doorstep and sad, stained, once-white wall. "This will be our garden." I can see she's been thinking this through when she adds, "Not all at once. We stake a claim by planting something here," walking back and planting the pick at a spot about three feet out from our doorstep. Where our plastered wall ends is where the cars make their turn to get to the tourist villa. "It has to be something hardy that will grow while we're gone. Something prickly, to make the tourists swing wide past our house so they don't scratch their precious rental cars."

In her khaki shorts and faded blue camisole Mindy nevertheless looks like a general surveying defensive terrain before a battle. Hefting the pick high above her head, she brings it down hard on the packed earth. "We're going to plant a rose."

Chapter Fifteen
Who Kills a Rose?

In New York that fall, we carried Belle Île like a lucky rabbit's foot. Our boy had the glow and physical grace that comes of being out in nature for weeks on end. We were pretty lean and loose-limbed ourselves, *en bonne forme*. Within a month of our return, Mindy found herself interviewing for a new job, her first since Rory's arrival, and was quickly snapped up. (Because of her sun-streaked russet tresses, no doubt.) Now she spent her days working to preserve undeveloped forest, beaches, and watershed, good for the bank account and good for the soul.

The April publication of *Hot Water* was still far, far away, but I walked in a fog of daydreams and acute sensitivity to the great changes to come in my life. And then suddenly here it was, just around the corner. By mid-March I had an advance copy of my book (my book!) and carried it with me on the subway for the first few mornings, thinking this was the way to build word-of-mouth until the *New York Times* wrote about it. Then I began to worry that someone would recognize me from the author jacket photo on the back and wonder at my shamelessness and the *New York Times* would write about that.

The day arrived. At lunch I walked over to the Barnes & Noble at Grand Central and browsed the stacks. There it was!

One copy, but still. I was torn by the desire to buy it or go up to the desk and request it (but then I'd have to buy it). In the end I explained my dilemma to the clerk who agreed to order two more copies to have in stock.

That Friday I was at my desk when the phone rang. There was a business contact on the line. "Go now," she said, "and buy the *Washington Post*. The culture section. First page."

※

By July, *Hot Water* has come and, bookstore clerks apologetically tell me, is going, going…gone. My, that was fast.

But the rave *Washington Post* review is on the wall at *Success*, where my editor in chief put it with a goading glance at his two right-wing minions. It's a funny world; I think he's actually proud of me. When I ask again about going to Belle Île, he waves a hand and says, "Whatever. Go. You know, I saw a lot of *Success* in your book."

"Let's keep that our secret," I say.

We shake on it. And with that pat on the back, I go back to the mines and start coining more of my Belle Île currency: freelance articles. My output is at an all-time high. That has to be good, right? While I may not be working at a Manhattan name-dropper's job, at least I have the satisfaction that goes with all the work, the interviews, the cover stories, the editing, on top of which are the freelance book reviews, essays, and stories. In trying to get ahead to pay for Belle Île without shortchanging Rory, I've found another gear. Watch me zoom.

But in truth I'm unhappy, at times desperately. I published a novel and it didn't change my life one bit. Meanwhile I feel I'm shoveling shit into my brain and dishing it out in 1,500-word chunks for predigested consumption. In this I'm not alone, nor do I delude myself that I'm any different from my friends sweating out their lives in cubicles next to mine. Journalism is a messy craft, and its temporal quality rebukes any pretensions of writing for the ages. Instead of immortality, we get to bitch, colorfully and extravagantly. That is the joy of a newsroom. But you can't take it with you.

My one shot at immortality—okay, at making the back wall of the Strand Bookstore—seems destined for the same fate. Too late to ditch my dreams, I can only hope there's a second act down the line.

❦

Around this time we get a letter from France:

My dear friends,

A very nice couple from Paris rented the new villa behind your house over Noël and fell in love with the village. They would like to write you to ask if you'd be interested in selling your house. I hope this does not derange you, but I told them to go ahead and gave them your address. They are charming and would make good neighbors. They have three small children but are willing to keep such a small house as yours. I do hope you will entertain their offer. It is important that the village center have life, and your house is quite forlorn now.

With my best wishes,
Gwened

So, dear muse, it's good-bye, Belle Île, just like that? Thanks for the memories? *Je ne regrette rien*, or maybe, *je regret vous?*

We haven't recovered at all when a letter comes from the young couple of Paris. To our dismay Gwened is right and they *are* nice. They seem acutely aware of the pain their inquiry must be giving, and choose their words carefully and compassionately, a delicacy of temperament that is explained further down in the letter when they mention they are psychiatrists. Of course, being Parisians, they can't resist exclaiming that they love New York.

Mindy refuses to reply. She has had to write so many letters in French to France, to Madame Morgane and Suzanne and Gwened, to the Mairie de Sauzon and our insurance agent, to Denis LeReveur and all his crew. Every single letter that she has written has gone toward the realization of the house, our dream. I can tell the thought of this one rips her heart out.

I take it upon myself to ease her pain. Taking down *Le Petit Larousse*, I laboriously construct what I conceive to be a graceful letter, explaining our deep attachment to the house and how much we hope to one day spend the night under its roof, and ending with a jolly "We love Paris!" Later, of course, I will be informed that I have called the husband a woman and the wife a man in the coarsest possible terms. I've also apparently claimed that Paris loves me more than them.

Regardless of my illiteracy, the answer is still no.

But we don't dismiss Gwened's letter. She's right. This may be her version of shock treatment, but we deserve the bucket of cold water in the face. We *are* letting down the village. But we seem stuck. We can go back to Brigadoon or finish the house, but we can't do both.

🌱

Traveling once again. Dreamlike France. Dream in French. Dream = *rêve*. So, a reverie of repetition. *Rêve, rêve, rêve* your boat, gently down the stream… Like a filmstrip run backwards, we retrace our steps and movements from the years before.

In a sleep-deprived daze we hum hymns to the beauty of transatlantic planes and trains so various and reliable. We grunt along with the shudder of the ferry *Guerveur* when her blunted steel-riveted parrotfish prow bites into the first big ocean swell, and the next, and the next. With the other passengers we crowd the rail as the island comes in sight. Adult restraint falls away and we join everyone in cheering the two blasts of the ferry's horn. Inside the harbor's tight basin, behind a narrow mole, our captain spins the ship in her length, bow thrusters and screws churning up boils of yellow mud. The cargo door in the side clangs open onto a stone ramp that rises from under the harbor waters to the *quai*. We're here.

We could almost raise a chant: "We're here, we're here," as we march shoulder to shoulder with the other passengers to street level, like the Communards of *Les Soixante-Dix* to the barricades. Meanwhile the ferry disgorges cars, trucks, bicycles, and even a silver motorcycle with a sidecar.

The *quai* is lined with waving, smiling friends and family. Although they're not here for us, that's all right. Because we're not tourists or visitors who need a welcoming reception; we live here, sometimes. We have a house!

We're feeling buoyant; the universe feels generous today. Even the taxis look good—"It's just so France!" I say, inanely, at the sight of the drivers (two male, one female) leaning against the hoods of their cars and smoking. But this year we're renting a dented Citroën Deux Chevaux, exorbitantly priced. So we pile in and urge it, chug-chug, up the hill leaving Le Palais, then cry "Whee!" as it rattles like a roller coaster down the other side, and then up and down, swooping over the vertebrae of the central plateau. The twists and turns of village lanes slow us to a crawl until, *enfin*, we're pulling up in our little, white-powdered dusty square. We set the parking brake with a jerk. The car door creaks an awful protest. Stretching our backs, we take in the village.

But then:

"The rose is dead!"

☙

Poor rose, we stand over you, flattened into what once was mud, now baked into the hardpan. A sad, twisted stalk and a couple of tiny branched arms, no bigger than when we planted you. You look like a fossil or a stillborn from a Neolithic barrow grave.

"It never even had a chance." Mindy sighs. "I guess the renters didn't see it in time."

We stand over the fossil rose. Rory crouches and touches the ridges of mud squished up by the tires of a car or truck and then frozen by winter temperatures and dried in the kiln of spring and summer. There are a lot of ridges and herringbone tire tracks, a crisscrossing, as in multiple times driven over the rose. A lot of times.

"Someone did this on purpose," says Mindy. I've already had the thought.

Who kills a rose?

Back in June when we'd written Madame Morgane about accommodations she'd regretfully informed us that her son had a friend come by with a tractor to drag away the *cabane*. He was afraid it would detract from the pleasure of the renters as they sat in their cheap plastic chairs at an outdoor table under a beach umbrella and stared across the stubble field. What kind of man sees a forty-five-year-old wooden cabin, cunningly crafted and tight as a drum, barely large enough for three people, hidden away in a grove of trees, as a threat? A man who knows the price of everything and the value of nothing.

Perhaps, we think, *a man whose tractor-driving friend kills roses.*

We trail the offending tracks up the road to the edge of our house. Rory is like a tawny two-legged bloodhound, narrating: "Then they drove up here. These are wide tires. There are five different mud squishes here, so they must have had to back up and go forward to get around the corner. This was a big truck."

We think he's imagining things. We should know better. When we come around the corner and look, again blatantly breaking the rules because (again) outraged, we see the most horrifying sight yet: Madame Morgane's hundred-foot-long stone house is gone. As in *gone*.

Gone, from left to right: the stone stable and cowshed; the barn, with its exterior staircase of stone to the upper hayloft, a fixture now rare on Belle Île; the main building with its bedrooms and sitting room. Parts of that house dated to the mid-1700s, parts to the early 1800s. All that's left is the far end, the all-in-one Breton kitchen where we would sit during the winter of 1980, squeezed between an armoire for dishes and an armoire for M. Morgane's elderly parents.

In its place is a raw dirt hole with fallen beams and crushed interior paneling sticking out. It looks like a bomb crater. "Poor Madame Morgane," says Mindy. "She didn't even mention it in her letter about the *cabane*."

We stare and stare. Then Mindy gives herself a shake. "Let's go," she says. "We shouldn't be looking. What if Madame Morgane were to see us?"

It takes almost all week to worm it out of her, but Suzanne does tell us how Madame Morgane's son's friend with the tractor returned one day with a clamshell-shovel backhoe. He said he was going to use the clamshell to lift materials, new slates and two-by-fours, up to the roof for repairs.

While Madame Morgane was in her kitchen making coffee with Suzanne and listening to the radio, there came a powerful shake and shudder. A cloud of plaster dust and stone chips billowed in. Hitching up their skirts and running outside, the two old girls found the house collapsed right up to the kitchen wall.

An accident, said the backhoe operator. Then he began dragging away the old stones, some of them scavenged from the Neolithic tumulus that was built in the field five thousand years before. A friend came by in a dump truck and hauled them away. What else are friends for?

There had also been no room for us at Gwened's inn this summer, but we can hardly complain, as she has packed her house and barn with students of *kyudo*, the Japanese way of the bow, most of them Belgians. We see them wandering through willow-hedge mazes and pacing the edges of threshed fields, in couples and in small groups, heads bowed, often dressed in white *gi*. They seem to regard Gwened as a guru. (Ah, yes, where have we heard that before?)

We stay away from her property at the back of the lane, not from wounded pride but for safety's sake. Sometimes Rory and I tiptoe close enough to hear the creak of a bow, the twang of a bowstring, the whoosh of an arrow. Red flashes fly across Gwened's *jardin* toward a paper bull's-eye pinned to an old horse cart leaning against a hayrick. But, Rory snickers, they rarely hit. They don't even come close to the target.

As much as we keep our distance, Gwened keeps hers. It's as if she doesn't want any reminders of her life before donning the white habit of a *shin-zen-bi* (truth-goodness-beauty) archer. Fine. Whatever keeps cancer at bay. And it does seem to be working.

So where are we staying? Our house, out of desperation. There's nobody we can rent from in the village. Though the kitchen-dining area's rotten floorboards were trashed and hauled away when the workmen renovated the upstairs, the back bedroom still has a floor of sorts. In our absence, the new neighbors of last year threw out a sofa, which somebody, perhaps Denis LeReveur, has dragged in.

Denis also donated two rickety chairs and an equally unstable pale wooden table from a failed *boîte de nuit*, nightclub, he's redesigning. An old futon mattress is waiting for us, donated by Franck and Ines, who, it turns out, relocated to town and now live above the small business they bought. No stove, no sink, no refrigerator: we'll continue to cook over our Bleuet Campingaz stoves and run cold water (no hot) in pots down from the upstairs bathtub.

It's quite a comedown from Gwened's immaculately appointed kitchen and comfortable hobbit-burrow bedrooms. Our one piece of good luck is marvelous weather—*beau temps*, Suzanne assures us when she comes by for an inspection. She doesn't seem to find our squalor disagreeable. Then again, her own hut is a layered midden of paper and kindling and open sardine tins, dark and smoky, hopping with skittish kittens.

We notice a pile of cans and dirty implements in a corner, covered with old newspaper.

"*L'homme*," says Suzanne.

"What man?" asks Mindy.

Suzanne shrugs. The man who lived here for a while before Denis booted him out.

We are living a true upstairs-downstairs life; the funny thing is we're playing both roles. Downstairs life is dirty, uncomfortable, and lacking in modern conveniences. Upstairs, once we've climbed the twenty-foot ladder, the same relic we cached in the tall weeds last year, we're in a shining magical treehouse. We've got two bedrooms with those big dormer windows; ceilings of bright, varnished knotty pine; and a bathroom with a deep tub and a skylight overhead. The clean white walls have never been blemished by so much as a fingerprint in all these years.

There is no question of sleeping upstairs, however. The ladder is giddy-making and the drop from the top of the second floor, which has no railing whatsoever, is vertiginous. Just the thought of Rory wandering around in the dark with a twenty-foot fall awaiting him is enough to cause my stomach to do a flip-turn. We will sleep on the futon on the ground floor and make up a pallet for Rory to sleep near us.

That we are emulating the homeless *homme* is a thought to keep far, far from the surface of our minds.

❧

Lucky us, we can stay out all day—which stretches for eighteen hours—if we please. This is the longest spell of *beau temps* anyone can remember. Every night we go to bed thinking the beautiful time is over; every morning we wake to that preternatural stillness and clarity.

Excellent lizard weather for Rory, it inspires Mindy to start digging a trench, twelve inches wide, alongside the house. I take over when her back and palms give out.

"What are you doing, Don?" asks Gwened, drawn out from behind her screen of hydrangeas by the clink of the pick on hardpan. She's in a white *gi* cinched tight at her waist by a black belt, quite fetching. We've noticed several of the Belgian youth are also quite fetching, in a Flemish school of painting, ca. 1540 AD, sort of way.

"Preparing the soil," Mindy says, stepping from the interior shadows into the doorway.

Gwened waits for elaboration. "For what? Are you planning something?"

"Trench warfare," I quip. This doesn't go down so well.

"Mindy, this is not your land to do with as you please," says Gwened gently. "It's part of the road and the square."

"You mean like the other road?"

Gwened smiles beatifically. It's like she flipped a switch; suddenly she seems to emit rays of goodness. "I can understand how you would like a garden. Why don't you come up and use mine?"

Poker-faced, Mindy nods, but her sidelong glance at me is devilish. It's a funny thing—when we're confronted, insulted, even mocked, all I have to do is look at Mindy. We exchange a glance, and it's enough. "I think a little grass and some flowers will improve the look of the place," says Mindy.

Gwened shakes her head.

"We already have weeds," I point out. "We'll just put in some nicer weeds."

"I'm afraid if you do, someone in the village will report your *fosse*."

Wow, is this a threat? It has always rankled Gwened that we went for a common septic tank instead of buying the famous nuclear-powered feces furnace like the legendary old lady of Le Palais. Still, our *fosse is* perfectly legal.

I'm trying to not forget my manners when Mindy replies. "You mean the same person who killed our rose?"

Touché.

Gwened draws back visibly, surprised that we know it was no accident. Connect the dots and it becomes obvious that she's one of those who didn't speak up. And now that she knows we know it, she can no longer claim ignorance the next time someone decides to murder our rose. She will have to ask herself if she's become *un collabo*, a collaborator.

"I see," she says. "I'm afraid you will be disappointed again next summer when you come, but I see."

✿

With the long bout of *beau temps*, the ocean this year seems different, too. We've been used to rows of snarling, chaotic walls of white water marching up and down the sand. The crisp, glassy tubes Mindy compared to Pupukea in Hawaii during our first winter must've been a one-time event, or even an illusion. Or so we were beginning to think, until now. Suddenly we find ourselves pausing in our sand castle building and Frisbee throwing to stare in rapt concentration at waves, real ones. We turn to each other and chatter excitedly. Yes, this is definitely surf. And it looks good. *Cowabunga!*

Lacking boards, we still can bodysurf. At first we take turns heading out, the other keeping watch. There are no lifeguards and nobody else around who looks like they can swim more than a stroke or two. Despite the *beau temps*, the water is shockingly cold—59 to 61 degrees Fahrenheit—but having to constantly kick and stroke and duck dive at least provides some heat or distraction. It's a strong swell, with swirling currents. The waves are quick, shifty, hard to gauge. Afterward, comparing notes on the sand while shivering under towels and sweatshirts, we agree that we need better tools. Swim fins, definitely: we use them in the big surf of Hawaii and California.

What about surfboards? No, no, no. Really. Mindy is wistful. Sure, honey, eventually. (I'm lying.) Sure, really. (Let me get this straight: You want to haul a surfboard on a New York City taxi to JFK, then take a plane, a Paris taxi, three trains, a taxi to the port, then a ferry, and finally one last taxi? With a five-year-old in tow? *Are you crazy?*)

Of course not, dear. I want you to haul it. (Mind reader!)

A couple of days later, Franck and Ines come out for an *apéro* and to see the old village. When we mention that we've been swimming at Donnant, Franck pales. "That's crazy!" he shouts. "You will drown. Every year tourists die there, swept away." He sputters and stares and shakes his head—we are dumbfounded. Finally Ines calms him down while saying to us in her tiniest voice that the reason Franck is so upset is that a good friend drowned horribly right in front of his screaming family, after being swept off the rocks of Donnant.

Belle Île's best baker, Momo, was collecting *pousse-pieds*, the great delicacy of the European mid-Atlantic region. Americans at the seashore never give these goose barnacles a second glance, let alone consider taking and eating them. But off the coast of Portugal and Brittany, locals and itinerant crews have harvested them down to the lowest level exposed by the super-lowest of tides. This creates a situation ripe for disaster, as extreme low tides often come back up fast and hard.

We try to explain how surfing makes us safer than the average *pousse-piedophile*, because we know waves and aren't scrambling around on rocks to start with, but in vain. Franck keeps shaking his head and growling. This seems odd, considering he built his business on windsurfer rentals. But his beachfront shop was on the calmest, sweetest Continental side of the island, the Côte Douceur, on a wide beach of powdery white sand. There were never any waves except during the rarest of storms. His clientele was timid and respectful of Franck's authority. And in those early days of windsurfing, the boards were little more than small flat sailboats. It had all worked very well for Franck and Ines, although they'd ended up exhausted and selling the business.

The idea of wild Americans opening up Belle Île's western frontier, the Côte Sauvage, is the last thing they needed to hear. Publicly we make our reassurances. Privately, after they've gone, we laugh. What wimps. The whole point of surfing is going out when it's big, even a little scary. In Hawaii and California the best-formed waves often come out of a wicked storm, rolling out like shiny, smooth sculptures from a howling maw.

When we go back to Donnant the next day, however, we find we've caught Franck's fear. Objectively speaking, the beach can be fearsome. First the ocean's energy, gathering for weeks across a 2,500-mile open fetch, is funneled by steep cliffs into a bulb-shaped bay. All the while, tides of up to forty feet sweep up and back, turbocharging the rollers. They turn the bay into a boiling cauldron at high tide, and at low, expose the sands all the way to the entrance, where gray-green closeouts slam the door. Finally, the half-mile-long horseshoe of sand is cleaved at the middle by a large rock ridge that divides the waves, setting up a refractory backwash that sends giant waterspouts ten to twenty feet into the air.

We talk it over and decide to cool our surf fever until the following year, when we will bring the swim fins and, for Mindy, a wet suit.

Chapter Sixteen
The Dream Team

Our new life on Belle Île was taking shape in our minds. Around us was still dirt, dust, mold, exposed nails, and blackened greasy walls, but if we turned our faces skyward, a celestial city awaited. All we had to do was ascend, like Jack on his beanstalk. Why not now, we argued, lying on the floorboards that never got clean despite Mindy's daily scrubbing. Why wait, when Rory was strong and coordinated and fearless.

The next day I began scrounging two-by-fours and other pieces of scrap from the collapsed barn. No carpenter, yet still I trusted in the power of a nail, many nails—hammered in at all angles, linking up struts and cross-pieces—to create a barrier around the L-shaped edge of the second floor. Done, I surveyed my work from below. It looked like a logjam on some Western river. But that was okay. Beauty wasn't the issue; safety was. And Rory would have to use a crowbar to get through that wall.

Now, at night, we climbed the ladder as a family: first Rory, then me with my body arched over his as we climbed in unison, step for step, handhold for handhold, with Mindy hovering just below, arms open wide, ready to spring into action.

Going to bed with the dormers wide open to the soft night air, we cuddled and said our good nights and turned out the little electric lantern. Up high, we could really appreciate the quiet and peace, and it might have been a beautiful night if either of us could've fallen asleep. Instead we waited in the dark for Rory to rise and wander. When I finally drifted off, it was to wake up in silent dread, uncertain if I was dreaming or reacting to a scream.

The next night we brought rope. Stringing it from pillar to post, we created a web that might catch Rory, he of the innocent "Who, me?" eyes, if he should outwait us and then, when we were asleep, bust through the flimsy barricade. Yes, flimsy. In the mind's dreaming eye I had appraised my work and found it lacking.

Short of tying Rory to a doorknob, what were we to do?

For now, put him to bed between us and the wall, so if he tried to escape he'd have to crawl over us both.

❧

A long tramp on the moors, heading north along the Côte Sauvage. Rory has reached the indefatigable stage and his little legs pump as we follow the trail, narrow and bounded by blue-green succulents, dark green pincushion mosses with red ruby flowers, and ankle-biting gorse (flowering bright yellow as if to draw us closer). But heading down on the shaded side of the little valleys we swim through fields of softly waving ferns, head-high in places where the rutted path has worn itself five feet deep into the hill.

Up and down goes the *côtier sentier*, the coastal path. The sea shines like silver out to the horizon, an electric blue-green at our feet—well, fifty to sixty feet below our feet. The cliffs of the Côte Sauvage are no joke, and once again we wonder what possessed us to bring Rory into the presence of such great heights. Mindy covers him as closely as she can, short of tying a rope around his neck. But he's motoring on, strong and agile as a mountain goat.

After a couple of hours we're tired and hot. Fortunately the trail dips to the edge of a white, rocky beach with an enticing grotto and a *roche percé*, pierced rock. These demand to be explored. We spread our picnic out on a shared towel and take off our sweaty shirts, lying back on the hot, white, polished stones, emitting little yelps of pain and pleasure. Within moments we're up and racing for the big, brilliant blue.

Beau temps has now reached out and stilled the sea. We head inland on the path we think will take us home: there are no signposts. Up a verdant green valley of ferns and marsh rushes, we find a welter of paths, some for cows, some for sheep. One is for us—but which one? The moor is open for miles. Over the top of a nearby windbreak of cypress we think we see the top of the *moulin blanc*. Triangulation makes it possible to devise a course. We come to a road, barely a track, but rutted by car tires.

There's a shoal of cypress trees, yanked to one side by the wind. Their green-needled branches twist together like the tresses of a goddess. As we walk past, we see a glint of silver under upswept boughs: a gleaming motorcycle with a classic 1940s sidecar. A spiffy khaki rainfly roofs the sidecar; it looks designed, like something L. L. Bean would make if he joined the Hells' Angels. Another tarp covers a collapsible safari table. A blue bubble tent sprouts like a psychedelic mushroom off to one side.

"Campers," we tsk. Tsking because camping is illegal, but who are we kidding? We've been there before—living rough. It just feels different when it's your rough, your island.

The scene is tidy, nicely laid out, no trash in sight: well policed, as my Boy Scout father liked to say of a clean campsite. Still, the farmers are tired of campers messing up their fields, and the island's self-appointed conservators also are vigilant. Birdwatchers see everything. You can get away with a night or three, but...

"Want to bet how long before somebody runs them off?"

"Or maybe not." There's a stake driven into the roadside ditch and a little homemade mailbox of wood is attached to it. This is somebody's home. Or will be, one day. Looks like we have some competition in the rough-living department. And it looks like they're ahead.

❧

A drive into Le Palais on a crisp morning to shop at the open markets.

Bags weighing us down, we stop at Denis LeReveur's *atelier* on Place du Général Bigarré. Now that our accounts are settled, he doesn't try to duck our visits. He has time to talk, to reach behind into the wall of cubbyholes and bring out our rolled-up plans. We spread them out on the drawing table. And sigh.

We never get past the sighing. But, today, Mindy clears her throat after studying the graceful lines of the staircase, the spidery tracery of the downstairs with an imaginary armoire against one wall and a set of see-through furniture waiting for the ghostly perfect family.

"We've waited long enough," she says. "Can we get the job finished by next summer?"

I repress a big *whoa!* and squeak out a little one. "Um—Mindy—I mean—?" Pause. "Shouldn't we think it over?"

"I've thought it over," she says. "It was seeing that motorcycle camp. I don't want to end up like that. If we wait until we have the money… we'll never do it."

Mindy does look spooked at the thought. I can see the picture in her mind of us huddled around a sooty fire blazing on the ground floor of our house. Like after some kind of apocalypse.

Good thing Denis has the same relationship to English that I have to French. He doesn't know we're sparring over our very financial future. He simply goes on nodding, but in a restrained way, not overplaying it. In fact he looks serious, *très, très sérieux*. That's smart; I could learn from that, instead of always turning everything into a joke. But Americans don't have the same natural gravity of the French, Bretons, *Bellilois*. We have to work at it and I'm here on vacation.

Mindy is explaining in French now. I am coming around. After all,

200

this is something we should've done five years ago. We'll find the money. *Blasé blasé*, as the cooler black cats in my high school used to say.

"There is a problem," Denis says. Even I can translate that one.

We wait. He inhales and tries English:

"Monsieur Borlagadec is *retraité*." Retired.

"Surely we can find another to do the floor and stairs?"

"These old houses require an eye," says Denis, switching back to French. "In the old days they didn't use yardsticks or levels, just strung a piece of string along the wall. The modern ones, they use"—he raises his hand and points it, makes a beeping noise—"*les outils électroniques*."

I nod. I'm following. My construction experience fills in the gaps. He's saying that today's construction workers are like those in the United States, little more than installers of prefabricated shells. For an 1830 stone house we need a craftsman.

"The new eye does not the old house do." Denis, trying English again.

"Well, who has that kind of eye?"

"Monsieur Borlagadec."

"Ah."

"*Retraité*," I say, helpfully.

"*Oui*."

"Can you talk to him?"

"I have."

"And?"

"*Retraité*." Denis extends an arm and swings it across the ceiling, squinting. "Pheasant. *Boum!*" He aims at the door. "*Lapin. Boum!*"

We leave with an understanding that, though Denis is out canvassing among the old and doddering artisans of Belle Île, we are essentially doomed to a frustrating process and unsatisfying result. When the new construction workers see an old house, Denis says, they don't want to spend a couple of weeks cutting and shaping each piece to the irregularities of a nineteenth-century stone wall. So they shrug, say, "Yes, I can do this," and when you're out of sight, they bring in a backhoe and yank it down.

"*Une accident, oui?*" he says, and we hear his anger at the loss of the old houses, the old skills and, worse, the lack of shame.

"*Oui*," we say. "*Une accident.*" Thinking of Madame Morgane.

❧

"Don! Come! Come now!" cries a breathless Mindy, gripping the doorframe and sticking her head inside the house. Then she yanks it back outside.

Rory: my first thought, followed by guilt. We've trusted him too much. He's gone and hurt himself. Fallen down the well.

I run after Mindy into the square where she waits, hands on hips, staring down our *allée*. Just as suddenly my panic wanes. Rory's on his knees in the white dust over by Gwened's stone wall. He's pushing a toy truck with a little Playmobil man in a hard hat at the controls. Phew.

I sidle up to Mindy. She has an eager air, like a hawk facing into a strong wind and hovering, waiting to plummet and pounce. "What?" I ask.

"I saw a car going down the *vallon*. Pheasant hunters. The season hasn't started yet."

"Did they have guns?" I ask. She shakes her head. "So what's the big deal? We can't stop them from scouting the terrain?"

"I think I saw Monsieur Borlagadec." She takes a deep breath. "I'm going to talk to him. Wait here." She looks at Rory. "No, come. Leave Rory. He's fine."

We race down the unpaved *allée* and turn right down the slightly larger road, down into the *vallon*.

After emerging from the cypress tree tunnel at the throat of the tri-angular pasture, we pause and pull ourselves together near some baby cows, *les petits veaux*, that cluster around a rusty steel water trough. *Look casual*, we tell ourselves.

"He's not here." Mindy spins around. "He must've turned."

There's a dirt road or a couple of narrow car tracks to choose from. We take the road. A long 180-degree pan of the stubble fields and hayricks turns up nothing except, ironically, a brood of pheasants picking grain out of the chaff.

"Wait. Listen." Mindy pricks up her ears. She turns this way and that. Her chin lowers. A half a mile away a screen of trees shelters a couple of small, white houses at the outer edge of the village. "I hear voices." We scoot back up the road to a muddy driveway, which we've never taken because it seems to go nowhere except into somebody's front yard.

We round a corner into terra incognita. A burly, mustached older man in a plaid wool shirt jacket is talking with a young workman, the two of them chatting easily while standing atop a newly laid concrete foundation. So there's a new house going up here. I'm disappointed. But then I'm always disappointed at new construction anywhere.

"It's him," says Mindy, looking at the older man. "Here we go."

Neither man acknowledges our presence until we draw near enough that it's obvious we're going to speak to them. "*Bonjour*, Monsieur Borlagadec," Mindy starts, and soon she's introducing herself to the workman to refresh M. Borlagadec's memory: "I am the American woman with the house that is not finished."

But it's evident he needs no reminding. He seems taken aback at our sudden arrival, but not offended. His strong mustached face hardens as Mindy asks if he's come to see how his pheasants are doing. "What pheasants?" he asks.

Mindy smiles. "The ones Denis LeReveur says you're going to come back and shoot, *bien sûr*."

The black eyes glitter. It occurs to me that he knows what's coming and is not going to make it easy on Mindy.

But then she switches tack and launches into an earnest apology for not continuing the work. She keeps her explanation to a minimum: *la catastrophe économique mondiale, le bébé. Mais maintenant...*

"*Je suis retraité*." Blunt and to the point, that M. Borlagadec.

"Yes, I heard. Congratulations."

He likes that. Though she's overmatched, in his mind, Mindy staying in the ring is the sort of thing a *Bellilois* appreciates.

"I do not wish to intrude now," she continues.

"You're not," says the workman, who is also beginning to enjoy this. Mindy may be his first fluent foreigner. Her Tourenne accent would ordinarily come off as *un peu snob* in a Frenchwoman, but being of no discernible class, Mindy gets a pass. The workman raises a bottle of wine and offers it to her, a drink from the spout. Mindy knows better but laughs at the teasing. The workman turns to Monsieur Borlagadec. *"Etes-vous prêt, Papa?"*

Ah, father and son. It registers with a shock of pleasure. We feel new warmth in the air, now that we know, but Mindy keeps her cool. She steps back and lets the two of them make the next move. Instead of leaving, they step up to the new foundation and pour a libation on the ground just inside the southwest corner. Nobody says anything for a little while.

"Bon," says the son. He turns to us. *"Pour la maison. Afin que personne, n'aurait plus jamais soif."*

For the house. So nobody will ever be thirsty.

He offers the bottle again and I immediately get it—he's offering us the first swig, so no germs, quite a courtesy—and say yes before Mindy can recoil. It's port. No, something else sweet, more alcoholic... I squint at the label: *Pineau des Charentes?* The Borlagadecs are watching so I take a second swig. They like that. Then I tip the snout to Mindy who sees the look in my eyes, laughs, and takes a sip.

She hands the bottle back, saying, "Perhaps you would like to come up to our house for a drink?" Before the "no" is out of M. Borlagadec's mouth, she adds: "I would appreciate your opinion at what must be done to complete the foundation and the staircase. Perhaps you could even recommend somebody."

We know damn well M. Borlagadec has refused to give Denis even one name. He's apparently proud that he was the last of the best and there is no one left with his skill set. But he's leaving behind sad, empty houses that will never be finished without him.

But the son, he doesn't know. He's curious. Which house is it?

Chez Jeannie.

Tante Jeannie? Son turns and gives father an amazed, delighted look—a look of love and wonder. *Tante Jeannie! Tante Jeannie!*

M. Borlagadec heaves a sigh, and when his broad shoulders settle, there is a new expression on his face. Mixed in with a slight lowering of his guard, I think I detect a real curiosity about Mindy. And wry, if still grudging, respect.

We walk slowly up the *allée* to the square. Rory is out in front, bent over his plastic backhoe now, pushing it around, shifting a tiny pile of dirt by the door. M. Borlagadec stops to watch. He smiles, really smiles, for the first time. Nudges his son and points. His look needs no translation: that's just like you when you were a boy.

Rory chooses this moment to turn his head and look M. Borlagadec in the eye. His expression is very serious. It is not an appeal, but something more imperative. M. Borlagadec understands. He squats and inspects the toy backhoe. He doesn't touch it. Then he looks at Rory and tilts his head at it. Rory nods, yes, of course.

M. Borlagadec extends a hand and with the tip of his index finger pushes the backhoe toward the pile of dirt. Rory's head is bobbing, yes, yes, yes. His body tenses, eyes widen.

With a gruff laugh, M. Borlagadec ruffles his hair and rises. *Un bon homme.*

We step into the house, Mindy and I filled with trepidation. It's such a disaster, but of course to a construction worker that's normal. Father and son move slowly around, touching and pointing, clearly remembering how it looked when it was Jeannie's. *I sat here, you there.* Then they turn their attention to Denis LeReveur's upstairs renovation, starting with the ground floor ceiling, which instead of being completely replaced contains both new planks and old. One half of the roof beams are original, too, ca. 1830, probably handsawn over trestles in the square.

Mindy explains that this was our decision, taken with Denis. Only some of the wood had dry rot.

"You took a risk." He waves at the new wood. "This could all rot because you left one bad board. One bad board! *C'est fou.*"

"Denis was careful. I trusted him."

M. Borlagadec gives a grunt that would be easy to read in English, but has extra levels, flavors, in French. Maybe Denis, that wild roving boy, is famous for taking risks. Or maybe he's cheap and spun a good story about saving us money while charging us for new wood and using only half. Clearly a house is doomed when a fool mixes old wood and new. M. Borlagadec turns to his son: "Much better to pull it down, *oui?*"

Mindy breathes a shocked little "no!" and he smiles at the success of his cruel joke. But to Mindy he's opened a door.

"*Le maison du Madame Morgane,*" she begins, but at a look goes silent. A touchy subject, naturally. Maybe it's not proper for an *étranger* to discuss these things with an *îlien*.

The exchange seems to have darkened M. Borlagadec's mood. He shows impatience. Looks a question at his son—shall we go?—who shakes his head. The son, we sense, is on our side, rooting for us. But the decision lies with Papa. And Papa is *retraité.*

Everything could still work out, I'm thinking, when M. Borlagadec takes hold of the ladder. He frowns. Smacks a rung at head height, watches the termite dust slowly sift and fall. *Faible. Foutue.* After that he shrugs and climbs halfway up.

He stops, frowning. "What is this? Did Denis do this, this *thing?*"

"Ah, no," I say, adding a little proudly, "I did. It's a what-do-you-call-it, not a wall, a barrier…"

He snorts. Climbs another couple of rungs until his head is level with the floor. He sees the futon, the sheets and quilt. "What's this? Why is it here?"

"We up there," I say in broken French. "We sleep. Bed."

"Nobody should be up here," he says. "It's not safe. *Pour le sécurité. L'enfant.*"

He climbs back down, slaps his palms on his pants, and stares at me, not Mindy, giving me his full attention for the first time since we tracked him to the new house. All day he's kept me at an angle, aslant, on the periphery of his vision.

Now I wish he still considered me beneath notice. Seeing myself with his eyes, I cringe at the danger I've put my family in. Only then does he slowly stalk out.

"Well, that went well," says Mindy, "until he saw your *barrière*."

"You mean my *derrière?*" I halfheartedly joke.

She smiles, but I feel exposed and small. We mull it over, the odds. Not as much of Rory falling, I'm sad to say, but of M. Borlagadec getting on board. *Not good*, we think.

Then we think: *can't risk it*. We move our beds to the ground to sleep on the floor.

Pounding on the door, early the next morning, way too early for anybody civilized. I'm still boiling water for coffee. Rory sleeps. Mindy is upstairs washing her face and brushing her hair, having mounted the ladder groaning at the indignity.

I open the door. There's no one there. Oh, great, a prankster. But out in the square a white panel truck sits with its rear doors swung open. A moment later, M. Borlagadec comes around from behind the truck, T-square in hand. He's wearing denim overalls and a worn leather tool belt polished to a high shine by decades of use.

His son pokes his head out of the back of the truck and waves.

An hour later, the second floor has a proper temporary barrier and *père et fils* are gone, having politely refused repeated offers of *un petit café*. My handiwork, the old barrier, is a mess of kindling in the fireplace. It looks like Popsicle sticks.

During the last days of our stay, a team assembles: Borlagadec *père et fils*, still the best concrete men (the son has the foundations of a dozen Parisian second homes to pour but puts them on hold); the plumbing team (also father and son with matching ponytails); the best electrician (fingers alarmingly bandaged, but, it turns out, from chiseling *pousse-pieds* off the rocks, not from being electrocuted).

Denis LeReveur shakes his head in quiet satisfaction at each addition. The best. At a team meeting in the house Mindy explains, at Denis's prompting, how we do not want to change a thing that can possibly stay the same. We want a Breton house, a *Bellilois* house, a *saine* house, a house Jeannie herself would recognize, were she to return.

"No gold faucets?" asks the plumber.

Everyone bursts out laughing. They're antsy, shifting from foot to foot, smiling, flexing their busted knuckles like cowboys ready to saddle up and head out one more time for that last roundup. Who knows, this may be the last old house they ever get to rebuild in the old style.

⚘

Before we leave, once again the pickax comes out. One more rose from the nursery goes in. If we can just force the tourist cars wide of our front door, it opens up a space for a garden along the wall.

The trench of turned-over soil running alongside the house gets a scrawny little red-tipped *sauge*, sage, and a cutting from one of Gwened's hydrangeas. Both should require no watering. Gwened thinks the corner is too shady for the hydrangea, but then Suzanne comes by to inspect and Mindy draws her into the conversation. She gives a snort. Hydrangeas grow wherever you want in Kerbordardoué. The question is, what color do you want? Bury a grapefruit with the cutting if you want blue, leave it as is for pink.

"I think some grass here would look nice," says Gwened, pointing.

We nod in silence. Instinct says not to mention Gwened's change of heart.

Flower by flower, beam by beam, we're going to win this thing.

Chapter Seventeen
The Parent Trap

As the house neared completion we'd made plans, schemed, and saved for an entire year to spring ourselves for a full month. Yes, a month off from work: unheard of in America but typical in France. After years of wrangling with bosses, pleading with editors, and bluffing with no cards, we'd vowed it was now or never. We had good reason. The visit would be an exorcism of our initial folly in buying this house, because, for the first time in eight years since we took the plunge and signed away our lives, we would be spending the night under its roof.

No more staying in Gwened's cramped attic guest bedroom, no more renting Madame Morgane's unplumbed migrant-worker shack in the fields. No more cooking on a mountaineer's Bleuet Campingaz stove, no more bathing Rory in a tin washtub surrounded by clucking chickens. Well, we'd miss *that*. But now the floor was poured and the staircase to the bedrooms upstairs finished. Eight years after signing away our financial future, we could move in.

And then my mother called. "We're coming to visit you this summer," she announced.

"You are? Here? New York? Great."

"On your island in Provence."

Eight years and she still hadn't gotten it right. My mother, the comparative literature PhD, less one thesis defense. Not an accident. "It's Brittany, Mom. But what brings you out? One of your golf tours?"

Other people's parents travel with airplane tickets in their hands, dress in clothes from their closets, drag their luggage or tip the porter. Mine go in officially coordinated tours of twenty and thirty, all in bright red logoed windbreakers and stretchy nylon pants with matching red shoulder bags, their giant suitcases and golf club cases similarly rouged and stickered, the whole herd manhandled by large former football players in red blazers and security earpieces. They are alpha American golfers, my folks. The Greatest Generation mustered into Arnie's Army and conquering the world.

"No," my mom replied. "Just coming to visit."

I wouldn't have been surprised, really, if they had announced they were golfing Stonehenge, Antarctica, or Guadalcanal. But coming to Belle Île without clubs? Something was fishy. They'd already made their feelings clear about this place.

When I'd called to break the news that we were buying the house—"A cute little ruin on an island in the Bay of Biscay," I kept saying, as if repetition would make it sound better—my mother had asked "*Where?*" while my father listened in stony silence. I'd hoped he'd see the fun, since all through our childhood he'd bought odd-shaped land parcels to hold for resale in some future when Disney needed that exact strip (three feet wide and half a mile long) to build their next Magic Kingdom. (Actually, that deal broke even when the strip was bought for a freeway widening.) I thought that my dad would be tickled. "Chip off the old block! We Wallaces, we're *always* buying ruins!" Hoped, evidently, for approval.

Instead, when I had finished, he was curt: "I know why you're doing this. It's so that, when you're at a Greenwich Village cocktail party and you run out of things to say, you can always talk about your little house in France."

Now my dad's familiar growl came on the line again, but Mom jumped in, "Now, lover, this is exciting. You remember how everyone in the country club is excited? Jimmy Wagg was impressed. You know Jimmy is now a *Chevalier du Tastevin*, Donny? He wears his burgundy robes at the annual wine tasting society dinner. He says Provence is very chic. The ladies in my bridge club are just going ga-ga about helping me choose the decor…"

I winced. I winced *on so many levels*, but just to mention the first, Mom's taste and ours were diametrically opposed: froufrou and chenille versus jeans and T-shirts, country club Republican versus ultraprogressive, dinner dancing to "Tie a Yellow Ribbon" versus flailing to Talking Heads's "Psycho Killer." *Qu'est-ce que c'est?*

"Mom. You are not choosing the, um, decor. Any of it." Not that we had any, but still.

She ignored me. "Where is it in Provence, again? Everybody's asking."

That last phrase was a clue to their change of heart, from ridicule to this sudden giddiness. I recalled how, at Christmas, we'd been on the receiving end of an assembly line of copies of *A Year in Provence*, Peter Mayle's memoir of food, wine, and no-guilt, no-budget overseas living. It had been on the bestseller lists all year, spawning a fad for bright, pastel Matisse-like wall coverings and drapes, and faux-naive painted armoires and tables. We who suffered in a dark one-bedroom in New York, rueful owners of an uninhabitable ruin in unchic Brittany, felt a trifle put-upon to get even one copy. But as we opened another one, and yet another, the wound grew more raw.

Now I got it: since *A Year in Provence* had shot to the top, my mom must've been telling everyone "she" had a place there, too. Only, when pumped by her all-a-flutter bridge and book club friends, she'd drawn a complete and embarrassing blank on any details.

I consoled myself that this visit was a kind of revenge by farce, but the joke was on us. By the time we coordinated our trip with theirs, they'd trimmed our four weeks on Belle Île to two. Because we must meet them at the Paris airport and ferry them and their bags to the hotel. Because then there would be two days of shopping. Because then we would visit the châteaux of the Loire. Because then we would go to the island and, after two weeks, reverse our steps to Paris for more shopping before escorting them back to the airport.

Still, I was game. It felt like an impending breakthrough, rapprochement between the generations. Mindy was slightly tragic—she'd be making all the arrangements and doing all the translating—but a good sport.

My parents, on the other hand, turned out to be brats. We'd begged them to come straight to Belle Île, because Paris is notoriously hot and smoggy in August, and many museums would be closed. I mean, that's why Parisians go to Belle Île. But no, Paris it had to be—Paris in the midst of a searing heat wave. Naturally, they complained about it.

Dad refused to try to speak any French, even in restaurants. Instead, he used his menu Spanish from El Torito. For breakfast each day he ordered *huevos rancheros*, always with the same result: bewilderment, embarrassment, a bellicose refusal to eat anything else, a squabble with Mom. He treated every waiter as an adversary, barking in the universal language of the surly tourist. Only the wine pleased him. Another reason to thank God for good Bordeaux!

Dad had always been the sweetest man, a gentle giant, loving, interested, intelligent, and wise, forgiving of his children and man's foibles. Was it only France that had set him off, or something else? A downside of the Greatest Generation, I've found, is a resistance to speaking about their feelings. All I could get from Dad was: "*Huevos rancheros.*"

At least Mom was a happy camper—what woman wouldn't be in Paris—until we got to Belle Île and Kerbordardoué. "But this isn't at all like *A Year in Provence!*" she wailed as we pulled up. (I know: How *could* she?) But, to give her her due, she'd insisted on spending a day in Vannes buying us fabulous Provençal-parrot-patterned duvets, quilts, sheets, pillowcases, and towels from a Pierre Deux–like boutique. There was no stopping her. She was in a zone.

What hurt wasn't her shudder and desire to flee immediately to a hotel, instead of waiting for me to assemble the Trois Suisses mail-order beds. I'm a ham-handed man under the best of circumstances, and my only screwdriver was a Swiss Army knife. No, what hurt was that Mindy and I didn't get to celebrate finally seeing *our* house finished after eight years. Instead we got their frowns of disappointment.

Our little bubble burst, over the next week we drove them around the island (five-minute drive, stop, get out for a photo, get back in car, five-minute drive, and so on), ate at restaurants for every meal (all of them "terrible," plus every morning a scene involving *huevos rancheros*), and browsed the handful of shops (no Gucci, no Louis Vuitton—what did Mom expect from A La Providence, a consignment store with a plywood cutout of a French sailor standing on the sidewalk?). Criticism pitter-pattered down like acid rain: these croissants are too hard, the *crêpes* are rubbery. Jimmy Wagg at the *Confrérie des Chevaliers du Tastevin* would not approve of this cheap Muscadet... What were we thinking? Belle Île was too small, too rural, common, nothing to do here, no museums, no glamour.

"President Mitterrand flies in on his helicopter to eat a *crêpe* here every year," I said meekly. The look I got in return said I'd just proved her point.

It all came to a head at the Hôtel du Phare, where the service is so slow it feels existential and can only be survived by getting a prized outdoor terrace table. We'd scored the table—the view of the pretty little harbor of Sauzon was postcard-perfect—when Dad launched into an assessment of our adventure, his voice dripping with sarcasm. Mom sat behind her sunglasses and didn't deflect or moderate a single remark.

Mindy began to tremble. I tried to change the subject: Rory was sitting here, reading his little book with a stormy brow. I said: "Dad, Dad..." Then, when he wouldn't stop, "You don't sound like yourself here."

"How dare you speak to your father like that!" snapped Mom.

Oh boy, here it comes now, I thought. But at that moment Rory glanced up. "Grandma," he said, in a calm little voice, "you and Grandpa are not treating Mom and Dad very nice. They planned this trip and drive you around and speak French for you and order food like *lotte* and sole at restaurants, which is very good for you, and very fresh, and they showed you the Grotto of the Apothecary and the Trou du Vazen and where the German gun emplacements are"—he gave a suppressed shudder of excitement at this—"and all you can say are mean things about them.

"The service is slow at the Hôtel du Phare," he continued, "but we can have langoustines and oysters and read our books and Huna can read his *Herald Tribune* that Dad makes a special trip into Le Palais to buy every morning. Do you know that when you're at your hotel, my parents are always talking about how to make you happy? But you don't even care." He looked at his grandfather, whose nickname he'd bestowed. "Huna, you should behave better."

The benefits of a progressive preschool education.

Chapter Eighteen
The Sole of Solitude

Serene and focused, Rory was a writing parent's dream from age five on—at least for the first few hours of the weekend or vacation day. But at some point, usually around lunchtime, he'd look up from his toys or book and glance around impatiently for a friend. On Belle Île, a look of disappointment would come next. For the rest of the day, no matter what else we were doing, our main hope was to find someone to keep him occupied, with the fate of the vacation—and our careers—hanging in the balance.

And finding playmates was a chore. What's easy at home is difficult to impossible on an island where you aren't a native speaker and a lonely cove or epic stretch of beach is a typical unsupervised playground. Yet we had to try. It's obviously important to the child and a game changer for the parents, who otherwise will be pressed into service to do endless vulture voices and Monty Python imitations with action figures.

For a portion of the first two summers Rory had Leo, son of our doubles, Bruno and Valerie, but after the second year they didn't come back (although we continued to see them in Paris). Just as the weather

seemed a lot colder back then, the island more raw, the pickings for
playdates underwhelmed to the point of seeming grim.

I remember three or four years of hopeful hangouts with other
expats, British mostly, in other half-completed houses in other villages.
These followed a pattern: cups of cocoa for the kids and tea with hidden
hits of Scotch for the parents, stilted conversation, heavy sighs over the
cost of finishing the renovation "next year," and the whole thing coming
to an end with a brutal attack on somebody's favorite stuffed animal or
Star Wars figurine.

In many respects the hunt for a friend for Rory paralleled the search
for a food he would eat. In New York City he was single-minded and
phlegmatic. Early days, give him his Gerbers and "mup" (milk) and
you'd never hear a peep. But in France during his first visit, at eighteen
months, our increasingly desperate question every single day was, "*Avez-
vous du* baby food?" In the early years the answer from Madame at Les
Quatre Saisons was a bewildered gesture at her four walls of canned
mushrooms and asparagus, *tête de veau* and *boudin noir* (that unctuous
pudding of blood), cheeses and wines.

Bretons seemed politely incredulous at the idea that children might
require a different cuisine. We asked for applesauce. (Try Normandy,
three aisles and a hundred miles to the north.) For a couple of years,
meals were nerve-racking. When he hit four and a half, the next new
must-eat arrived: "*Avez-vous du* peanut butter?" We learned it was called
beurre de cacahuètes, and that nobody carried it.

So we tried crushing peanuts in an improvised pestle. We tried
Nutella. (How he could turn down chocolate-laced hazelnut butter is
beyond me, but he did.) What saved us was not applesauce, but apple
cider. In our exhaustion one afternoon, we forgot to pack Rory's box of
juice before leaving on a drive to one of Belle Île's wilder coves. He sat in
his car seat growling away until Mindy spied a village grocery, hopped
out, and returned with a familiar dark glass bottle. "It's *doux*, the nonalcoholic kind," she said. Rory was in a famous mood the rest of the day,
napped eagerly, and ate his picnic lunch without the usual imprecations.

Attributing our son's instant conversion to some mystical affinity for Brittany, we lay on the sand imagining a more vacationlike groove. At last, we could have an occasional undisturbed afternoon. Rory burbled along, quenching his thirst with an occasional pull at the stuff he called "bubby." Just like a good Breton boy.

That evening, when Franck and Ines stopped by, they observed Rory's glass of fizzing cider and asked us if it was an American practice to get our children drunk. *Cidre doux* did not mean soft, as in nonalcoholic; it meant "sweet," as opposed to dry. Ah! The (unlabeled) bottles we'd been giving Rory ranged from 1.5 to 4.5 percent alcohol. Oops.

᪲

And yet I date the education of Rory's palate from that fateful first sip. For whatever reason, perhaps because it made him a little loopy, after that he didn't complain about the lack of peanut butter (or our pathetic alternatives). It's also true that the following year we took him out to dinner with one goal: to procure a plate of edible french fries. This might seem like an easy quest to fulfill in France, but Brittany, after all, is land of the galette and the *crêpe*, and a french fry from a *crêperie* tends to flop about on the plate like, well, a *crêpe*.

We arrived at the Hôtel du Phare and girded ourselves for the usual three-hour marathon dinner. That *frite* had better be good. We worried. Would a French french fry meet his standards? Or would he drive a stake through our hearts and say, "I want McDonald's"?

At the last second I had a brainstorm and, before offering him a *frite*, fed one to the officious seagull standing like an avian *maître' d* on the far end of our table. Rory was delighted by bird and fry.

Our table on the terrace overlooked the tiny port of Sauzon. The gull edged even closer on the balustrade as Rory tried his first bite of a golden-brown fish that lay, head to tail, across his plate. Rory eyed the bird warily; this was *his* dinner. "What's this called?" he asked, chewing, a frown of concentration creasing his forehead.

"Sole…" we said and held our breath, waiting for the tirade.

"It's great. From now on"—his knife and fork were sawing furiously away—"I want sole. Lots of sole."

Mindy and I leaned back and raised our glasses of Muscadet. "*Le* breakthrough," she sighed.

Forgetting that you must be careful of what you wish for, I nodded. "What if he grows up to be a child gourmet? Wouldn't that be something?"

Rory's ringing voice pierced our happy haze: "Dad, don't eat all your sole. I'm going to need more."

"I didn't order the sole. I ordered the *lotte*."

"What? Are you crazy? You must always order the sole!"

We sighed. I had a feeling this wasn't going to end well.

The following year, Rory took a marine biology class in school that not only turned him on to the world of fishes, but convinced him that it was his duty as top predator to eat his way down the marine food chain. In our first weeks back on Belle Île, his appetite for seafood was satisfied by sorties in a neighbor's boat for mackerel, bass, *vieille* (grouper), *aiguilles* (needlefish), and *lieu*, as well as low-tide expeditions to collect mussels and those siren *pousse-pieds*, whose white beaks, extruding from wrinkled black necks, protect a succulent morsel of flesh. It was the barnacles that told me that things were getting obsessional. The sight of Rory scrambling over a cliff with a butter knife in one fist and a lust for *pousse-pieds*—goose barnacles, for heavens' sake!—in his eye will always stay with me.

Rory's sea hunt caught the eye of an acquaintance of Gwened's, the sporty father of a very proper *famille en bonne forme* who had rented her house for a couple of weeks. I'd whittled a spear at Rory's request so he could go after the fish he'd seen in a small fjord. The father, Hector, came up to us after our unsuccessful expedition and without a word handed Rory—age nine—a spear gun. "This will work better, I think," said Hector.

Of course Mindy and certain other parents (okay, myself included) were rather nervous at the gift. We debated returning it. But that felt so…so…wimpish. What would a real man of Belle Île, a Denis LeReveur or M. Borlagadec, think?

To calm our frazzled nerves, Hector took us aside for a dry run and safety tips. As Rory loaded his bag for a return to Port Scheul, Hector smiled at me. "He will find out how hard it is to shoot underwater, to track the fish, the angle of deflection, everything," he said in his perfect Touraine French, so clear it sounded like English. "But he's so passionate he deserves real equipment."

We drove back to Port Scheul. I was still laying out our towels when Rory waded in, spear gun pointed straight ahead. Several mothers with small children near him turned to stare disapprovingly. "Be careful of the children!" I shouted to him. He kept on wading, like some kind of merboy in his mask, snorkel, and fins, gun cradled against his chest, tip pointed in the air as he'd been instructed.

The women rushed to their children—who were on dry land, let it be noted—and hustled them away from the water's edge with accusatory glances at me. Rory submerged. He began to cover the sea bottom in a methodical grid, snorkel spouting every twenty seconds or so. He moved a bit farther away, where the bottom dropped off, and switched from sand to rock.

I was so absorbed in watching Rory, worrying about him shooting himself, that at first I missed the arrival down the fjord's dirt road of a white horse with a yellow mane, ridden bareback by a long-haired gypsy-looking man wearing nothing but, I swear, a Speedo.

He rode the horse straight into the water. I started to rise, to shout—but what? I didn't have the French but also, it felt foolish; surely Rory wouldn't shoot a *horse*. At least, not one with a Speedo-wearing gypsy riding bareback.

Rory was now fifty yards offshore anyway. Maybe the horse would go away soon. But no, the gypsy rode out until the water was up to midthigh, then slid off and began splashing and rubbing the horse's back. His long black hair trailed down like his own mane. The scene felt magical, yet creepy, like an encounter with a troll.

Now Rory was heading back, facedown, snorkel spouting, fins slowly fluttering. Everyone watching from the beach was enthralled by the scene: the gypsy, the white horse, the converging unaware merboy with his spear.

Suddenly the horse clenched and dropped a half-dozen green turds, each with a splash. The reaction on the beach was international and audible: "Eeeeuuuuu…" I sensed a shift in sympathy. This guy was gross.

Blithely quartering the sandy grid, Rory headed off to the far side of the fjord. He stopped kicking. Floated without expelling water from his snorkel. There was a flash, a splash; he twisted his torso violently, then launched himself forward, feet churning. I started to run toward him.

A moment later he was standing up, a shining bloody mullet in his hands. "Dad!"

The mothers on the beach were now looking on with admiration. But the gypsy in the Speedo just kept splashing water on the horse's back.

One day, we treated ourselves to the island's acknowledged citadel of cuisine, the cozy Contre Quai. As Rory blithely speared and ate a lagniappe of raw sea snails called *bigorneaux*, our boy informed us that he had been thinking about how to improve our dining experience. No longer would Dad order the 215-franc menu as in the past, leaving Rory the child's portion of sole.

When the waiter arrived, we listened in growing consternation as Rory asked for the fresh sardines on a bed of steamed potatoes, roast garlic, and fennel, followed by *two* grilled sole fillets in lemon butter. He wanted tastes of Mindy's braised sea bass and my grilled dorade. He also chose all our desserts and sampled them all.

What could we do? He'd done his best to speak French, pass out napkins and snacks at our cocktail parties, and tolerate too many pats on the head and being told he was a *un petit joli homme*. We let him order.

The following summer, hoping to divert Rory's attention from *le menu du jour*, I brought a Wiffle ball to Kerbordardoué.

It is said that baseball doesn't travel well, except to Japan and the Americas. Certainly this was true for our Wiffle bat. It had to be hand-carried, over Mindy's objections. (The morning we left, she hid it in the closet, where I chanced upon it while searching for a sack of American fishing lures I wanted to try off the Côte Sauvage.) The French security force at our charter's terminal didn't blink at the garish, big-eyed, scarily hooked poppers. But they studied the plastic tube judiciously.

Heading for the Breton coast on the TGV—the *Train à Grande Vitesse*, or high-speed train—that bat was eyed, discussed, and analyzed by our seatmates, young and old. I finally stashed it overhead so we could get some sleep. By the time we had settled ourselves on the ferry for the last leg of the trip, the bat had assumed totemic status, as if it knew it would be keeping company with the monumental Druid menhirs and dolmens.

꒰

The game began shortly after we arrived. The village was full of children from rental houses that summer. They peeked out at Rory and vice versa, exchanging shy *bonjours* and pantomimed invitations to go bicycle riding or lizard hunting. Like Rory, they were in Kerbordardoué all summer, and their days were of their own making.

One lazy afternoon Rory picked up the bat and ball and started chopping line drives down the road. The news traveled fast: the American boy was doing something unusual. At first the children were content to chase respectfully after the ball and return it, cupped in their hands as if it were one of Madame Morgane's hen's eggs. Then one or two dared to throw it, gently, underhand, a few feet. Next Rory and I decided to put on an exhibition. Halfway through, they were lining up for batting practice. At this point the season began.

It startled me, the delight with which everybody took to the sport.

Villagers watched from dormer windows, from vegetable gardens, on trips to the garbage Dumpster at the edge of town. Suzanne paused in her magical flower propagation and brought her knitting over to watch. Even Kerbordardoué's center of gravity, Madame Morgane, altered her customary evening stroll to take in the later innings.

Rory couldn't get enough, which caused me an equal measure of wonder, because in the spring he had again refused to join Little League. To stir up some enthusiasm we had gone to a classmate's game. Fathers and mothers with clenched smiles barked orders and networked avidly with each other or over cell phones. I gleaned that "our team" had been assembled through insider trading and organized to win—which they did. Rory didn't take to this approach at all.

Baseball in Kerbordardoué, on the other hand, offered Rory an endless variety of angles from which to appreciate our national pastime. For both of us, baseball proved to be a fine way to practice our French, requiring endless choices for exploring argot and slang. For example, in my attempt to explain the pitch (*le jet*), I demonstrated *la fourchette*, or forkball, and *le tire-bouchon*, or corkscrew, a name substitution for the "scroogie" that referred to the joltingly slow train from Auray to Quiberon. For the fastball, a natural choice was *La Boule à Grande Vitesse*, or BGV, after the French TGV train.

Of course, the children ignored me and my flashy offerings. That was another thing to savor about baseball in Kerbordardoué—it belonged to the players, not the owners. These boys and girls of summer needed no contracts in order to play, nor were there owners to lock up the field. Night and day, the Wiffle ball and bat were left out by a drystone wall that enclosed a garden of herbs and annuals. If you were in the mood to play, you played.

At first Rory and I struggled to explain the rules, then gave up and watched a system evolve that took into account Kerbordardoué's peculiar stadium, French dining habits, and each player's personal style.

In the village square, "square" was a misnomer and every hit an adventure in following the bouncing ball. Often, watching children pursue a hit ricocheting among the rooftops, I was reminded of the time I first saw, as a child Rory's age, the movie *The Red Balloon*. Our left field was a downhill-running dirt road that led to a ruin. Center ended abruptly in "our" stone well in the shape of a beehive. Right went deep but was interrupted by a low drystone wall that served as second base and bleachers. Our house was the left foul line, and third base a sack of potting soil that gave a satisfying thud when kicked (prompting Mindy's Franco-Bronx cheer from inside the house: "*Arrêt! Ne touche pas le sac!*"). Home base was a tuft of grass between big-headed hydrangea blooms.

Another reason for baseball's popularity became apparent to me the time I asked six-year-old Juliet what she'd had for lunch. "Fresh tomato soup, grilled fresh sardines, pork cutlets, beets, salad, cheese, tart, espresso," she reeled off crisply. Adults need to doze off these meals; not so children. Baseball gave them something to do while waiting for the parents to rise from their comas.

All these, I realized, were the old virtues of the game. Without the siren cacophony of Nintendo or hypnotic vacuum of cable television, the possibilities in a bat and ball become endless. Direct observation leads me to suggest that true baseball expands to fill the time left in a day. Only the television version of the game worries about "going over" its allotted period. We had all the time in the world.

※

Around this time, we were encouraged to hear that a new family had moved in. They'd bought a parcel on the edge of the *vallon* the year before and built a house. Rumor had it there were three children, two close to Rory's age. Hearing this, he looked at me and we nodded sagely: more ballplayers.

Bumping into them accidentally on purpose on the main blackberrying lane, we did a double take upon making introductions. Yes, it was the young couple of Paris. The same family that once wrote at Gwened's instigation and offered to buy our house. The twin psychiatrists Gwened had chosen to take our place.

And this is how we became friends with Celeste and Henry. It was as natural a friendship as could be: talking and walking, we discovered Celeste and Henry were kids of the sixties, like ourselves. In them we quickly envisioned coconspirators. The older boys, Marc and Michel, were smart and their funny-sarcastic Paris wisecracks made a New York City street kid like Rory feel right at home. The young one, Auguste, was by some peculiar genius already speaking phrases in BBC English and had us all wrapped around his *petit doigt*. With them, village life often veered into a deadpan comedy of manners.

As far as we were concerned, the rest was gravy—and of an excellent kind. But it didn't hurt that the family had friends and that, most considerately, all these fine people had children. And the children had bicycles, as did Rory. Soon they were on the loose, shooting across the moors, pedaling madly from village to village, just for the joy of it. Our constellation of five hamlets was like a solar system, with villages as planets and kids slingshotting around them like comets.

Celeste and Henry's friends included an almost shockingly large contingent of summering psychiatrists, not to mention spouses who were attendant art curators, ad men, lawyers, and even a journalist. All seemed to be in the process of buying or building homes in the adjoining villages. We, who had never been analyzed, couldn't help but feel a little baffled. We also sensed a turning point for the Côte Sauvage—could the rest of chic Paris be far behind? Searching for their shrinks on the beach?

The island was changing. Who knew where it was all headed. At least, in the meantime, we had plenty of playmates for Rory. And if it sometimes seemed that they'd all had found one spot to congregate—in Kerbordardoué, in the square in front of our house, directly under Mindy's window as she was trying to write—it was because it was true and because of me and my gosh-darn American ideas of fun.

Baseball Kerbordardouénnaise opened the eyes to smaller pleasures. To watch a pop fly land on a slate roof, travel down a rain gutter, bounce off a well, and land amid a profusion of honeysuckle blossoms is to taste what Gwened's Zen poets would call be-here-nowness. Such surprises drew out a quartet of shy little girls, who emerged one day from behind their house's impenetrable hedge and sat primly in their blue-and-white frocks on a stone wall, giggling and picking favorites among the boys. Although we were on an island painted by Monet, I'd have to say that this was more of a Norman Rockwell moment.

The idyll continued until early September, when the time came to say good-bye to our teammates, who had to leave on *la rentrée*, the return. One by one they left. We would stay on a little longer, hoping to snatch one more week of sun. At least, after so much activity, Rory didn't seem to mind being left alone.

Then came one morning toward the end of our stay. A rising sun cut slowly through the salt-laden haze. I stood in the doorway watching the gray dissolve to blue, the dull walls turn to white, the many-petaled hydrangeas shift to brighter hues, like a black-and-white photograph being hand-tinted. Even the dirt of the square, lately our diamond, became richer, a faint reddish-orange.

Suzanne strolled out, hands clasped behind her back, inspecting her hydrangeas, the fuchsias, the square. She looked at me sidelong, asking in her robust Breton way, *"C'est tranquil, sans les enfants, oui?"*

For a moment I could almost swear we saw them: gap-toothed Pierre, a lefty flamethrower from Perpignan; our psychiatrist kids, Marc and Michel, the one large, the other lean, who didn't shrink from a fastball and were capable of blasting towering home runs (*coups de maison*); Laure of the long blond pigtail and infield cartwheels and ripping speed on the base paths. Then, really hearing Suzanne's words, I was suddenly stricken with a terrible doubt: I had been too dense to notice that baseball had become an all-American nuisance, disturbing the peace of the village.

Suzanne scuffed her toe in the dirt. She placed the fist of one hand atop the fist of the other hand, cocked her head, raised her shoulders. A pause. She took a cut with an imaginary bat. Checking out my response, she let loose with a gust of a laugh.

Baseball had come to Kerbordardoué.

Chapter Nineteen
La Chienne

H appiness is almost always best appreciated after the fact—recollected the morning after or while dozing on the plane home or, even better, years later as the two of you are standing side by side in a cramped New York City apartment kitchen, one measuring coffee, the other slicing a baguette, and the senses awaken with memories of Belle Île.

An exception to the rule is to observe happiness not your own, and that secretly from concealment. Like the time when we were lying in bed with the lights out and Mindy heard a sound. We held our breath, listening hard. Mindy reached out for my hand in the dark. Because it was our boy and his cousin, lying in their beds in the next chamber, singing Sly Stone songs. Not just one or two. An entire Greatest Hits collection. "Nah-nah-nah-nah-nah-nah-nah-nah…"

The best concert ever. But—Sly Stone songs! The pioneer of funk from the sixties, the best cruisin'-with-the-top-down-and-radio-blasting music of my high school years? However did that happen?

Well, a random cassette came to the office as part of a promo. I threw it in the bag marked for France that is kept open all year until it's time to go. Forgot about it, until it came time for the first ride down the bumpy road to Port Scheul for the morning spearfishing excursion. The instant I slapped it in the cassette player, the tape became a soundtrack. Soon the boys, bare-chested in bathing suits, were hanging out the window and calling out to all the cows and funky chickens in the dusty village by-lanes, "*Boom*-shaka-laka-*boom!*"

Years of trips have followed, always to the same tape on the same bumpy road, the boys getting bigger, but never too big not to sing: "IIIIIII love everyday people!"

More than once on that bumpy road I think we all sensed that we'd gone through some mystic portal and entered a golden age, but we also had the sense to not "mouth it up," as Ernest Hemingway once said. "Isn't this great!" is one sign that decline has already set in.

So we pretended we weren't there yet. Wherever we were, though, it sure was good.

When we arrived that second year after the house was completed, the whole village was talking about our witch. She'd always been a flamboyant enigma, Sterenn—a woman of a certain age, face painted and rouged like a Kabuki's, swathed in pastel scarves. Usually we saw her at twilight floating and flapping like a golden ring-necked pheasant around the 3,500-year-old standing stones, cousins of those at Stonehenge and Carnac, on the road that linked Sauzon and Le Palais. But this summer she defied convention, common sense, and even reality by popping up miles away on the most remote dirt tracks, barefoot and twirling. Everyone wondered if Sterenn had finally gone mad.

"*La femme de* Marlon Brando," Le Vicomte had confirmed when, having disbelieved the rumors, we asked if he knew anything about her. Brando's lover! We had to accept Le Vic's word. He'd seen it all—war, love, and celebritydom—and was honest as an anvil. Still, it was a stretch: Marlon Brando, here? When we'd first seen Kerbordardoué, the village had seemed tired and forgotten, not to mention rude and muddy.

Early one morning, we headed out to the morning market at Le Palais with the night fog still clinging to the ground. Sterenn came out of the mist, holding up a hand palm out, blocking the single-lane road. She walked to the passenger door and opened it. "Hello, my American neighbors," she said in arch BBC English. "Could I trouble you for a lift to town?"

By the time we let her off, we'd formed an entirely new opinion of her. We also had an invitation to dinner. Sandwiched between another house and a stone barn, her cottage was low-ceilinged, little more than a pair of whitewashed rooms. Like us, she had no yard. Unlike us, she'd filled the right-of-way with a mosaic of shells and colored pebbles from the island beaches. The designs were intricate but not unfamiliar. As we stepped over them, I made out the Celtic knot and cross, the Assyrian solar disk, the universal labyrinth, and the inverted Tibetan Buddhist cross that resembles a swastika. All familiar but not surprising to one who'd grown up in the psychedelic sixties.

Sterenn proved an easy and down-to-earth hostess. There were hors d'oeuvres, olives, gherkins, and little toasts smeared with *pâté*. Sardines and boiled potatoes—the basic Belle Île meal. Butter and salt the only condiments. She assumed our interest in the early expatriate society of Kerbordardoué, so incongruous, and explained that there'd been a time—yes, in those crazy, wonderful sixties—when she and some friends had settled here. They'd just wandered into the village and rented or squatted in abandoned cottages. "Like you," she said.

So we'd been observed.

"Kerbordardoué is a spirit center," she said. "You know it was marked on the old maps as the place of the devil. But that was the Christian missionaries' doing. The pagan belief here was too strong for their crucifixes and rosaries. They were afraid. Shall we do the Tarot?"

The deck was at hand. She began laying out the cards.

Mindy and I stayed up after we got home that night, comparing notes. Sterenn had been elusive on the subject of Brando. But her other famous ex-lover was the film director John Boorman, whose witchy Arthurian drama *Excalibur* we'd seen (along with his Southern gothic *Deliverance*). He and she had laid out the mosaics in front of her house—under the influence of a magic potion, of course. "You see Kerbordardoué in his work," she said.

"You are writers," she added, "so you will want to know there are influences here that are unavoidable. The spirit world that was centered here in the Gulf de Morbihan seven thousand years ago had followers in the dark forests and deep glens of Ireland and Scotland in the north, down to Spain and Egypt in the south. People in Brittany still accept that profound darkness is necessary for summer's golden light. It makes no sense to try to avoid the dark, or its king, Mister Death, known as Ankou... And so the culture is defined by fatalism, ghost stories, and harvest rites, such as the one that celebrates the opening of the door between life and the underworld. This is Samhain," she intoned, "which falls at the end of October—"

"Our Halloween," we chorused, well-schooled by Gwened's library of Celtic literature.

Sterenn spoke of the root myth of the hound of hell, which Arthur Conan Doyle borrowed for *The Hound of the Baskervilles*. And there was much more: birds, beasts, mists, cries in the night, apparitions, and strangers met on the road who stop your wagon and ask for a ride...

The way we'd met Sterenn.

And so, in a way, we were warned. If we could've but read the signs, understood what it meant when the fog settled only a foot or two above our heads, followed by the mackerel clouds of sunset, the hoot of an owl. But after all the obstacles and rejections and disappointments that had come between us and our house, we felt we had a right to rejoice. This year, the second since we'd completed the house, would be the summer we finally kicked back and enjoyed. And looked forward to years more of the same.

That was when the cold spirit of Ankou, Mister Death, accompanied by his familiar, known as *La Chienne*, blew into town. Howling across the moors, the Great Bitch, as they call the hound of hell in Brittany, came calling one evening in August.

We'd arrived a couple of days before and were almost over our jet lag. Our friends Celeste and Henry had bought and assembled a "picnic table, ees that what you call eet?" We were invited over for grilled merguez and chipolata sausages. The table of honor had been placed by a screen of young alders, beyond which our host's gravel driveway ran through a tunnel of trees. Behind that was the small forest of elms at the rear of the Vicomte's yard.

Henry had come to our house to get us. We walked with him down the *allée* to where it met the village road. Le Vic was sitting on his slate stoop, smoking his pipe. We hailed him, as we do. He gave a nod and a grunt. As we walked past the elms, Henry nodded at their ghostly trunks in the dense greenery. "Next year they will all be gone."

"What? Why? Is he going to cut them down?"

"No, but he should."

"Why?"

"The malady. Do you have eet? *Les ormes sont condamnés.*" The word was easily grasped, but the meaning sounded more dire in English: condemned, like a prisoner who's going to the guillotine.

It took the rest of our walk to sort it out. Dutch Elm disease had come to Europe. No, wait, it's called Dutch for a reason, so we guessed it must have returned. We watched the kids set the table (Rory and Devo watching as well, not being well-brought-up compared to French children). Food came out. Sausages sizzled. Lemonade and wine. Meal done, the table cleared off, the tablecloth flapped to shoo away crumbs, we all moved up to the house to go indoors, have a coffee, and sit at the long table and talk. The kids could even watch TV—a huge decision for Henry, who has a vision of Kerbordardoué as a haven from electronics.

At last there was only the bare blond picnic table at the edge of the dark forest in the rear of the Vicomte's yard, and Rory sitting alone, reading his chess book.

We were at the door to the house when for some reason we all turned: me, Mindy, Henry, and Celeste, who said affectionately, "*Rory lit toujours.*" He always reads. Then we heard it—and a moment later, saw it—a disturbance in the blue, transparent yet roiling. Next an immense gust of wind came out of the north, bending the tops of the trees. *La Chienne.*

From the ghostly trees, I heard a crack. It wasn't even a loud crack, more of a mushy crunch. It conveyed the rottenness of the tree way down to the roots, a totality of dead wood. Then one of the towering white trunks began to fall, at first almost silently, with just a whooshing sound. When it reached the living trees that screened the driveway, though, the sound became a muted roar of breakage, an oncoming freight train.

And this is what we will remember after: we barely had time to see the falling tree, let alone calculate its direction and sprint across forty yards of uneven grass to get to Rory. We never moved.

The tree roared forward now, snapping first at the ten-foot mark, behind the driveway. It must've been four feet in diameter, but the break was clean. The rest of the tree kept on coming. The trunk snapped again at the screen of alders. Now the great white Y of its forked upper trunk was flying forward, freed of the bottom half, like a twenty-five-foot-long ghost with outstretched arms. It was heading straight for Rory, who sat, head hunched over his book in the failing light, completely absorbed.

Doing the math, I'd already realized it was too late. My one hope was that it would fall short but I knew it wouldn't. I considered yelling, though there probably wasn't enough time—just enough time to pray, *Please, please…*

The tree hit the ground and exploded in a rippling motion. The sound filled the air like armies clashing. As the great Y slammed down on either side of Rory, its limbs shattered and the crotch of the Y kept moving, sliding forward, reaching out, stretching for Rory. A cloud of white rotten wood fragments blew up and swept ahead. The main branches, fragmented, still more than a foot in diameter, bracketed the picnic table. As they hit the ground, they bounced up and down and around like the bones of a dancing skeleton.

Smaller branches lashed the ground all around Rory. A white cloud of chips and fungus-ridden wood engulfed him. As the cloud settled, it revealed Rory sitting untouched in a little clearing. A spinning woodchip flipped slowly end over end and bonked him on the side of the head.

We finally were running.

He hadn't noticed a thing.

There would be plenty of tears and wails. But only for a little while because, as Mindy and I agreed, exchanging a look over Rory's head, it was better if he never knew how close he'd come.

Nobody could really talk after that. We stayed together in the living room and watched the television for hours, until the sound of Rory and the boys laughing at some idiot police thriller gave us permission to unclench, relax, exhale. But nobody talked about it.

Terror is one more thing best recollected in tranquility.

❦

The next day the woodcutter arrived with his chain saw, his apprentice, and his expertise. He had a slicked-back Elvis hairdo and wore rather fashionable slacks and nicely polished shoes—not your average lumberjack. A styling *French* lumberjack.

First the bottom third of the tree was cut, because it blocked Henry and Celeste's driveway. Their car was actually trapped. Henry decided he deserved the wood. The woodcutter explained that he took away half as part of his fee.

Henry was scornful. "Half! Well, I'll take the other half."

The Vicomte begged to differ. He was paying the lumberjack, so he got the wood.

"But it fell on my land."

"But it is my tree."

"Yes, and it nearly killed Rory. Maybe *he* should get the wood."

Up to that point, things had been getting testy. Hearing the previously unspoken outcome finally voiced put a different spin on the issue. The discussion became calmer, civilized, and finally exquisite. We left them to it.

A couple of hours later, Henry arrived at our door out of breath from pushing a wheelbarrow up our *allée*. It was full of wood: logs, branches, twigs, all neatly sorted—a survivor's portion. There were also two enormous cucumbers. "From Le Vicomte," said Henry. We invited him to stay and have a drink of whiskey.

Later, after he'd gone, the Vicomte's two grown sons stopped by. They nodded when they saw the wood. "Oh, good. Rory gets his share," said Thierry, whose English was now better than my French. "And you, Don, get *les concombres*." We served them whiskey, too. They were happy to get it out of sight of Maman.

The next morning we gave the cucumbers to Suzanne. After that, I took the longer pieces of wood outside to cut with a saw. Suzanne came out to watch and laugh. Waving me aside, she grabbed a large bough and broke it with a stomp of one blucher-shod foot. Gesturing, she shamed me into doing the same. *Ow!* screamed my knee. She watched, delighted, as strapping Young Strudel hopped around on one foot.

After lunch we visited the site. There was a white sawdust silhouette, like a crime scene's chalk outline, where the deadly elm had fallen. The picnic table was gone, too. Henry was concerned about *his* children now. He'd already moved the table far away, far from any trees, to a bare rise overlooking the moors and fields.

Over the next couple of days, there was some village ire directed at the Vicomte for his forest. People said he loved it too much to cut it down. There were too many children in the village to indulge him. We stayed on the sidelines, happy that ours had been spared, but in the end, Gwened, Henry, and others felt there should be a discussion of all the rotten trees. After some hesitation Le Vic joined in. The village walked the wood.

The following week the woodcutter returned. An entire small forest fell that day.

The averted tragedy had unlocked something. The village had had to decide if it was more than a collection of nice houses and pretty flowers. The village had made the right call. Any doubt about that was laid to rest when the Vicomte and Yvonne threw an *apéro* for *les propriétaires*, the owners of village houses. Then Celeste and Henry held their *apéro*, and then the married professors held one. Even Gwened held one.

When we got to her secluded patio, the first to arrive, Mindy and I looked around in puzzlement. Finally we realized what was different. Where were the beautiful Belgian youths, the white-robed acolytes drifting about the *jardin?* Gwened smiled at our covert inquiry and careful expressions.

"I sent them home," she said, adding, "I have met a beautiful man." She nodded at our expressions. "He is coming here this weekend."

Chapter Twenty
Beau Temps

H ere's one for an omen reader or Chinese soothsayer: happily warbling, a bird flutters into my dreams. An instant later I open my
eyes to see a real swallow backpedaling in midair confusion above my
head. With an anxious squeak of disapproval at the sight of our stunned
bodies under the twisted sheets, it flees out the open dormer.

In dreams begin reality, a poet once said. Or was it responsibility? For
me, the swallow shakes the slumbering beast of worry. "Ohhh…" I can
barely move my lips from jet lag. "We didn't have swallows before, did we?"

"No… They don't…" My wife clears her throat. "*Ruairrrrriiii-
aaaddddhhhh.*"

Mindy sounds like she's wrestling a yeti under the tangle of sheets,
quilts, and that impossibly configured French duvet that took us twenty
minutes to figure out last night, when we finally went to bed after seventeen hours of travel from New York and another five of opening the
house and walking down to the beach and fixing a spartan supper of
tinned sardines, bread, and butter. But I can sense a smile lurking somewhere under the duvet. After all, we're here. Back again. At home.

Mindy tries out her voice again: "Swallows don't like…living places…" Catches herself. "I mean, where people are living. They prefer ruins."

Oh.

Now the bird irks me. It must be confused. This house is no longer a ruin. Both upstairs bedrooms look snug as a ship's forward cabin, up near the bows, an illusion assisted by the slanting roof and nautically ruggedized skylight opposite the dormer. This is our ark. That's why we're here.

The sky outside the window is baby blue. A soft cross breeze flows from the skylight. I look at Mindy, eyelids closed and trembling during a brief dream sleep, russet hair wild and long. She looks like a Rossetti—no, a Matisse—against the rose-green-yellow pastels of the parrot-patterned duvet and pillowcases. *Eyes, be my camera!*

The bedding set, a present from my mom, turned the room into a tropical hothouse the moment it was unfurled from clear plastic cases. Five years on, everything is still bright as the day when she spotted the linens in a Vannes boutique. Got to hand it to the mom. We may not always agree, and our tastes are an ocean apart, but here she got it spectacularly right.

"A lesson to always listen to your sainted mother," she'd growled when I told her, her playful mood and high spirits a total change from that first visit.

Her taste made a revolution in more ways than one. Thanks to the check she wrote us for Christmas following The Dreadful Affair at Hôtel du Phare, we'd ordered a handsome armoire in the old Breton style from Madame Morgane's grandson. We didn't know it, but that was his first commission. It came out beautifully for him and for us. We got a place to store our clothes where they wouldn't mildew, and for him, our house became a convenient showroom, which meant it got a regular dusting and cleaning the whole year long. So the house didn't mildew, either.

We also earned the extended Morgane family's approval, which manifested itself in a curious way. No sooner had we returned to New

York than we received a letter from Madame Morgane's sweetest niece. She lived on the mainland now and was getting married on the island. She wondered if she and her fiancé could spend their wedding night in our house. "Just the bedroom," she said. "With the sheets and duvet. We would be happy to pay."

Of course we didn't charge. Our reward was to hear, on our return to the island that summer, how the village filled with over two hundred *îliens* and mainland Bretons, eating galettes and drinking *cidre brut* long into the night, singing and dancing in a serpentine line to the droning bagpipe, huffing accordion, and thudding hand drum. These sorts of events are held in the late fall or winter and, I get the feeling, pop up like flash mobs so tourists and *étrangers* like us won't stumble upon them. It was nice to think of the village reconstituted, time rolled back. We felt lucky to play a small part; it was the next best thing to being there.

The following year, another Morgane relation, this one a niece from the mainland who'd seen the bedroom while attending the wedding, wrote to ask a similar favor. Though we didn't know this niece—and wondered if all two hundred of the guests had trooped up the stairs to stare at Mom's Matisse parrots and would soon be requesting conjugal visits—we said yes, of course.

Next, a friend from New York, traveling with his girlfriend in France, wrote to ask if they could stay. Sure! When they returned to the United States, they announced their engagement.

Was it just our imagination, or did our little house have a certain aphrodisiac effect?

❧

While the house gained a reputation for having the power to make villagers and other lovers happy, it all would have been for nothing if our parents had continued to disapprove of us and our folly. The first to come around was Mindy's mother, Dolly, just after the Dream Team had finished the staircase and floor. We'd barely digested the news that she had a new boyfriend, Brian, when she called to say he was taking her to Europe—and wanted to visit Belle Île.

Not having seen the finished job, we said yes with real misgivings. Dolly was nobody's idea of a country girl. But off they went, and in the moody month of October, too. Brian managed to turn on the electricity and the water all by himself, and even made a few home improvements. (A towel rack! Now why didn't I think of that?) Of course, no sooner were they back in Hawaii than they, too, got married.

That left my parents. The year after they ruined our seeing the finished job for the first time, they decided to give us a second chance and come out again—a total surprise.

What had made the difference? For my mother, there was the ongoing influence of Peter Mayle's *A Year in Provence* and the unflagging curiosity of the Bixby Knolls Book Club, her reading group. Mom and Dad were also taken by Rory's stern lecture at the Hôtel du Phare, which grows funnier with each retelling. It's now part of family lore.

But those weren't difference-makers. No, it took a peculiarly French moment that befell my father on the last full day of their first trip. It didn't seem like much at the time. But it came to mean everything, in a way, to me.

We were running out of things to do with the Great Sulky Ones, so we'd gone in no good mood to the cliffside shingle beach of Pointe des Poulains. Here, under the worn pink battlements of Sarah Bernhardt's once-grand mansion, we tore apart rotisserie chicken with our fingers and drank cold alcoholic cider, just as Monet and John Russell did, and maybe also on another occasion a young Van Gogh and his paint-around-pal, Paul Gauguin.

Maybe, just maybe, this was even where *jeune* Marcel Proust waited in vain, smoking neurasthenically, for an audience with The Divine Sarah. It definitely was the beach off which the Prince of Wales anchored his yacht one day in 1901 and paused to have himself rowed ashore to visit his old lover, before returning to his yacht and setting off for his coronation as Edward VII.

All this I rattled off, hoping to impress, as I tend to do when faced with imminent disaster. It wasn't working. (It never does.)

Then a French family arrived and, with a smile, took the next cove over in the rocks. When they opened a wicker picnic basket and produced not just a checkered tablecloth but linen napkins and silverware, bottles of wine and Perrier, I braced myself for criticism of our feeble attempt. Instead, my grumpy father finally melted.

"Here's a nice family," he said, as if such a thing simply could not be found in France. "The father, the mother, and the teenage daughter." We stole covert glances as we ate our ruder but no less delicious lunch. It was hot; the cliff blocked the wind. A seagull walked slowly up. My father tore off a piece of baguette and tossed it. The seagull decided he might as well get acquainted and hopped onto the rock next to Dad, who was almost childishly delighted. My mother and I exchanged glances. It had been a rough recovery from his heart attack, not only physically but mentally. Afterward, a sense of play was lacking. Nice to see it back.

Lolling in the sun, our two families exchanged smiles and hoisted glasses to each other.

"This is a normal family having a picnic," Dad said, falling into his Edward R. Murrow radio broadcast voice. He did this sometimes. "The girl is well-behaved—look at how she offers the Perrier to her father first, then her mother, before helping herself. Now she pours the wine for her father…"

The day got hotter. We flaked out in bliss. The girl got up and from a soft, cloth shoulder bag took out two juggling pins. Dad just kept narrating. "The good daughter is now going to juggle for her father and mother. See, they don't have to go to a circus, she's going to put on a show right here…"

The girl stopped after a couple of minutes and mopped her face with her sleeve. Her father held up the Perrier bottle and she took it, drank, and with a flourish, added it to the juggling rotation. My father sat up and applauded. The father nodded in appreciation; the mother smiled; and the girl dipped a quick knee and kept her eyes on the pins. With a flourish, she stopped, mouthed "Whew," and sipped from her Perrier bottle. Her now-prostrate father raised his glass of wine like a toast to the gods.

"That's the way children should treat their parents," said Dad.

"You wish," I said.

Mom added: "You just want a juggling girl of your own."

After taking a breather and sitting down for a spell, the girl got up again. We shifted on our towels and prepared for the next act. She picked up the juggling pins and tossed them slowly into the air, flipping end over end. It was a warm-up; she caught them in midair and set them down, rolled her shoulders and reached down to the hem of her blouse, gave it a tug and pulled it over her head. She threw her blouse aside, unpinned her chignon, and gave her long hair a shake as it tumbled to her shoulders. Her breasts were small and perfect.

"Oh no," said Dad. She picked up the pins and tossed them into motion. "She shouldn't be doing this." With the slow, sensuous air favored by jugglers, she prowled around the picnic tablecloth, stepping around her mother and coming up to her father—or, should I say, "father." Because she continued her performance directly in front of him, slowly, hands a hypnotic blur, the flipping pins encircling her rosy nipples.

"No-no," said Dad. "Her father should stop her—the mother should stop her—oh, dear! He really shouldn't be watching her."

"But you're watching her," Mom observed, deadpan.

With an effort, he wrenched his head away to stare blindly out to sea. "They seemed like such a nice family."

By the time we'd gathered our things to head home, the father was reclining fully clothed with wineglass in hand, wife and daughter, both topless, on either side: *le déjeuner sur le rocher.*

Later, after we'd climbed back up the dirt road to the top of the cliff, I was careful to pause to let Dad catch his breath. He stood silently, staring along the rugged, carved-out coastline topped with moors twinkling with points of light. It was calm and still.

From nowhere a sadness came over me. My father seemed so old, suddenly frail. His gaze over the shimmering Côte Sauvage and mirrored ocean seemed to see all the way across the sea, toward England and the coast of Cornwall, where the souls of the dead lined the northward cliffs, waiting to be ferried to the mythical island of Avalon. I felt our loss of days together, living so far apart. My fault.

He sighed, smiled.

"I can see why you like this place," he said. "I think it's good for you."

He turned to go, then stopped to look one more time. "Reminds me of Carmel. If they put in a golf course, your house could easily double in value."

✼

And lo, it would come to pass the following year that my sister Anne, the golf writer, would track down the rumor of the famous golf course, allegedly founded by Sarah Bernhardt in 1900. Yes, it actually existed, in crude outline. And it was lurking in the heather on the very moor we'd been surveying. The newly roughed-out links were originally played, it is said, by Bernhardt and her lover, the same Prince of Wales, while the latter dallied en route to putting on the crown and, with it, the burdens of a king.

Abandoned during both wars and frequently storm-racked, The Divine Sarah's *Champs du Golf* had lost five holes over the past century to cliff collapses. Its tortured fairways wound through daunting tunnels of gorse and blackberry. Our golfers—Dad, Mom, Anne, and her son, Devo—nevertheless fell in love, viewing it as their own private Pebble Beach.

Mindy and I, needless to say, were nonplussed. It was a little humbling to realize that we weren't enough of a draw on our own. But beggars can't be choosers. So we waved gaily whenever the golfers announced they were going rogue for the day—"for the day" because, with only thirteen holes, the course could be done two or three times in one of our long Nordic afternoons. One hole in particular drew them back again and again: a pool of grass marooned on a narrow spire two hundred feet above the churning sea. My mother needed to get down on her knees and crawl across the narrow spine of rock to play her ball. But she did, and loved it.

Over the years, the addition of golf to the island repertory has proved to be a kind of safety valve for many American visitors, who occasionally need a break from our notions of rough summer sport, but its most important role will always be how it led to the parental seal of approval. The favor was returned by the louche crew at *Le Club House*, a one-room box with artichoke and tartan-plaid wallpaper and a clientele that dressed to match.

When the British Open was on the television one afternoon, my father made a calculated entrance in his full regalia of canary yellow pants, red and white saddle shoes, bright green polo shirt with white Titleist polka dots, thistle-and-rose cashmere vest, and a floppy Augusta National Golf Club hat. There was a hush. And then we heard a gentle pattering of palms—applause, the kind that ordinarily follows a model's strut down a runway during Fashion Week. Dad couldn't buy a drink that day. When my sister Anne returned to the States with tales of the knee-crawling *Trou de Sarah B.*, she promptly hit up her editor at the golf magazine and wrangled a story assignment in order to return.

Given a green light, Anne took her boyfriend. The marriage that followed was almost a foregone conclusion.

※

Meanwhile, here it is, our first day back in Kerbordardoué this year, and we're still in bed. We used to be such warriors! Now it's the height of luxury to loll and nap—and watch the swallow dart in, beating his wings hard to brake, hover, and warble indignantly.

I roll out of bed, feel the pine paneling graze my head, and realize that, while I may have forgotten to duck, my muscle memory of this place is already returning. Mindy growls again. "Stop it!" she snaps, not fooling.

"I'm just seeing if the rental house is occupied."

"Stop looking out the skylight. If Madame Morgane sees you…"

Still rigorously observing the village rule, I see. Even if every renter and tourist who walks by our house on the square cranes their neck to peer in—*Regardez la maison rustique et authentique Bretonnes! Regardez le rosier! Les fleurs! Les paysans!*—we'll not return the favor, at least not on Madame Morgane's side. Mindy is of course correct, but the reason she's so fierce is that she has her heart set on a second skylight, in Rory's room. This would directly overlook M. Morgane's house and was thus out of the question in the original plans. The negotiations have been going on for years. Favors pile up. Nothing changes. Mindy doesn't quit. She knows the business of acquiring land, rights over a well, access for a driveway or a road, even a wall's shadow; it's never over.

Poor M. Morgane, she has larger worries than a fifteen-by-fifteen-inch pane of glass in our black slate roof. She is suffering from the vacation renters installed every holiday in the new house attached to the remains of her old stone one. Separated by only a door, the tourists carry on without regard for her presence—playing the TV at high volume all day, holding conversations at a shout. Everything already echoes in the cheap, prefab plasterboard and lath chambers.

"I'm a prisoner in my own home!" she cried to Mindy last year, when paying her ritual call for *un petite café*.

"*Pas bon*," muttered Suzanne, inconsolable on behalf of her childhood best friend. "*Dommage.*"

Mindy holds two coffees each summer, one at the beginning and another at the end. At each she bakes her chocolate football, as Rory calls it. The two old girls arrive and I make my hello, and Madame Morgane listens incredulously and then remarks that my French hasn't improved. (She's the only one in the village who doesn't lie and say the opposite.) With that out of the way, I take my leave. But I know how it goes.

The two of them will perch on their chairs, alert as birds, and pretend to look around as if they don't know the house, haven't spent a part of every day sitting in our *salle de cuisine*. They'll exclaim over the lace on the windows, even though it's Suzanne's. They'll talk about the *buffet placard*, the poster on the wall, Tante Jeannie's old Jubilee card.

Mindy will play along. For many years now, we've never questioned what went on in our absence. We used to figure that Suzanne would let herself in every so often, as we requested, to air out the house. Maybe she'd sit and knit a bit.

We were charmed, too, when the first lace appeared one summer, and each year waited to see if a new window would get the treatment. Unlike the elaborate tourist lace sold for a fortune in Le Palais—which, rumor has it, is sourced in pieces from China and finished in Brittany— ours is made from rough cotton thread in a pattern unique to Belle Île, and possibly Suzanne. A fancy Belgian woman who once insisted on visiting—to be able to report back suitably sordid details of the hovel of the Americans, we belatedly realized—took one look at the lace and laughed, saying, "It's the work of a drunken spider." That told us all we needed to know about *her*.

But we couldn't dismiss so lightly the warning of one of the village's second-home people—from the Continent, not Paris—when he took us aside.

"I hesitate to bring this up," he said, and of course we knew he meant the opposite. "But do you know those two old women go into your house?"

"Yes, of course. We've asked Suzanne to air it out when it's sunny."

"But they're there *every single day*. Two of them. Did you know that?"

"Yes," we said simultaneously, faking it.

He didn't buy it. "Look, they're in your house when you're not there. All year! A violation. Everyone thinks they're putting one over on you."

"We think it's kind of wonderful," Mindy said firmly.

A spontaneous reaction to being pressed, this nevertheless felt true: I felt a warm flush, the kind you only get when you find out you've brought about a mitzvah without any knowledge or intention. Not a random act of kindness, exactly; an unconscious one.

"*Pah! C'est fou.*" He gave us a look of pity mixed with exasperated admiration, and off he marched, shaking his head.

When Mindy and I discussed it later, we agreed. We didn't want to feel that the old girls were putting one over on us. We decided we liked having them here, as if in their girlhood, evoking the memory of Tante Jeannie.

※

Finally deferring to Mindy's dream of another skylight, I withdraw my head, but not before taking a quick peek around: no changes, big or small, no signs of work being done. The northern end of the village seems quite deserted.

Even after padding downstairs and putting water into a battered pot on the stove for coffee, I can't bring myself to open the door. I'm afraid to look. It's like Christmas morning. What if the presents aren't there under the tree? What if this is the glance that pops the balloon? What if a year's absence has stripped away the last pretense? What if reality has finally shattered the fragile illusion of belonging?

Instead of the door, I open the window, the one that overlooks the rose. The moment I undo the latch, the two halves of the window swing inward from the pressure of bunched-up branches. A thick tangle of dark green leaves, fresh reddish thorns, and bright green rosebuds pushes its way into our kitchen like an aggressive Christmas wreath.

"*Whoa!*"

"*What?*"

"The rose has grown. I mean, *really* grown."

A moment later, there's a decisive thump: Mindy's two heels landing on the floorboards beside the bed. She's up.

I peer into the heart of the rose, which has filled the frame and actually blocks all but a vague filtered light. It's like having a hedgerow in our kitchen. There are creatures living inside, an ecosystem of spiders, ants, praying mantis, lizards, moths, midges, probably a mouse. But that's all right; the window will stay open as long as we're here.

Although the coffee is poured, Mindy insists on an inspection tour. We split up and circle the open kitchen–dining area from opposite directions, calling out questions and findings. Is that cone of black ash in the fireplace a natural accumulation over a year's time, or should we call the chimney sweep? It seems harmless. Does the puddle by the refrigerator mean it's leaking? A miracle it's even running, as we bought it used twenty-four years old. We'll keep an eye on it. Does the closet smell of mold, or is that just me? Or my socks?

At the built-in cupboard, I take out the rusted tin that a single malt Scotch once came in, now full of plastic baggies of spices: cumin, coriander, curry, turmeric, chipotle, cayenne. Spotting a handful of tiny brown beetles swimming in the dull orange cumin powder, I sling the bag into the trash. Have to remember to buy more before the annual *Concours du Guacamole*. Next we move along the walls, feeling the areas of discolored plaster to see if they're moist. We stand under the old cracks and debate whether they've grown.

Finally, we step into the other downstairs room, which is both a guest bedroom and a study. A beautiful armoire gleams against the far wall, but first we visit the three surfboards hanging from the rafters. Their blue-green nylon hammocks, which I cut from washed-up fishermen's nets, are striped with tar and entwined with dried seaweed.

All in all, a most satisfying inspection. No major structural issues, the musty odor already clearing out, just the one bag of cumin tossed. Time for coffee?

Mindy unlocks the armoire and sticks her head inside until it disappears. Then she starts handing out wool sweaters and socks, fleeces and heavy cotton shirts, tees and blouses and socks. "I'm going to start a wash," she says.

Our tiny French washer receives its instructions and sits awhile, thinking existential machine thoughts, while we drink our coffee and eat buttered Krispy Rolls. Finally, with a clunk, the washer begins to run. Another miracle. You never know when you've been away for a year what will work and what will require a stern talking-to.

French washers are worth talking to, anyway. Ours runs much longer and more gently than American ones, uses less energy, and gives a longer life and softer feel to our clothes. Mindy has already written this up in her newsletter, and it will one day make it into her book, *Do One Green Thing*. She's come to rely on France as a good source of green lifestyle changes that will wash up on U.S. shores in a couple of years: clearly labeled organic foods (*biologique*); organic beauty products and clothing; energy-saving appliances; fuel-efficient cars; an efficient train and bus system; and, last year, the phasing out of plastic bags in the island markets, which went off without a hitch.

The Breton kitchen has also taught us much. Breton cooking is elemental, even plain; it owes everything to ingredients. Brittany is the land of the buckwheat galette, farm-fresh egg, and grilled tomato—it's like hitting the Refresh button every time we go back. Whenever we visit Crêperie Chez Renee in Bangor, I'm whisked away to those nights sitting across from M. Morgane's old father, listening to his dreamy reminiscences of his younger days.

In the morning he would put away a dozen buttered galettes made from the wheat of his own fields, threshed in our *place*, milled by the wind-driven *moulin blanc* up on the hill. He'd work until sundown, chow down another dozen galettes, then walk two hours to Le Palais, where he would dance, drink *cidre brut*, and finish off a dozen *crêpes de froment et sucre* before walking back home to start the new work day. When did you sleep? I once asked. High noon, he said. In the shadow of a hayrick. He winked. But not alone.

The weeks we've spent in Kerbordardoué tending a yellowed stoneware bowl full of bubbling, temperamental buckwheat batter has shown us how simple doesn't always mean easy. But that hasn't stopped Mindy from tackling classic French dishes out of *Tante Marie*, France's equivalent of *The Joy of Cooking*, now sadly out of print.

Over the years, we've both grown bolder but have never deluded ourselves about mastering French cuisine, which is justly renowned for complexity, for being rich, diverse, and informed by an obsession with *terroir*, freshness, and technique. We take to heart the only remark by President Charles de Gaulle that will go down in history: "It is impossible to govern a nation of 400 cheeses." We know we will never claim citizenship in the Fifth Republic of *Fromage*. We've barely scratched the surface and will never get very deep. But we're not sad. For us, it just means that wonders will never cease.

These days we set our sights low, mind our ingredients, and enjoy gratifying results. We notice and borrow how Celeste packs barely seasoned ground pork into a hollowed out garden tomato for *farci*; see how a head of frisée from a neighbor's garden can change from a salad to an entrée after a quick toss into a pan of seared *lardons*; listen carefully when the fishmonger, having sold out of *lotte*, recommends the other ugly fish, *le grondin*, roasted in a pan with butter, shallots, and *fenouil*.

Sadly, the ugly fish never tastes the same back home in the United States (if you can even find it—we don't do ugly very well). But the recipes can travel and, in an American kitchen sourced from a farmer's market, do just fine.

The cultural rules of French eating travel even better. We paid heed to them after noticing that we always returned home thinner and healthier despite all the butter, cream, and other indulgences. (The only time I fit into my old Agnes B suit was the week after Belle Île.) What was up with that?

After years of polling Celeste, Sidonie, Yvonne, and the other women on the beach, Mindy thinks she has the formula: no between-meal snacking, no processed foods, no sweets (except a square of dark chocolate on the half hour when writing), smaller portion size (and no seconds), no soft drinks (including, at my insistence, diet cola—Mindy's one weakness), lots of greens and vegetables, plenty of olive oil, and fruit or cheese, or both, for dessert.

I've told Mindy that I can accept all of the above, with the occasional forgivable lapse, if there's a loophole allowing tarts, cakes, and other *pâtisserie* on a more-or-less daily basis. *No? Then why did you take me to France in the first place—to torture me?* Yes, there has been give-and-take on the topic. When my argument was about to prevail due to superior logic, Mindy called in my *ami* Henry to betray me.

"But, Don," he said, "you know, one does not eat the special dessert every day."

"Come on," I replied, man to man. "Don't tell me that you aren't tempted when you walk home from the office, passing all those glass-front displays of *Gâteau Bavarois* and *Bombe Chocolate*, not to mention the cute little chocolate mice, *Petit Souris*, and those gorgeous *tartes*, oh my god, *aux fraise* and *au citron* and, dear me, those of *mûres et framboise…*" (I'll take one of each, please, by the way.)

"No, Don."

"You really need to have some special sort of occasion?"

"Yes, that is true," Henry said.

"Like what?"

"Like when you visit with your famous appetite."

All of this has gone into the pot, grist for the *moulin*; it has inflected our shape, our health and, in subtle ways, our careers.

Meanwhile, in our adopted country, nothing stays the same. *Plus ça change* is no longer the rule. France has only 300 cheeses now, I hear. The long siesta has been curtailed by European Union membership, hurting small bistros and shuttering many. The women we so admire for their knowledge and culinary *savoir-faire* shake their heads at us, saying that we're idealizing a role they are glad to give up. It doesn't reflect the reality of a France where women began working longer hours decades ago. I remember Gwened's complaint, going on almost twenty years now, about the toll of living up to the French feminine ideal. Our friends still resent the pressure.

During the same time in the United States, attitudes toward food and diet have changed dramatically—going in the green, ingredient-based, if not exactly French direction—while on the Continent, McDo and BK have made real inroads. At least we have yet to see a *food fast* joint on the island, or an obese *îlien*.

C'est le même chose: a Frenchwoman, even exhausted, can still out-cook us all.

❧

With inputs like these that she gets on Belle Île, green journalism has suited Mindy well. Combining our sixties idealism and writing, it allows her to put her law degree to use without the drudgery of a practice. It's a good fit, too, with her Tiger Mom's obsession with what exactly goes into what: chemicals in fish and breast milk, pesticides in applesauce and baby food, hormones in shampoo and herbicides in genetically modified plants, and so forth.

Moving from The Trust for Public Land (TPL) to the Natural Resources Defense Council (NRDC) to Mothers & Others for a Livable Planet, before going out on her own, Mindy has worked closely with scientists and researchers and honest-to-god farmers literally in the field. She's done global, local, and urban green; worked with Kennedys and Rockefellers, Martha Stewart and, in particular, Meryl Streep, cofounder of her newsletter. Mindy's affinity for sifting and blending the input of all those experts and practitioners has won her national honors.

So we live the green life. Not as a once-a-year Earth Day thing, like those special issues in the mainstream magazines (where Mindy is often asked to contribute), but as a conscious daily practice. I'm cool with that. Sure, I used to get tired of the constant grilling about my food shopping choices—that, and lectures at the dining table—but now I'm up to speed. Ask me anything. Go ahead, ask me about my butt. You see, I use this special French crème...

Only on Belle Île can we and she relax the cycle of constant vigilance and interrogation. The fish come straight from the sea, the lamb from the fields. Even the beef (which she avoids) is culled from island bulls. She allows me to gnash the occasional *contre-filet* to keep my incisors sharp. Toss in cheap organic vegetables from the farm at Kerzo or

Gwened's garden, and all the *cidre brut biologique* you can drink; now, that's a real busman's holiday.

Visiting Belle Île is like visiting some breakaway green republic. Okay, the French still smoke; but we're working on it.

$\mathcal{H}$

As for my own career turnaround, or evolution? *Hot Water* became a one-pound résumé. It took me places. Opened doors. When my former colleague Tom hooked me up with Evan, who was leaving some indescribable but very upscale-sounding gig at Condé Nast, it was the novel that became the convincer. That and the *Washington Post* review.

So I made it past HR, whose Cerberus had her doubts, I could tell. Going in to meet the editor in chief, I knew I still lacked the inner *je ne sais quoi* of a fabulous person who belonged in The Land of All-Black. I looked at Mindy. She nodded her head. It was time for the suit.

I put my fate in the hands of Mr. Agnes B. Homme, who slid like a flat, black matte silhouette up Madison Avenue. He got off the elevator at the twenty-second floor and charmed, I'm told. It was only the second or third time I ever wore it, and it felt a little tight at the waist and at the ankles, but that suit hugged my chest and shoulders like Spandex.

As books editor, my job was to read books. And be fabulous at it. Not a stretch. Well, until I had a few too many long literary lunches, and then, *malheureusement*, popped a button and had to buy something roomier to accommodate all the dunnage.

Chapter Twenty-One
La Fontaine Wallace

In the spring of our thirteenth year, we made the momentous decision to add an outside faucet to rinse sand from our feet after the beach and to be able to attach a hose for watering the garden and washing down wet suits and surfboards. Mindy called a plumber. The first summer after making the decision, the plumber almost came. The second summer, never almost.

Laurent was a fine guy, a *Bellilois*, who'd taken over the business from his father, who'd plumbed our lines years ago. We occasionally saw him surfing late in the evening after a day of rushing from tourist and second-home jobs. In the lineup, with the sun low on the horizon, the points of surfboards serrating the horizon like shark fins, he'd make promises that we both knew he could not keep. Then he'd paddle away.

The rumor of a second plumber came courtesy of our *maître du bâtiment*, Theophile, who'd started as apprentice to our first master builder, Denis, and had eventually taken over the business, including our own slow-motion renovation. (Here insert a TV announcer's voice: *Now in its **twenty-seventh** year!*) Theophile was a young man with a bright glint in his eyes. We were not great clients from a financial perspective, and certainly not as a means of furthering one's reputation, given that we owned a former ruin that still looked as if it could lapse any day now back into ruination.

But, he asked, weren't we the Americans who had introduced surfing to Belle Île? Well, Theophile had watched us in the waves when he was a boy, and now he was a surfer, too. Was it true Mindy was Hawaiian? *Superbe!* And you, Don, you will have to go out fishing on my father's boat. We know where the sea bass sit in their holes. We will get drunk and sing to them until they come out and bite our lines.

There was no decision to make; we'd already adopted each other.

But even Theophile couldn't summon a plumber. Instead, one day he asked us if we'd heard the story about the Midnight Porsche. How late at night, long after the last restaurants and bars had closed in the three towns, a blinding streak of light occasionally went flying down the central route from one end of the island to the other, all eleven miles of it, Locmaria to Pointe des Poulains. Like a mirage, or a silver bullet.

My ears pricked up. Yes, I could've sworn I'd heard the redline screaming of a fast car's gearbox being rammed through the changes. It was a sound hauntingly familiar to me, who had lain in bed as a child listening to the ecstatic love moans of candy-colored, dual-carb, super-hemi funny cars floating up the Los Angeles River's dry concrete bed all the way from Lions Drag Strip in Wilmington.

I remembered one such night late in the fields of Kerbordardoué when we'd walked out to watch the Perseids. Instead, Rory sidetracked us into looking for the glowworm that lit each summer in the same spot, year after year, climbing the same stalk of tall grass (or so it seemed). And there she was, shaking up a booty cocktail of luciferin and luciferase, lighting the old green lantern for the boy worms on the prowl, when suddenly a streak flashed up ahead like horizontal lighting: the phantom Porsche. Or else a giant rival she-worm.

To Theophile I said I recalled spying, while on a rambling bicycle ride over and through the hamlets and farms, a sleek silhouette covered by a tarp in a graveled driveway. Theophile affirmed that this was not just a phantom Midnight Porsche, but a plumber's Porsche. He gave us his number and name: Benedict.

"He is not *Bellilois*," said Theophile, which we understood to mean he understood that we wanted this faucet badly enough to risk going outside our established island network. But we ought to be careful that word did not get around, especially in the surf. Laurent would be hurt. It might actually affect his mood in the water. And he might never come when we *really* needed him, not just for something trivial like a faucet.

Mindy made the call and charmed Benedict, not a small thing, given that this was such a small job. He said yes because he was curious, we suspected, and we prepared for the *Bellilois* ritual, long and glacially paced, of getting to know each other before work would start. I filled the coffee filter and put on water, Mindy set out a bowl of the archaic sugar cubes so beloved of *Bellilois* and the blackberry butter cake she'd made the day before. When a panel truck came bumping up the lane and parked a safe distance from Gwened's barn, we sighed. We really had hoped he'd roar up in the Porsche.

Benedict was large, with a rugby player's torso and a big, handsome head. His hair was styled. He had the well-brought-up French person's social distance that makes conversation astringent until, without warning, it erupts into hilarity. With Benedict the moment came after polite offers of coffee and cake, which he declined once, twice, three times before giving in "*avec plaisir*"—but only, he insisted, after inspecting the job.

That took all of five minutes, including a visit to his truck for a length of pipe, tools, and a butane torch. Then he decided he wanted to work first and have coffee later. Recognizing that once again we'd been out-mannered, Mindy excused herself to go upstairs and write. I settled into a wicker chair to watch. Our son, age twelve, toyed with a chess problem on the dining table. Unable to keep up my end of the conversation without Mindy to translate and make excuses, I reached over to the cassette tape player and punched Play.

On his knees with a wrench and a rag, Benedict raised his head.
"Joe Cock-*aiiiiiiirrr*?"

"*Oui*, Joe Cock-*aiiiiirrr*."

"*J'aime* Joe Cock-*aiiiiiirrrr*." He inhaled deeply and shook his head.
"*Pour vingt ans, j'étais un chanteur du rock.*"

"*Vraiment? Mais, je suis un chanteur du rock!*"

Rory, whose French was already considerably better than mine, was
aghast at this development. Particularly as, unbeknownst to me, my reli-
ance on an ever-present tense had Benedict thinking I was actually the real
thing, a rock singer, hiding from my public in this tiny hamlet. Even after
we got this straightened out, with much laughter, Rory dreaded what was
coming next: a comprehensive shout-out of our favorite groups.

Rolling Stones! *Oui!*

Kinks! *Oui!*

Cream! *Oui!*

Benedict knew them all and soon was reeling off stories of his life
on the road in a van with a band, playing clubs and *discothèques* all
over Europe.

He finally stood and, instantly grasping the acoustic potential of our
tiled kitchen floor, joined me in a reverberating chorus: "Do you *need*
anybody? I need someone to love. Can it *be* anybody? I want someone
to love."

We looked at each other and grinned: we both had *the big rock voice*.
Mindy came scrambling down the stairs at the commotion, and Rory
covered his ears in protest.

This was our cue to twist spasmodically, knock-kneed, a la Cock-
airrrr, and to bellow: "I get *high* with a little *help* from my *friends…*"

※

At last we had an outdoor faucet. We also had an invitation to an aperitif at Benedict's house—*un apéro*, as it is called here, by second-home
owners. (The *Bellilois* don't do *apéros*.)

The tradition of the *apéro* on Belle Île can feel like tyranny. For many second-home owners and renters, it is the chief form of entertainment during the summer—not only for the conversation, but for the gossip surrounding who invited whom. Of this we were blissfully unaware for our first eight years, because we lived in such a state of disrepair that entertaining never crossed our minds. (*Please come by the Wallace lean-to at 5:00 p.m. for peanuts and cheese breads served on a Frisbee.*)

The few invites we had to accept—from Gwened, Franck, and Ines—were reciprocated eventually, as in years later. When we did, we were inevitably observed pointedly by those whom we owed an *apéro* for some kindness they'd done us (we borrowed a lot of stuff, beginning with rides to the market) when we couldn't return the favor. Others whose invitations we'd declined now moved us into the category of fair game and began laying snares.

This led us to formulate the concept of the damage control *apéro*— one dreamed up to forestall hurt feelings. Since we owed or were in arrears for *apéros* with everybody, we tried to clump ours together, only our efforts never seemed enough. It was like a rolling credit card balance, gathering more and more interest despite your efforts to pay it off.

The problem was the Belle Île *apéro*'s resemblance to a certain Pacific Northwestern tribal rite, the potlatch. "Drinks at home" among my parents' generation when I was growing up—and as lately revived by hip young things inspired by retro television programs—featured a spartan if punishing lineup of martinis, peanuts and olives, crackers and cheese roll-ups. For the rest of us in the States these days, it's enough to meet in bars or just fall by for a beer on the deck. Jars of salsa and bags of chips are opened.

Such a lack of effort would never do on Belle Île. With very few exceptions, such as Le Vic and his wife, Yvonne, whose soirees are a model of moderation because they're followed by a real dinner, the *apéro* is often an unending onslaught of nibbles and delicacies, both plain and elaborate, lasting for hours and frequently extended by the merging of rival *apéros* from other residents in the village and even other villages.

Once an evening of *apéros* kicks off, you won't be able to extricate yourself until the last can of sardines in the back of the pantry is pried open with a Laguiole folding knife, and you can count yourself lucky that no one cuts himself trying.

By this point in our story, the Season of the Outdoor Faucet, we'd recognized that the chief hazard of the *apéro* was, surprise, the morning after. The resulting slowness and inertia was incompatible with our quest to take advantage of Belle Île's eighteen-hour summer sun. The *apéro* also interfered with our surfing, since windless evening glass-offs, while unpredictable, were glorious when happening.

With Benedict, we knew there was no way out. Of course the chosen evening was a perfect, hot, calm one. Naturally our *Bellilois* surfer friends were all out in the lineup between the cliffs of Donnant. And where were we? Dressed up and sputtering along in our rattletrap Renault, looking for a well-hidden house in another village. The gray shrouded silhouette of the Porsche in the graveled drive gave it away.

Benedict's girlfriend, Annette, led us to a back garden table set with glasses and plate upon plate of *hors d'oeuvres*. A voluptuous blond with a touch of Marie Antoinette playing milkmaid at Versailles, she uncovered a tray of charcuterie. An hour later we were still being introduced to new dishes, some whisked out of the oven. Benedict and I were warbling snatches of song to each other. At the two-hour mark, Mindy tried to suggest we really should let them go. "But wait," Benedict cried, "Champagne!" It had been in the sun for a while and popped with a spray of foam. A perfect plumber's drink, we all agreed.

At three hours we tried to find the door. Our boy is waiting for us, we pleaded. But the French don't fall for that one, ever. We all laughed. No, we agreed, he was probably delighted to be out in the never-ending twilight, going from *apéro* to *apéro* with his village pals. Benedict raised a hand to get our attention. "It is time for you to see…" He gestured to their bedroom. We blushed. Annette pulled on a velvet rope, and purple curtains parted.

It was a vision of ancient Greece straight out of a Maxfield Parrish print that hung on my grandmother's guest bedroom wall, a fresco of robin's-egg blue sky and fluffy pink clouds at sunrise, flanked by the real article, Ionic columns in *bas-relief.* And beyond those, inside, a ten-foot-tall pink scallop shell made of plaster of Paris whose base ended in the gold faucets and tap of a spa tub and Jacuzzi.

"*Pour l'hiver,*" said Benedict. For the winter. He winked at Annette.

"*Elles sont longues, les nuits,*" agreed Mindy, with a giggle. Winter nights *are* long.

"With the bubbles of the bath," said Annette. "Like Champagne?"

"*Avec Champagne, parfait,*" I said. "*Parfait pour un chanteur du rock.*"

"Don't you get any ideas," said Mindy to me. Then, of course, she had to translate and Benedict had to promise to draw up plans for a proper bath for a fellow like me, which is to say, a fellow like himself, a man with *the big rock voice.*

✣

We may have woken one of the old Druid water spirits with the faucet—and not a benevolent one, because on a day not long after Benedict's *apéro* we were roused from our siesta by screams in front of our house. The whole village came running. We stumbled out our front door to find a distraught tourist, a wild-haired woman who'd rented a house for herself and her many, almost uncountable children. She was standing on tiptoes beside the beehive well—the well that had once been ours—peering down into its dripping darkness. Shrieking the name of a girl. Sobbing, she started to climb up the stones as if to plunge down after, we assumed, her lost child.

It was a horrible moment.

"Mama?" asked a small, curious voice. A little girl popped her head out from under a large, tentlike hydrangea next to the well. The mother took one look and nearly fainted.

Back at the house, we found ourselves shaken and spent some time reliving the incident. We hadn't given the well a thought for years. Once it wasn't ours anymore, it had merged into the village scenery. But now we realized that, yes, it was a terrible accident waiting to happen. We decided to speak to the "owner" the next day about installing a door or barring the well completely.

Then Mindy broached a worry that, we had to admit, only an American would think of. What if a child fell in the well and the *gendarmerie* asked who owned it, and our neighbor did an about-face and swore it was ours? What if some tourist drank the polluted water and got sick? What if they sued? And who would they sue—a French person or an American?

It may be important to note that Mindy had trained as a lawyer and passed the California bar. Though she'd never practiced, Mindy was, as they say, *sensitized*. We knew the French were not lawsuit-minded. But why not protect ourselves, since we'd already given up the well?

We decided to not approach the Mairie's office. But we'd recently received notice that our old insurance agent, whom we'd never met, had retired and passed our account along to a M. Grancoeur. Unlike his predecessor, M. Grancoeur had written us a personal letter wishing us the best and hoping we would visit him.

We needed to see him anyway, he confided, to discuss our automobile, the first we had purchased in France. We could insure the car, satisfy our curiosity as to why our predecessor had always included a cow in our home coverage, and find a way to specify in our contract that we did *not* own that well, no sir, nor had we ever.

M. Grancoeur's office was on the *quai* in Le Palais, overlooking the harbor's second basin, and enjoyed an uninterrupted view of the looming Citadelle Vauban, our island's grand, star-shaped fortress. A small sailors' café next door was, as always, packed with red-faced, stubble-cheeked men and red-faced, straw-haired women in cable-knit sweaters. Next door, a window display of naked chickens sizzled and bronzed under an artificial sun.

Our diffident entry into the insurance office was greeted enthusiastically with a raised hand from a mustached *Bellilois* in the back, while the female agent in the front tried hard not to smile. She looked like she'd been waiting for this moment.

And it didn't take long. With flourishes and the fastest French I've ever heard, M. Grancoeur ushered us to our chairs and got straight to business: Would we come to dinner tonight? No, how about tomorrow night? Okay, then, Sunday night. Settled. His wife, Marianne, would cook a fish, perhaps a *turbot*, perhaps a *lotte*. Oh, could she cook! His thick black eyebrows rose and fell with each declaration.

"Do you fish with a cane?" he asked me in labored English. At my double take, he smiled. "Maybe you are not so old. How about a pole?" Then he rhapsodized about casting from the cliffs where the waves crash. Now *that* was fishing.

Eventually we got down to our insurance policy. We'd simply paid our bill over the past thirteen years and stuck it in a file without knowing what it said, except that a cow was mentioned. It was our first insurance in our lives and at the time still our only insurance. (We were idiots, in other words.)

But M. Grancoeur began to show us how he would save us money, tsk-tsking over his predecessor's lack of imagination. Our annual fee, already quite reasonable, could easily be trimmed. Our car, if driven thirty days or less a year, could be covered on a pro rata basis. If we promised never to take it off the island, there was a special discount available. *Voilà*. Mindy and I looked at each other, impressed. All this *and* he was having us to dinner?

Finally, unable to restrain herself any longer, Mindy brought up the cow as a prelude to bringing up the well. M. Grancoeur waved the thought away. It was automatic, he explained. Every house had a cow because every house needed milk and butter. Times had changed, but the basic policy hadn't. He paused. "Do you wish to rent a field?" he asked. Because he knew where he could get us a cow. We shook our heads.

The tinkle of a bell. The next client was here for his appointment. Mindy looked a question at me. I shook my head, no. It would not do to bring up the well. She nodded in agreement. It would not be *sympa*. An all-purpose word used frequently on Belle Île, it meant to display tact *and* generosity, like what M. Grancoeur had just shown us.

So we'd never get the well back, and we'd never be truly rid of it. It would become a tale lodged in the village's tangled history. One day no one would remember, or care. Or it might show up as a set of cross-hatches on a map. *"Puits et chanteur."* As we were forever learning, such was life on Kerbordardoué.

※

Later that summer the waves got good and never stopped. We'd had a summer like this two years before, the first year that we completely forgot ourselves and lived like surf rats. For our Parisian second-home-owning friends, the change that came over us was alarming and unforeseen. Because during the previous fifteen years, as we'd worked to repair and renovate the house, we'd been earnest, attentive, respectful Francophiles, they did not recognize these feral new Wallaces. In our heedlessness, we made regrets to M. Grancoeur for his gracious dinner invitation and never did reciprocate with an *apéro* invitation to Benedict and Annette. We told ourselves we'd make it up the following year. We didn't.

Surfing was our folly back home, one we'd never expected to surface on Belle Île. Now it had made us do a graceless thing. The consequences weighed heavy on our minds. We talked about making amends the following year.

But the following year was 9/11, and we did not come.

※

A year later, the morning of September 11, 2002, found us sitting at our dining table in Kerbordardoué. Mindy and I were a mess. After living with the smell and sight of Ground Zero, we'd decided to go away from our neighborhood. If anyone needed a break, it was Rory, who'd lost his best friend at Hunter College High School in a hit-and-run on

Queens Boulevard at the beginning of the year. Another close friend from school, Sam, was coming along, as well as Devo.

By the time the departure date rolled around, we craved Belle Île. But in two short weeks the boys were gone, cutting it short. Following our painfully scripted instructions (we hoped), they'd set off for Paris and the United States. Nothing you can do once they hit the teen werewolf phase. Or so we told ourselves.

We stared at our coffee and a limp little bouquet Mindy had picked the day before. A little talking, a few tears. Then nothing to say.

A rap on the door. "Uhhh…" Company? This early? Probably a couple of the boys wanting to borrow the village scepter—Rory's spear gun. I got up and opened the door. M. Grancoeur stood in a coat and tie, cheeks freshly scraped, a profusion of Belle Île's glory in one hand and a bottle of wine in the other.

"Please," he said, "accept the condolences of France."

❦

No way were we going to blow this *apéro*. Getting to the market early (and not even pausing to check the surf), we'd scored the little, fresh Sauzon "*Chèvre Amouroux*" in all their varieties: *ciboulette*, black pepper, red pepper, rosemary. Not one day, but three days before, Mindy went to the Hôtel du Phare and dared to enter the kitchen below the stairs. There she bought enough langoustines to fill three supplement *plateaux de fruits de mer*. We asked our psychiatrists to recommend wines.

A brace of avocados came out of deep hiding to make Don's famous guacamole. A second wave, including lamb chops, would hit the barbecue at zero hour plus one twenty. And those were just the heavy artillery. We had tacky little cheesy wheels from the supermarket. We had puffs and doodles as only the French can make them. We had the tins of *Quiberonnaise* lobster *pâté*, mackerel *pâté*, sardine *pâté*…

An hour before M. Grancoeur and his wife and wonderful cook, Marianne, were due to arrive, Mindy began to scream from upstairs, where she'd gone to give the toilet one more swipe of the brush. I ran up to see her cowering in the doorway, a bath towel wrapped around one arm, trying to advance under it like a shield toward a geyser of water shooting up from the toilet and blasting off the skylight and varnished pine ceiling.

It took only a minute to shut off the water for the entire house. With fifty-nine minutes to go for the guests, Mindy ran to Gwened's to borrow her phone and call Laurent, the plumber from whom we'd been advised to hide our outdoor faucet, lest he never make a house call again. A moment later she came back, panting. "He didn't answer, of course. It's Sunday!"

"Okay. Well, we just have to keep the water shut off."

"Marianne will want to use the bathroom. I will."

"Look, Gwened will understand…"

"She's having her own *apéro*. She was not pleased when I asked to borrow her phone. If we send strangers over to piss…" We both knew the kind of village demerits that would earn. Mindy stared at the carefully laid outdoor table, the two interior tables, one laden with bottles and glasses, the other with plates and baskets.

"I'm going to call Benedict."

Then it hit us. The *apéro* we'd never reciprocated. The *Was-that-them?* glances we'd received from Benedict and his wife across the beach. "How can you?" I spluttered. "We haven't talked with him in forever. He'll never take our call!"

Without answering, she walked downhill to the Vicomte's to make the call. In five minutes she was back. "He's coming."

"On a Sunday? No plumber in history…. How did he sound?"

"Friendly. Polite."

The arrivals were near-simultaneous. First, a throaty rumble and silky gear shift. The silver Porsche leaped up the lane like a panther and slotted itself across the square. Then a stolid Citroën bumbled in, barely squeezing between the blossoms. As we were shaking Benedict's hand and beginning the awkward explanation of the last three years of neglect and social sloth, the Grancoeurs came up. Because Benedict was in his Sunday clothes, they mistook him for a guest. Awkwardness squared.

Benedict and M. Grancoeur recognized each other and were professionally friendly, but I suspected that our insurance agent was disappointed. Of all the guests we might invite to join him: a plumber. We had friends among the psychiatrists, professors, artists, museum curators, lawyers, and so forth. Did we honestly think that only people that he, noble-hearted Grancoeur, might feel comfortable with were…

Benedict never let it happen. *Of course, good to see you, too, M. Grancoeur, but if you will excuse me for interrupting your party, one has to see to a little plumbing emergency.* Once Mindy and I jumped in with the story of our watery disaster, hilarity ensured, inspiring a cascade of similar stories and fond memories. I'm sure Benedict could've blown us all away, as a maestro, a connoisseur, of the water closet. But he preferred to act more as a referee, arms crossed, chuckling, throwing out the occasional informed commentary.

What had just transpired? A romance of manners. If only the sincerity and, counterintuitively, the artistry with which the impeccable Benedict and the expansive Grancoeur became instant comrades could be bottled and shipped back to America!

With a shrug, turning down offers of drink and food, Benedict headed upstairs with his canvas satchel. I tried to follow, feeling obliged in case my assistance was required. He waved me back. "*C'est votre apéro,*" he said sternly. The show must go on, rock star.

The *apéro* was hardly halfway through when Benedict came down. "*Voilà,*" he said. "*La Fontaine Wallace est complète.*"

"*La Fontaine Wallace!*" exclaimed M. Grancoeur. He squeezed his eyes shut. "*Parfait! Vraiment, c'est La Fontaine Wallace.*" His wife giggled uncontrollably.

I looked at Mindy. "I don't get it. What's the joke?"

Benedict, M. Grancoeur, and Marianne roared. M. Grancoeur handed Benedict a glass and filled it with Champagne—he'd arrived with a wine caddy and vintages for every stage of what was supposed to be our *apéro*. "Call your wife," he said. "She must try this Champagne."

Annette made excellent time for driving a plumber's truck. The party rolled, each wave of food cheered and devoured. We made a lot of noise, I guess, because a steady stream of neighbors not having *apéros* strolled past just to crane their necks and wave through our wide-flung windows. Dusk donned her robes of purple velvet (unless those were wine stains from M. Grancoeur's excellent Burgundy swirling before my eyes).

At one point Gwened's departing guests filed past our windows like ten little Indians, if you replaced the feathered headdresses with identical coifs from Le Palais's Elle-Lui Salon du Coiffeur, each woman of a certain age and impeccably dressed, if a little prim. They nodded and smiled and made little hand waves. We waved back over the necks of the empties.

"Madame Guedel will think we are drunk," said Mindy, in French.

"*Ainsi, nous sommes!*" we cheered back. Well, we are!

Pop went a Champagne cork. "*La Fontaine Wallace!*"

Even an *apéro* must end. Ours did, after several false starts. At midnight we were doing the dishes and bagging the trash when there came a rapping on our window. "Oh god," said Mindy, but when we saw Celeste's and Henry's wide-eyed faces pressed to the panes, we had to laugh. Who better to analyze the party than our very own psychiatrists?

They burst in full of questions: How did it go? Everyone in the village was talking about our *apéro*. M. Grancoeur, he was our insurance agent? He was reputed to be one of the island's true gourmands. And the owner of the Porsche, who was he? A very chic fellow. Our plumber? *Non, non*, you are kidding. He drives a *Porsche*?

Mindy tried to explain. Benedict came for our— "*Fontaine Wallace*," I interjected.

Henry and Celeste looked very respectful. Of course, *La Fontaine Wallace*. A very important part of France's heritage.

"Oh, my, look at this label," Celeste cried to Henry, holding up a

268

bottle among the several that she was putting into a black garbage sack. "Is M. Grancoeur a collector? This vintage is very rare. Extraordinary." She nodded approvingly at us. "You have had a distinguished evening. A great social success."

Mindy and I looked at each other. How could we begin to explain?

"Ou est votre Fontaine Wallace?" asked Celeste. Her expression was earnest and delighted. She wanted to see *where* our "fountain" was?

The jumbled conversation that followed went a bit like this:

"Celeste, Henry… Perhaps you can help explain…"

"Yes, yes, Mindy. Yes, Don, what is it?"

"Well, our toilet broke today. It just popped and shot water up like a…bottle of Champagne."

"Oh, but what a terrible thing! And this before your *apéro*? But you shut off the water. You might be able to get a plumber in a couple of days. They are impossible all vacation. That young Laurent is very unreliable, worse than his father."

"Actually, Celeste, we did get a plumber to come."

"On a Sunday? Never! Laurent? But you are surfers, and he is your friend. That explains it."

"Non, non, Celeste… You see, Benedict really is a plumber. With a Porsche."

Silence.

"A plumber with a Porsche," said Henry at last. "This makes perfect sense. Psychiatrists cannot afford Porsches."

Henry and I cleaned up the tables and stacked the dirty dishes next to the sink where Celeste and Mindy were doing the wash and dry. When all was done and the tables sponged clean, shining for the morning fast approaching, and the giant black garbage bags stacked by the door, we sat down to a knuckle of Scotch.

"La Fontaine Wallace?" asked Celeste, never one to leave a thread unexplored.

"That's what Benedict called our exploding toilet," Mindy said.

"But of course," said Henry. "Everything makes sense now."

"It does?" we asked.

"Yes, of course," said Celeste, twinkling.

"You're not telling us something!" Mindy exclaimed.

"This is true," said Celeste.

"It would spoil things." Henry made a sad clown face. "Anyway, the village needs a mystery. Kerbordardoué has nothing right now, no great curiosities."

"Except the flowers," said Celeste.

"Except the flowers," echoed Henry.

Celeste smiled. "And now, *La Fontaine Wallace.*"

Mindy and I scratched our heads. We still didn't get the joke.

In the morning, when I couldn't stand not knowing any longer, I strolled down to the Vicomte's with my coffee and joined the old hero, his wife, and their sons and girlfriends in sitting along the slate-topped stoop in the sunshine. We discussed our *apéro* and the *apéro* of Gwened and the satisfaction of seeing the mysterious Midnight Porsche parked in our own village square. Le Vic heard my faltering question and dispatched one of his sons inside the house for a book. It was one of the old-fashioned kind, with bound color plates for the architectural connoisseur. Le Vic flipped a few pages, a few more. "*Et voilà.*"

I leafed through page upon page of the familiar, elegant cast-iron public water fountains of Paris, designed, the captions said, by someone named Sir Richard Wallace and given by him to the people of the city after the German siege of 1871, so that the poor might have a supply of clean water. For this, Sir Richard was rightly revered.

There it was, mystery explained. At least our glorious fountain had a distinguished pedigree.

"Are you related, Don?" asked the Vicomte's wife, Yvonne.

I was tempted. Here was a harmless way to claim a little reflected glory in my adopted country. And how could I be sure it wasn't true?

But Mindy is always scolding me about my tendency to overembroider, especially in France, so I shook my head. No.

"Didn't think so," said Le Vicomte gruffly in French. "He was a bastard son of the Marquess of Hertford, I believe. A great collector, the Marquess. Never acknowledged his son, but the boy inherited the whole pile, just not the title. Gave all those fountains to the city. Didn't leave Paris during the Siege. Founded that museum in England."

"Don't be too sad, Don," said Le Vic's son, Thierry. "We won't tell anybody."

"Yes," said Yvonne, "we are proud to have had our very own Fontaine Wallace here in Kerbordardoué."

"Even if for only a day," said Thierry, puffing a smoke ring into the blue sky.

"*C'est vite, la gloire*," said Le Vic.

Chapter Twenty-Two

Trop Beau

*B*eau temps means beautiful weather but also beautiful time.

What I love is how *beau temps* comes out of nowhere and catches you unaware. You pause while scrubbing a scorched pot in the sink. *What's that sound?* And you realize: *it's nothing*. The purest nothing that there is.

Later that morning, you hear crystal voices tinkling in your ear. *Who's talking? Where are they?* You can't see anyone. Perhaps you're imagining things. Anyway, you keep on and turn down the *vallon*. The light suffuses everything. The air grows humid, and the sunbeams glint off spiderwebs like gold thread.

That afternoon, leaving a gummy fish dish to soak in the sink, you walk—same old, gray scrubber in hand—to the open door. You feel drawn to step outside onto the single flagstone, mossy at the edges, the ground moist as a spring from the lilies Suzanne planted there. The entire village slumps into the most profound silence. Even the swallows are asleep.

This is it, you think. *Listen.*

Down the lane comes the movie actress, humming. She has changed over the last couple of years. No longer a starlet, she holds her young daughter's hand like any other mother. She is famous for her provocative roles, for showing some skin and a lot of décolletage, but her choices lately also delve deeper. Although a bit of a media frenzy attended her divorce from her husband, a famous movie director, Luc Besson, here she walks without self-consciousness or fear of paparazzi.

We smile at each other. We will never mention that day at the beach, when for all of five minutes she lay on her towel next to me and asked me to help her with her English. Ah, the memories... She strolls on, scatting a snatch of some pop song with her daughter.

And this, too, is *beau temps*.

But not everyone is on vacation, not everyone is at the beach, not everyone is singing, because some people have to work. And you tend to feel sad and a little guilty when you see them, say, across a freshly threshed field. You can barely pick out the solitary old tractor and its disker, paused on the edge of a ravine that overlooks the sea.

But then you remember that *beau temps* is for tractors, too. There was that time you surprised a boy and a girl in the cab, going for a slow cruise, clutch in, tractor shuddering, while they stopped for a kiss. Once you passed a young man and a woman, still in the first flush of marriage, sharing the single seat, feet on the fender, opening their brown bag lunches. Several times you've come across a crusty old farmer of Kerhuel who has whisked his bride of forty years away from the village for a September adventure, a tractor ride to the outermost limits of their land to pick blackberries from the brambles that line the ravine.

It's all *beau temps*, and it's all good.

But it's fleeting. Nobody with a head on his shoulders wastes *beau temps*. As Madame Morgane likes to say: "*Profitez.*" One must profit.

This kind of profit means enjoy. It has nothing to do with money, and yet, at its root, yes, there is a financial calculation. As in: forget about the money, honey, and *profité*.

We wake early and dash to the market in Le Palais, hoping to beat the August heat and tourist crowds. We go first to buy *palourdes* before they run out, greeting Shra-Shra and Mumbles, as we've nicknamed the swaying, bewhiskered duo whose words never quite make it out of their wild moustaches. All that emerges are alcoholic fumes, enough to knock you down. So hammered are they at eight a.m. that they can barely count out clams, let alone change.

Then we hit the *Bellilois* corner of the fish market to check out *lotte* and *bar*, striped sea bass, and say hello to the tall, striking blond in the yellow full-length rain slicker who cleans your sardines while standing on a box. She's the best-ever advertisement for a sardine, but she does have a rival: the tall Danish blond who sells the sea bass her husband catches. What a knockout! She, too, cleans and also scales. Both women are elegant and poised, a little salty in conversation and always with a sharp, wet knife in hand. They flip purple fish intestines over their shoulders to the low-flying seagulls behind them with all the insouciance of a bride tossing a bouquet.

After that, I slip away to solo with the goat-cheese queen, who guides me through my halting French. Mindy discreetly withdraws from these *tête-à-têtes*. I have made it clear that my relationship with the goat-cheese queen and her wares is not open for discussion. Mindy is especially not to read anything into the fact that my lady friend's round cylindrical cheeses, so fresh they quiver, bear a label that reads *"Chevre Amouroux Belle Île."* That horny goat looking out from the label with such a stern expression is sending you a message, Mindy. Butt out.

Back by 9:30, we load up the car for the day's first surf run. A swell is running, so we ignore the aching muscles and the twitching calves, the sinus pain and the sun-fried skin that feels like pork cracklins. No time to lose.

We put a lot of pressure on ourselves, as we have during every summer when the surf is good. *Profitez!* We're still superstitious—we remember the first eight years when, even when it was hot and calm back in the village, the beach wind blew cold and the sea was gray and choppy. It has now been eight years of fine weather and good surf; we suspect that the day we don't respond to the call, the waves will die and not come back.

It can oddly feel like work. We even joke that the ocean is our office. One day a couple of summers back, we realized that there'd been ten straight days of surf. Our heads were rolling around on our shoulders. Ten days of surf doesn't mean an hour or two of surfing a day; on Belle Île, with its Nordic light that goes on until ten at night, it can mean two daily sorties that last from two to three hours each, sandwiched around a nap and meal break.

Of course no normal mortal can withstand that pace. It takes true dedication to do that. But as soon as we arrive, in the beginning of our month, we are working our way into shape. Rolling out of bed in the blue morning, fueling on coffee, fried eggs, and baguettes buttered and slathered with blackberry preserves that Mindy makes in our first week.

After an hour of writing, we roust the boys. (In addition to Devo, there is usually at least one of Rory's American friends visiting while his parents scoot footloose and fancy-free all over France.) While Mindy is yelling at them to get their suits and towels off the line, I pull the battered old Renault up and yank the parking brake. Now the boards come out, to be snugged into the roof rack and lashed down. With the three heavy boards on top of the Renault, a strong gust of wind will raise the car's front wheels off the road like a rearing stallion.

The parking lot is at the bottom of a *vallon*, with a tall grassy sandhill to the left and thirty-foot sand dunes directly in front. We load up and trudge across a wooden bridge over a stream, between green rushes and cattails, then follow a narrow path through the dunes. We emerge overlooking the bay. Though golden and already warm, the beach is almost completely deserted. God bless the French and their rigid social protocols: the lunch hour must be properly observed. They won't arrive until after.

Not so the surfers. There are already a couple in the water and a few perched on their bicycles or mopeds, checking things out from up on the cliff. There are those who call themselves surfers but prefer to watch. Not us.

Time to grit the teeth and pull on the black rubber, our wet suits still damp from the evening before. Then, with groans and shrieks, we pile into the white water and begin to paddle-battle out to the third break, where the ocean meets the bay. Ten minutes later, we're there, breathing hard—eyeing the horizon and each other, jockeying for position, one big happy family turned happy rivals.

At noon we're back at the house. "Food!" shouts Rory, throwing himself on the *fauteuil* and reaching for the nearest chess book. Devo growls, head buried deep in the refrigerator.

While Mindy soaks in the tub to warm up, I make salami-tomato-butter baguette sandwiches. Yesterday we had *pan bagnat*, soppy tuna-and-hard-boiled-egg salad spooned with plenty of capers and sliced tomatoes into puffy round rolls.

At the same time I collect rations for the picnic to come: chocolate and apples, biscuits and a thermos of hot Earl Grey go into the straw basket we'll bring back for Round 2 at the beach. Pausing at the bookshelf, I decide to grab a novel from the stack that we mailed to ourselves once the house was complete. I had sent fifty pounds of books three months in advance—by ship, in a dingy USPS canvas bag—for just twenty-five dollars.

I dawdle over the titles: Poe, Melville, Proust, Anthony Powell... Or perhaps a thriller is in order? We have Alan Furst, Chandler and Hammett, John le Carré, and Philip Kerr's Berlin Noir trilogy. Then there are those books that I return to and reread every summer. Which shall it be: *The Name of a Bullfighter* by Luis Sepúlveda, Andrei Platonov's *Fierce and Beautiful World*, or *Some Clouds* by Paco Ignacio Taibo II?

It turns out to be an unopened *Times Literary Supplement*, still wrapped in plastic, from years ago. The very definition of exploration—diving into a time capsule of late-1990s British high culture. For me, 'tis jaunty, arcane, and absurd. Like our summer days.

After lunch, there is a pretense of reading. Soon everyone stretched out is snoring.

At one forty-five Mindy groans and shoves herself up on one arm. "Coffee?" Less than half of the day has passed, with hours to go before we sleep again. Time for a little writing, then back we'll go to our office on the sands.

Profitez.

꽃

After lunch, everybody goes to the beach. Young and old, Parisian and farmer. I've never seen farmers at the beach anywhere else in the world. But in Belle Île, the flocks of sheep are sometimes driven across the beach at Donnant at low tide. Sheep at the beach: just when you thought you'd seen everything.

Even the lifeguards don't show up until one p.m. With heavy-lidded eyes, they raise a flag to indicate the danger level: today is *jaune*, yellow—caution for everyone but us. They set up a board on which they write the day's *météo*, weather. Today there is a small ceremony: the water temperature has soared to 19 degrees Celsius (66 degrees Fahrenheit). Temperatures we'd think twice about before going in anywhere outside Belle Île feel positively balmy here.

Villages re-form on the sand in circles of towels. Look, there's Kerledan—shall we visit? I think I see Goelan. Oh god, don't look at Kervilahouen—we owe them a drink.

Some days I roll over and see Gwened and her new husband lying back toward the dunes. They like it just far enough away to not belong to any crowd, except to us who know her. She gives a little wave. Her man sucks in his stomach and carefully adjusts his floppy sun hat.

The dunes are where our surfboards line up like a multicolored picket fence. The boards' noses are hung with full wet suits, black Neoprene tops and bottoms, and towels drying. Rolling at the base of the dunes are fully clothed amorous teenagers. Next to them are motorcyclists, slowly peeling off their leathers and helmets to reveal chalk-white skin and platinum-dyed buzz cuts. Next to them the *en bonne forme* family lies primly, legs and arms straight, on their crisp blue-striped towels. And on and on.

Here comes a long line of clean-cut adolescents in uniforms: khaki shorts, light blue shirts, bandanas tied at the neck, cute little hats. Boys and girls from a timeless virginal grove, they make their way down the burning sands, threading between glistening, oily, uniformly topless bodies lying as if in state. Scouts? Sea Scouts? Oh, really?

They're chatting in German. Their scoutmaster is short, roly-poly, and unshaven, but his uniform has much impressive braid and many medals. When they reach the wet, packed sand at the high-tide line, he blows a whistle. *Mädchen und junge Männer* turn south and march off toward Bangor, the round guy bringing up the rear, fanny pack bouncing.

We shake our heads and smile. What can we say? A French beach in summer is reliable entertainment.

A couple of little goat paths trickle down the cliff face like the tracks of tears. Down them now, tiptoeing, hesitant, come families from the north end of the island. Then a new band tops the rise, each carrying a surfboard under one arm and a beach bag in the other hand: the Kings of Donnant, our surf crew in full complement. They plunge down the cliff, sliding but sure-footed, their families following, letting gravity speed them along.

As they set up camp at the far end, we exchange waves. We may go see them in a few minutes, after they're settled; they probably won't come here. The *Bellilois* give Parisians a wide berth socially. I stand up and tug on my shortie wet suit, a concession to age after ten years of going without. I turn to Madame. "Coming?"

Mindy sits up, stares down the beach. She's waiting on the Kings. "They'll know when it's good," she says.

The gang is looking over at us as she looks at them. They rise from their towels and reach for their wet suits. Who knows if they think it's time, or if they just saw me getting ready and thought Mindy would be coming, too. Whatever, the Kings of Donnant are going out: Theophile, our *maître d'bâtiment*; Andre, the recently retired naval marine and his wife, Coco, who runs the spa at our one elite hotel; Yannick, the moody chain-smoking Sartre of Sauzon. The six of us have been surfing together forever, it seems, along with their friends Alain, Guy, and Roger. Mindy and I are twenty years older but it doesn't feel like it—the Kings' gift to us, and one we pretend not to notice.

All over Brittany a hybrid Breizh-Malibu surf culture has emerged, hardy and clear-eyed. There's even a Breton style of beachwear: think plaids and Celtic crosses. Thanks to the Kings, who represent the first generation of island surfers, Belle Île occupies a special place with an *Endless Summer* vibe.

Our local friends already led oceangoing lives, men and women both taking a few hours every week to go fishing in a guano-spattered skiff, spearfishing in the fjords, pole-fishing from the cliffs (during savage storms: the best time for striped bass), gathering mussels and *pousse-pieds*. Surfing fit right in, the missing piece. If we've had a hand in this—and we do occasionally claim bragging rights for introducing it on Belle Île—then let that be our legacy.

But, sad to say, surfing does tend to alarm our Paris friends. "You mean you fly 8,000 kilometers to France for thees?"

The short answer is no, of course not—but, you know, *profitez.*

The long answer? Surfing engages the natural world in a way a shutterbug's camera or a birdwatcher's binoculars never can. You live inside the tides with the sea state in your head, like a sailor or fisherman. You train body and mind to cope with conditions. The rules are up to you, and to make them, you learn to live with fear.

To surf well, you actually have to push yourself up to the edge and then, quite literally, go over. That brief moment of hanging upside down, head pointing into an imminent wipeout, is ironically what surfers live for. They call it "making the drop"—a phrase that can comfortably encompass our lives in general. Move to New York City at age thirty without jobs or prospects? We made the drop. Buy a ruin in a village on a tiny isle off the coast of Brittany? We made…(sound of idiot falling into a blackberry bramble).

The accusation that we are stuck in perpetual adolescence is harder to duck. Listen, surfing has a fairly stern code of law, an etiquette—but I can see you're not buying it. We comprise a society. No, it's not *Baywatch* and it's not teeny-weeny bikinis that draw us to the waves. This isn't about dudes, Malibu, or the Big Kahuna (though we enjoy them as kitschy *tropes tropiques*). We aren't about evading responsibility.

We try to be good neighbors on dry land. We bring a covered dish to supper. We recycle. And, of course, we don't bore friends or spouses by talking surfing (too much). A good surfer anywhere is laconic, cool. Pursues self-reliance in his life and appreciates competence in others. A really good surfer feels a responsibility to society and the environment. And has great hair.

⚜

Mindy and I slowly shake off the torpor of our nap in the sun to find ourselves the eye in a storm of passionate discussion.

The teenagers around us are studying for *Le Bac*, the great test that comes at the end of high school and determines your future in France. Even those who have two years to go are already studying, reading books off the list: Voltaire, Balzac, Thomas Moore, Flaubert, Sartre. Their mouths are pursed, brows furrowed. This discomfits Rory and Devo, who've always been able to count on Nintendo and Game Boy round-robins to fill the time when they're not in the water.

Our boys ask about the books. They ask to see them. They try a page and visibly recoil. The young-looking boy with the Apollonian curls asks what they read in America. "Do you read any French authors? No?" He looks sad. "Well," he brightens, "surely you've read Thoreau, Poe, Melville, Faulkner?"

Silence.

Celeste forms an "O" with her mouth and looks at Mindy, who nods. Our boys *are* savages.

The talk of books brings the teenage girls into the circle. Although they ask Mindy for her opinions about American authors, their own opinions—sassy, sardonic, and above all, *knowing*—immediately tumble out of their perfect, pouty mouths. Their hands fly about in languid arcs, as if holding cigarettes (which won't come out until Maman goes for a walk). They know books, and what's more, they can talk them. Better than *you*, their eyes say.

Their mockery reduces our boys to uneasy grins. But not Marc and the others, who fire back. Mindy and I are careful not to seem to be eavesdropping, or noticing Rory and Devo's forays back into the conversation. They're not used to being left behind. They seem energized by all the girls in the careful bikinis reading George Sand and Ronsard on the sand. The thought has perhaps occurred to them that there is more than one way to *profité*. Perhaps *beau temps* and *bons livres* will ignite a fire of a different kind. Not by coincidence do we happen to have those good books on the shelves in the house, back up the *vallon*.

✣

But the books don't fool our friends. Given that we Americans are all so *sauvage*, our Paris parents were a little anxious when we became Pied Pipers to the children of the villages, leading them out past the shore break into the wild ocean. We used Rory as bait—a bodysurfer since he was a babe, he could twirl, spin, and fly off ten-foot faces with aplomb.

The village kids were ripe for adventure, but Donnant is not for children, and their parents rightly worried. So while Mindy performed on the foamy stage—tempting and teasing the young *Bellilois* with her shortboard repertoire of Hawaiian-style drops and cutbacks—Rory and I spent a lot of time teaching the Parisian flock how to duck waves and deal with currents, while their parents watched from the water's edge.

We made bodysurfing our focus because surfing is so hard to learn, and nobody had surfboards to spare anyway. We decided that to join us, you also had to reject bodyboards, "*le peste polyeste*," and said it was for reasons of safety. As long as you're tethered to a foam floatation device, you aren't going to become a strong swimmer. You're also going to get dragged backwards, over and over. Then if your leash breaks, you'll be in trouble. But our real reason was aesthetic. Bodyboarders have no manners. They plow over people like bumper cars.

The rejection set us apart. It was our Aquatic Code. As anyone with any taste and refinement knows, we sniffed, bodysurfing is the ultimate form of surfing—nothing gets between you and the sea, the currents, the waves. It's pure.

Once our crew learned to handle themselves, we shared the advanced Hawaiian technique that involves dropping into the curl, gliding parallel to the wave, then spinning and carving using the planing surfaces of the body, like a dolphin. One by one, each had his "aha!" moment.

We also went big. Donnant pumping outside was a spectacle that beckoned. We ended up with a platoon of fearless wave hounds that came to include the lifeguards. At the fore were Rory and Devo and Marc. And Raoul. A quiet young man when I spotted him, fins in hand, at the shore break, I didn't know he'd just lost his father. I just invited him to ditch the bodyboard and come along. We've since been in the biggest surf of my life with shit-eating grins on our faces and looks that said: Can you believe this?

Too late, parents in the villages recognized the savage gleam in their child's eye at the sight of dark blue-green swells popping up on the horizon. But it really was too late. Once you've gone big, you never truly go home.

❧

Out of the water, warming up on my towel, I glance up the beach and—uh-oh. There is the man we call Man. Nicknames are our vice, in particular the iconic ones Rory gave to people when he was in his sixes and sevens. Because once they stick, you're stuck.

Man suits man. Wearing horn-rimmed glasses, the opinion writer for *Le Monde* is a serious person. Walking along the water's edge, hands clasped behind his back, deep in thought, he is the very image of French philosophy—despite or because of his pinstriped Speedo.

Man has been waiting for me to look up. He beckons, and I groan, pushing myself to my feet. Ever optimistic in the quest to improve my French to the point where we can talk books and politics, Man is my personal seriousness trainer.

I've come relatively late to seriousness. Like many an insecure grommet of Southern Californian origins, I cringed under the lash of my high school social superiors' drawled put-downs, delivered from Olympian clouds of coolness. I could only respond with the spoofy humor of the sixties inhaled from *MAD Magazine*, late-night FM radio, *Catch-22*, and rock 'n' roll. Eventually, like the old matchbook cover come-on, I found popularity through humor and became "the life of the party."

As a college student I tested an expression of profundity and, after graduation, had a couple of serious jobs. But humor was still my default when anxious. At times I felt it was eating away at my personality like some insect chewing up my brain.

Moving to New York brought a welcome brusqueness into my life, but the feeling returned and the predicament became chronic after we started going to France. Once again I was a social mute, helpless to order even a glass of orange juice without creating a ruckus. When people are laughing at you, there are only two responses: to get mad, or roll with it. Being a funny guy, I rolled with it—*Young Strudel!*—built on the misunderstandings, and played with words and pronoun agreement. Would it were that I'd been learning the subjunctive like Mindy did in Tours!

At age thirty I did begin working to learn French on my own, simply by ear and reading, but my progress was halting and the backsliding frustrating. Although it's actually fairly hilarious and a great icebreaker to offer to cut off your host's penis—completely unintentionally the first few times, I swear—it does wear thin.

Fortunately, Celeste and Henry began acting as unofficial conversation partners, bringing me along. And it was Henry who one day made the fateful observation, after I deflected yet another grammatical error with a quip:

"Don, you must be more serious."

"Don be serious," Celeste echoed, nodding.

I felt nailed. Of course, Henry was a psychiatrist. It was his job to nail people. And I definitely had the anxiety of someone who has never been analyzed. But still—he was right. I'd had a nagging, depressive feeling about my clown-as-avoidance strategy. It cloys, brings you down, when everything is a joke. That's why clowns are so sad, of course.

Man took me farther down the road. When we first encountered him at one of our gatherings at the beach, he was so delighted to meet American writers—and so disappointed with our lack of engagement in the affairs of the day, no, *hour*. Wilting under his monologue, Mindy soon ran off, leaving us together.

Man lived for earnest discussion and demanded details and attributions. I have that sort of mind, and we took to walking the beach chewing the fat, as they say *en Amérique*. He had no humor, so mine was worthless. He took the most facetious remark at face value. But he also was a friend to the point of partisanship. I remember his outrage that in America writers and intellectuals like Mindy and me weren't living high on government grants and university gigs. He took it personally that I had to work for such oddball magazines and scrape to get my serious work published. In France I'd be golden.

Over the years I've taken the Serious Challenge. During the eleven months away from Belle Île, I actually spend a little time each week composing my thoughts on the subjects of the day and then translating them into French, usually on my walks to and from the office. Yes, I know that sounds odd. Well, guess what? I also compose dialogues with other people—friends I'll be seeing in the summer. I've rehearsed for a hypothetical summer dinner party a whole year in advance.

It helps to cut my embarrassment to know that Oscar Wilde did the same, and in English, too. There is a tradition in France of Le Remark. Still—it's definitely eccentric behavior.

But did I mention that it works?

Learning a foreign language always starts with you talking, as it is a lot harder to listen. But too much talking is ungenerous, boring, isolating. When I embarked on listening, however sincere my vow, I found it almost impossible to follow whole stretches of glissading French phrases. It was hard not to break out my shabby old jokes. But if I had one of my composed-in-advance remarks up my sleeve, I felt calmer and, even if I was faking it on the outside, more serious.

※

At the north end of the beach, the mouth of our *vallon* meets the sea in a wide sandy wash. The steep cliff towering above has a pair of German gun emplacements, one for a machine gun, the other for a 75mm cannon, both still camouflaged after fifty years.

These remnants of Hitler's Atlantic Wall remind us of Belle Île's occupation during World War II. It was a harsh four years: the able-bodied men and boys were sent off to do forced labor on the Continent, many to build the bombproof submarine pens at Lorient. The elderly men and the women who remained, not by choice, mostly worked the fields and kept the herds. They had to turn over their milk, meat, eggs, and grain to the occupiers, who let them starve. Suzanne says she ate grass, *comme une vache*. To this day she does her best to ignore or avoid German visitors.

As a young boy in Le Palais, Denis LeReveur had a different kind of war. He mainly remembers the nightly B-17 bombing runs to take out the radar installation on the Côte Sauvage and the 88mm flak guns firing back. Sometimes the bombs fell inland, once even on the town. Sometimes the flak shells didn't burst in midair—a popular act of sabotage by women forced to work in the ammunition factories was to break the proximity fuse—and fell back on the island to explode or burrow deep into fields and barns.

At war's end the Germans honored the island's allure in a peculiarly disagreeable way by refusing to surrender, holding out until after the rest of Germany's armed forces capitulated. It may have only lasted twenty-four hours but they must have been long ones for the *îliens*.

I admit to a masculine weakness for fortifications, and Rory and I have explored the Côte Sauvage's installations. What a waste of concrete! What misguided ingenuity! But I didn't question my boyish attitude toward Donnant's casemates and gun slits until the day I accepted an invitation to lay my towel down next to the Majestic Madame.

Many decades ago, Madame and her husband had bought a post-war refuge on Belle Île, an entire village, one of the most peaceful and beautiful places I'd seen on an island full of them. The pair were very cultured and she had done something big in the Resistance—the Legion d'Honneur doesn't go to just any old hero, you know—and I worried about bruising her eardrums when I spoke my brand of French, though she never betrayed any discomfort. They had preserved their house and village, inside and out, in the old Breton style. This is what led to our acquaintance, actually. She was curious about our project, as it has been called, no doubt euphemistically.

She must've been pushing ninety when I came upon her that day. She waved me over. We talked. Sunning on the beach at Donnant with her left me a little awed and bashful. As we spoke—she so patiently—I happened to spot the tattooed number on the pale, *crêpey* skin of her inner forearm. From the cliffs on either side, the vacant eyes of those Nazi gun emplacements stared down on us. I'll never forget that sense of being watched. Or of how glad I was to be able to speak of other things, and so seriously.

❦

At the end of one summer—after the waves had finally played out—our psychiatrist friends cornered us at the end of a long group dinner and conducted an impromptu, wine-and-coffee-fueled intervention.

After a while, an elegant woman attorney, whose husband was also a distinguished international lawyer, took over the prosecution: "Why do you do thees surf? When we first met you, you did not use to. You did the garden, the shopping, the baseball. Now all you do is thees surf! And"—here came the clincher—"you don't come to *apéros* anymore."

When I started to explain, she interrupted me: "You do not come to France to surf!"

The following afternoon, to placate my inquisitors, I went with them to the all-weather courts of Gouerc'h and the *Club de Tennis*. We played a genteel game of doubles.

After a couple of points, our *avocat* huddled with her partner and then lined up opposite me at the net. We played several spirited rallies. She was good. Then very good. Too good. At the end of one quick-witted volley she caught me on my backhand and, with a slam, somehow broke my wrist.

Now I couldn't play tennis. But when the waves returned, I could go out with a waterproof splint—thanks to Docteur Pleybien, who entered into the spirit of my passion and empathized with my needs. Thus I resumed bodysurfing.

When Madame Avocat saw me on the beach again, she waved her hands. "*Pouf!* You did it all on purpose!" There's no pleasing some people.

❦

A couple of nights later, after feasting on Madame Avocat's excellent Algerian tangine of lamb, I felt I owed her one more attempt at an explanation.

Donnant was the magnet, the wave we'd spotted in that winter of 1980. It was part of the legend of our time there: a mystery spot. So surfing it was a matter of fulfillment of a task or quest. We saw it before it had ever been surfed. So then it became our duty to surf it. "Do you understand?"

"No."

Because it is the only obvious surf break on the island, these days Donnant can be overwhelmed in summer by crowds of bodyboarders. But—and I'd hate it if this got out—compared to California and Hawaii and Montauk, it is uncrowded. There are rarely too many boards in the water. The cost and time needed to catch a ferryboat and rent a car, all to check out a single sketchy beach, a rumor, discourages the surf masses that travel up and down the Atlantic coast from Spain to Brest.

"And?"

It feels like our own world here. A family affair. To know everyone in the water creates something special. A lot of surfers will pay through the nose to go 5,000 miles and surf with strangers in Bali and Fiji. Here we are with our friends. It is our break.

"So? We have our tennis here, too."

"I hope you will excuse me, but it is…not the same."

Her eyes narrowed and the whole table leaned in. Now the game was on.

I stood up and made my argument.

In the past Mindy and I may have been guilty of giving the impression that we were the first surfers on Belle Île, when it's better to say that we introduced the surfer to Belle Île who introduced surfing. This was back in 1984, when I was on assignment for the boating magazine. The story concerned a tribe of fierce, single-handed transatlantic sailboat racers who'd settled at a port fifteen kilometers across the bay from Le Palais. Imagine that! The best sailors in the world on our doorstep.

We found La Trinité-sur-Mer to be a hive of extreme sailing. Huge catamarans and trimarans sat on blocks or rested on sleds on slanting stone quays. Bearded men and women with sun-frosted hair hung off hulls in trapeze seats, scraping away sea slime and baby barnacles.

People ignored us to the point of being rude until one heard that Mindy was from Hawaii. His question—"Do you surf?"—changed everything. It turned out that when he wasn't sailing radical trimarans, Yves explored the rockbound coast of Brittany, pioneering the breaks. Every surfer's dream is to discover and explore one uncharted surf spot in his or her life. Yves had tried scores, maybe a hundred: reckless, even dangerous attempts.

Mindy drew a picture of Donnant for him, explaining what she'd seen: a wave that, at its winter best, resembled Pupukea on the North Shore of Oahu—that big barreling break next to the Pipe. Yves was swearing in excitement. He'd take the ferry over next weekend, hitch-hike with a board, whatever it took to be the first to give it a shot. *Merci!*

Mission accomplished, we later heard. However, for the next five years we didn't see any surfers at Donnant. But our friend Bill, surfing down at the Spanish border, did take the bait after hearing our tales of hidden wave treasure. He stayed in the unfinished house, writing back that Donnant in October was walled up and "spooky"—as surfing the Côte Sauvage alone would be. The next year Mindy tried surfing a windsurfing board rented from a gas station. Removing the mast, she paddled out. The board was too buoyant and fat, like today's stand-up paddleboards. She caught some white-water soup. Mostly she cursed.

By now we would catch an envious glimpse of a couple of surfers, a local and a *Bellilois*, enigmas in the gathering darkness. The *îlien* somehow surfed a board with a broken nose; the amazing thing was that he could stand up at all. The local surfed a red board like a madman. Seeing him out there was disturbing. Self-taught, gutsy, always alone, always in big surf, always pulling into the tube even when it was an obvious close-out. He just didn't seem like a normal surfer.

Then we learned he was the son of the baker who'd drowned at Donnant—drowned in front of him and the family, while hunting *pousse-pieds*. That seemed to explain the haunted style, a suggestion of mourning, as if he were looking for his father in those green underwater caverns.

Once we got our first board to Belle Île, there was no stopping us. At the end of our first surfing summer, Madame Morgane even suggested we paint our shutters *bleu marin* instead of green, because obviously we were sailors, not farmers. She seemed to appreciate our diligence, our seriousness, the way we approached surfing like a job.

"There," I concluded to Madame Avocat. "That's what this is about. Not surfing. About exploration, risk, testing ourselves, redefining the Breton coast, joining, mourning all the fathers that the sea has taken; and, maybe, almost accidentally introducing something that the young *îliens* could pursue instead of aimless scooter riding and drinking and— one hopes not, but—drugs. There are so much drugs these days. Belle Île is a transshipment point, you know."

"No, I didn't," she said. The lawyer in her was interested. "How does that work?"

"Go-fast boats come up from North Africa. They take immigrants. They take heroin and hashish, trade that in Spain for Ecstasy and cocaine, head up to France."

"How do you know this?"

"Don is a boating journalist," Henry said. "For him and for Mindy the Hawaiian, *c'est tout l'océan.*"

It is all about the ocean. Thank you, Henry.

The defense rests.

※

At the Feast of the Assumption on August 15, everything stops while the owners of boats bring their vessels into the harbor and back basins of Le Palais. There they line up, jostling in position with much shouting and many gesticulations, to receive the blessing of the priest from the Église Saint-Véran, who stands at a portable altar in the middle of the harbor.

Once I saw him on a motor launch, once on a *chaloupe*, a traditional sloop-rigged *sardiniere* painted in the deep rust-red called *rouge Breton*.

At least 15,000 people pack the small town. Cars are abandoned on the side of the road miles away. It is both the celebration of the death and elevation of the Virgin Mary and the unofficial but uniformly observed beginning of the end of *les vacances* in France. Within hours the great *rentrée* will begin, and by week's end the island will begin to feel emptied out.

In nearby Sauzon, one of the prettiest villages devised by man and nature, a smaller celebration takes place on that same afternoon, without all the folderol with the boats. But a priest is there, on the *quai* at the foot of the Église Saint-Nicolas, to bless all things afloat or in danger of sinking. It's a fluid and jolly affair, because you can move about, unlike in Le Palais.

Its small scale and stubborn local ownership are what save Sauzon. You can still walk down the *quai* to the lighthouse and not get run over by a moped. You can sit in cheap plastic chairs on deeply scored stones and get *un plateau de fruits de mer* and a glass of Muscadet to sip while you watch old-timers and children cast fishing lines into the murky green water. If you order the *palourdes*, the raw clams will have been raked out of the mud of this estuary by Shra-Shra and Mumbles.

We've managed to take in a couple of Assumption feasts in both towns, but the most memorable are Sauzon's because all young men in the canton are invited to take part in a diving competition. Going back to the nineteenth century, the prize was a cross thrown by the priest into the port waters. The water clarity must've deteriorated because now the boys chase a duck whose flight feathers have been clipped. The prize is the duck.

Once one of Rory and Marc's pals, Rex, won the duck. There was a great hoorah back in the villages—but then Rex looked at the duck and realized what was going to happen to it. His face crumpled. Fortunately a pardon came through at the last second and the duck took up residence in a local barn.

The long day concludes with a fireworks show that illuminates Sauzon's stacked houses and twisty streets like a flickering silent movie.

We've enjoyed lying on a threshed field at the top of a hill overlooking the town, keeping our distance from the crowds, getting the big picture and avoiding the traffic jam to come. Other times we are just too lazy to go. We find ourselves late for the blessing, late for the duck, late for the fireworks.

One of the most memorable such nights was when we decided not to go, then went out for a walk up the road to look at the Perseids. The night is dark on Belle Île and the shooting stars can look like grains of salt flying from a shaker. As we walked, faces turned to the sky, we saw a flashing storm of multicolored lights down where the edge of the field met the horizon. We heard a faint muffled rumble. The fireworks of Sauzon.

We kept walking, no need to watch for cars, no streetlights to blind us, the warm asphalt radiating upward through the soles of our shoes. On a whim we crossed the main road and picked up a country track that ran a mile or two through fields and dales before joining a winding single-lane road that descended to the back end of the Sauzon estuary.

This was certainly no night to walk to Sauzon—it would be all closed up by the time we got there. But we kept walking. Now the horizon was stabbed by headlights as each departing car crested the *vallon*. Then there were no more. Party's over.

We lay down on the warm asphalt to look at the shooting stars.

I may have dozed off. With a jolt, I realized there were lights coming up the road from the direction of Sauzon. If it was a car, we'd have to move fast—but the more I watched, the more curious the lights seemed. There must've been a dozen or more, shifting this way and that, waving like *Star Wars* light sabers, far away one moment, nearer the next.

We rolled over and sat up, silent, hugging our knees and staring at the silver-gray road and the black fields on either side. We could hear singing. Sweet voices, a choir unaccompanied. It seemed a simple song, like a folk or children's song.

Now we could distinguish them: a long line of children, walking and waving their flashlights and singing. Bringing up the rear were two adults, the woman conducting the choir. Her voice, at least, was familiar—Sophie, the mother of the *en bonne forme* family, whose father, Hector, gave Rory his spear gun and whose three daughters drove our boy into a crisis of fidgeting. They'd taken up a collection of village children and marched them off to the feast and the fireworks, fed them at Crêperie Les Embruns, and now were shepherding the little flock home.

They came upon us, still seated on the asphalt, too relaxed to move. We laughed when we heard their sharp intakes of breath. They laughed to realize who we were and, still singing, threaded through us and headed home.

We lay awhile longer on the empty, warm road. Now the island was nearly asleep. Far away a car whined up the hill, shifted into fourth gear, and streaked toward Le Palais.

At the tip of the island, north of Sauzon, the slow strobe circle of the light at Pointe du Poulains was suddenly joined by a whole new ball of flickering lights. We watched awhile, uncertain about what this might be. It looked like the beginning of *Close Encounters of the Third Kind*. Just as in the movie, the ball grew wings of cloud that began spreading out on both sides of the lighthouse. Heat lightning stroked the sky. A crisp white streak—the real thing, plunging into the sea—was followed by a faint rumble.

We got up without saying anything. *Beau temps* was over, and a storm was coming.

Chapter Twenty-Three

Ankou

Buildable land was at a premium. Fancy cars prowled the lanes, faces pressed to the windows, alert for stray parcels and outbuildings. When the occupants deigned to step out of a fancy Citroën Pallas, they often got straight to the point. Is that for sale? No? Is that? Tell me what's for sale. (Yes, I do believe the cow is for sale. No, I do not know who owns it.)

Daytrippers came in droves. Their looks of enjoyment were pure and joyous. But they were everywhere! You couldn't drive anywhere after a ferry landed, because two hundred bicyclists would be wobbling all over the roads, holding up cars, and causing near-accidents and real accidents. And we had up to twelve ferries a day.

Popularity is a curse, of course. When it comes to Eden, it's not enough to visit. People want a place of their own. When everybody wants in, villages fill out to the boundary lines, though the formidable law requiring a traditional Breton style once again proved its wisdom. (The best minds of an architectural generation still haven't figured out how to turn a slate-roofed cottage into a McMansion.) Some officials bent, it's said. A cookie-cutter subdivision appeared on the outskirts of Sauzon one day. How did that happen? Don't ask.

The centralized government bureaucrats who wrote the rules that protected Belle Île were long gone, retired to fine and private places. Their replacements were modern men. In 1987, they built a causeway to Île de Ré, an island only slightly bigger than Belle Île, fifty miles down the coast. By the Nineties, Île de Ré was "a popular weekend bolt-hole for Parisians," as one London tabloid cheekily described it. On a summer's day it was reputedly a zoo, its population swelling from winter's 15,000 to 220,000 *en vacances*.

Soon it was Brittany's turn for some fire-nozzle funding. You can almost see the technocrats and *fonctionnaires* sitting in a boardroom and throwing darts at a map. How about four high-speed superferries to Belle Île? Hydrofoils making 60 knots! How about a harbor for super-yachts so the film people from Cannes can stop over on their way to London?

No, no—wait! How about a causeway to Belle Île? A ten-mile bridge from Port Maria in Quiberon to Le Palais, with connections on the mainland to the D165 and *autoroutes*. Yes, perfect. And all the other stuff's a go, too. Cue the *Marseillaise*.

The causeway was all about delivering the Continent vote. Over the years President François Mitterrand had made several campaign visits by helicopter to Belle Île for the showy eating of a single buckwheat galette at Crêperie Chez Renée. The polling must've been good after, because that's when the causeway plan came up. Mitterrand stood down in 1995, but Brittany voted for his successor and rival Jacques Chirac, so the plan stayed on track.

Puffed up by all the national improvements, the Mairie de Sauzon took it upon himself to forward a mandatory village plan that included paving all our little paths and lanes and installing ugly concrete-pylon streetlights. *Streetlights.*

Gwened and Henry led that fight. But everyone was involved, from the Vicomte to Madame Morgane. We put our heads together

and decided that the petition should come from "the village of flowers." Everybody would sign it, *Bellilois* included and maybe even the
Unforgiving Couple. Gwened would appeal to the Mairie's vanity. She'd
take along all the postcards of Kerbordardoué that you can find in Le
Palais. Lay them out. See? They like us this way. We're a tourist attrac-
tion. In fact, do you know our postcard is the *number one bestseller*?

We won that round rather handily. But the bigger battle seemed
hopeless. But disaster, when it hit, came from an unexpected quarter. A
Maltese-flagged TotalFinaElf tanker, the *Erika*, broke apart seventy-five
miles from the island. As a huge oil spill approached, driven by a raging
storm, a thousand French high school and college students abandoned
their vacation plans and descended on the island to fight the oil in the
breakers and on the rocks.

In stormy and freezing weather they threw themselves into the fray;
the fight went on for weeks as giant new globs were released from the
sunken ship. Some young people we knew took leaves from university
to keep on task. Even from afar we felt how it had become a spiritual
battle for the island. They wore their hearts on their oil-stained sleeves.
Belle Île had given them so many little moments of heaven.

There's no doubt that those students saved the beach at Donnant.
But the storms drove the oil higher and higher onto the rocks and
undersea, into the crevices where all the littoral creatures lived.

Vacances the following year was depressing. The waters where Rory
used to dive stank. The rocks were slimy with oil. The once-flowing
seaweeds and kelp forests were dead, and there were no fish, of course.
We brought an Evian bottle filled with turpentine to the beach to clean
our feet and stationed another by the door.

Naturally, there was a steep drop-off in tourism. The magnifying
glass of media attention moved elsewhere. We did finally receive a
belated Christmas gift from the government when the causeway
was canceled.

In time we came to see the oil spill for what it was—a circuit breaker in the mad plans of those robotic fiends in the brooding gray bureaus overlooking the Seine in Paris. They shrugged and after that ignored us. But we didn't forget; *Erika* led to the growth and influence of an island environmental movement. Many *Bellilois* who wouldn't have called themselves green discovered it was their best hope of preserving their culture. Almost for the first time, *étranger* and islander could make common cause.

Yet another green boost we could've done without struck in 2003, when Europe experienced its strangest, hottest summer since 1540. Forest fires raged in Portugal; Italy baked for two months; glaciers melted under 100-degree temperatures in the Swiss Alps; and the Danube nearly dried up. France got hit the worst and longest, but the slow-rolling inversion didn't reach Belle Île until we were there in August.

At first we thought we would be spared; maybe this was *beau temps*. But it was so hot, too hot. All day and all night, the temperature and humidity kept rising. Within a couple of days, the very air we breathed seemed overheated, like when you open an oven door and stick your head too close. We didn't want to go out, even to the beach. If we did, the sand was a furnace. There were no waves and the sea, unnaturally warm, was full of aquatic lice that bit hard and drew blood.

One day we just stopped cooking. After consulting with Suzanne and Madame Morgane, we closed the wooden storm shutters for the first time in anyone's memory. The entire village went doggo. Stripped to our underwear, we lay on the cold tile floor with the lights out, reading by thin stripes of burning yellow sunlight boring in as if from the flare of a hydrogen bomb.

After a week we should've been going crazy. But our minds and bodies had gone into self-preservation lockdown. This is why 1,000-page novels are written, we told ourselves. I've always wanted to go on an all-yogurt diet. Let's fill the tub with cold water and lie there reading until it warms up and it's the next person's turn.

The nights were long and unbearably hot, but at least that damned sun wasn't overhead. We began moving around a bit in darkness, slowly, like spirits abroad on All Hallow's Eve. There were no parties. No visits. Social life was on hold.

Late one night, well after midnight, the heat reached an apogee. Staying indoors seemed almost dangerous. Mindy said, "I can't take it. I'm going down to the beach." We put on our suits—didn't even bother with shirts or towels—and shuffled like zombies down the *vallon*, through the grassy meadow, along the base of the tall sandhills, up to the gap in the dunes that overlooked Donnant. We did the entire twenty-five-minute walk without using our flashlights, even though the night was moonless. To our eyes, accustomed now to darkness, everything glowed like a photographic negative.

We walked the long sandy way toward the sea. A few dark figures moved at the fringes of our vision: somebody who must've had the same idea as us. There was no noise of surf. The ocean had been flat and still for over a week. We couldn't even see the water, just ultra-blackness, as opposed to the cobalt-blue horizon and night sky. Leaving our sandals behind, we slowly waded in.

Floating up to our necks, we looked around and realized we were surrounded by dozens, no, hundreds of floating beach balls. It took a moment to accept that these were the bobbing heads of people doing the cool thing. We were trading whispered impressions of the general weirdness when someone nearby spoke: "Mindy et Don? Ees that you?"

"Henry? Is Celeste with you?"

"Hel-lo Mindy! Hel-lo Don!"

Other voices chimed in: their children, Rory and Devó, and then from all around us, unseen in the dark, the voices of Kerbordardoué and other villages. The uncanny revelation kicked my mind into a warped place. To me, we were like those shades in the Underworld visited by Odysseus or Orpheus, or Dante in the company of Virgil— standing up to our necks in a boiling sea. Maybe that sounded like my imagination was running away with itself, but this was reality. The world had gone dreadfully awry, as if we as a species were like Icarus flying too close to the sun; now our wings were melting and our fall from grace had begun.

Mindy and I tried not to get nervous. I told myself that my doubts were undoubtedly common, given this unsettled time of war, terrorism, climate change, and political extremism. At least the economy was booming.

Still, I worried: Was our idyll coming to an end?

⚜

Brittany can seem a hard land. Its fields are a lovely gold in the fall, but much of the year is wet, green, and black. The Catholic worldview dominates, strong and grim, like my gloom-and-doom Scottish Presbyterian ancestors. We are sinners and we die; purgatory is certain, hell probable—you know God knows that you stole Tintin's butter from the cold safe by the spring! Do not be deceived by Gauguin's paintings of Brittany, those pure blocks of color. His most famous Breton scene, of country women in white lace caps, *coiffes*, pausing after church to watch the Angel Jacob wrestle Death, is a parable of you in your daily life, because your soul is always in the breach and someone, somewhere is wrestling over it.

In Brittany the nights are darker than elsewhere. I've never quite understood why. Fewer big cities, yes, but plenty of small ones. It's a rural quiet, a feeling that you are surrounded by fields and moors stretching all around you. Best to stay indoors. It's easy to see how the Bretons would sit around the hearth and tell ghost stories. They take Halloween seriously, though they call it *Kala Goañv*, better known throughout the Celtic world as *Samhain*.

When the portal opens between our world and the underworld, out pour the spooks, grabbing at the living, who dress up in guises to confuse their pursuers and go from tomb to tomb in the graveyard, demanding food that has been prepared by families for their departed ones. Even if you think you recognize your neighbor in that black shroud, face chalked white as a skull, you'd still better play it safe and give him a drink of milk and a winter apple.

※

The real specter of Death isn't bought off so easily. We've all heard the stories. Over in the next village, they tell the one about the sobbing, wavering cry in the fields at night that drew a farmer outside to look around and see if his cow was all right. We all know what happened to him. When the hound of death catches some poor devil, and you hear his howl of triumph, don't listen too long or you will be next. *La Chienne*, roaming the moors and bogs and desolate wastes, is not man's best friend.

Sometimes referred to as a great wind, *La Chienne* tears out a man's throat as he slogs through the marsh to reach the duck he shot—think *The Hound of the Baskervilles*. *Bidse an t-saoghail* is the root beastie but there's more to it. She's a whore who gets into a man's head. Like Stefane who went mad and drove his tractor straight onto the beach at Donnant, scattering sunbathers and screaming children. In his midthirties, he had never had a date, so he screwed up his courage to ask some tourist girl if she'd like to visit his barn. Because that was how it was done in his father's day. She pressed charges.

These are only stories, of course. Even that of *Ankou*, master of *La Chienne*, who hunts for him. Bringer of death and collector of the dead, Ankou drives a black carriage that had better not come to a stop before your house. If it does, resist the urge to pull back the lace on your window and stare. Because then you'll see him coming up your steps with his gnarled cane. If you encounter him at work in the fields between villages, he'll be sitting atop a cart piled with bodies, so many that the scrawny pair of white horses can barely pull it along. If he sees you—and he will—say your prayers. Because he's reaching for his scythe.

He has no face. That is known.

"Ankou" is also a season. When many die in a short time period, people say, *War ma fé, heman zo eun Anko drouk*: On my faith this one is a nasty Ankou.

The last weeks of the old year and the first day of the new belong to Ankou. This probably has to do with the simple biological fact that the old and infirm are most vulnerable in the dark of winter—when it's cold, damp, and smoky indoors. The air fills with animal dander from the cows and goats that share the living quarters; manure gets in the milk; and nobody washes their hands. The ergot mold that grows on the rye makes you hallucinate a black-shrouded figure out of a shadow—and then you die, hooting his name: "*Ankou! Ankou!*"

On New Year's Day, the old Ankou goes looking for his replacement. He's not particular. He'll take a stillborn. But if he can't lay hands on someone newly dead, then he'll strike someone down. That person then becomes the new Ankou, going door to door with his wheelbarrow for the next twelve months.

If you hear an owl's cry, it's an omen. Ankou is here in the village and will not go away empty-handed. If you hear the creak of a wheel at night, don't make a sound. It's him with his *karrigell an Ankou*, the wheelbarrow of death.

If nothing else works and he's coming for you in the fields or tap-tap-tapping up the path to your door, quick, pick up a tool. Not a weapon: a shovel, a plow, a spinning wheel. *Ankou* only fears honest work by patient men and women.

Ghost stories… What would we do without them on long winter nights?

※

As the years go by, Ankou makes his rounds. The amorous cowherd Dede, who'd proposed to Mindy faithfully every summer for several years, comes in from tending the cows, sits down to his dinner, and dies. Dede feels like a big loss; it's hard to explain how much just the sight of him, walking his herd daily up and down the side *vallon*, wool newsboy cap on that square head, meant to all of us. Of course we bought his eggs and, once in a great while, a duck or chicken. (He always let his sister do the garroting.)

He never married. That gold digger from Paris didn't last a week before her shrieks were heard all over the village and she was seen throwing things into her car and driving away fast. She'd wanted the land, of course. Got more than she bargained for, evidently.

Other news begins to trickle in—by letter, by phone, and lately, by email:

This summer Le Vicomte cannot come. It is pneumonia.

Suzanne, poor thing…her first time away from the island in her whole life and it's by air ambulance! The helicopter took her to the hospital in Vannes. She said she enjoyed the overhead view of the island, though. Said she'd never seen Locmaria—too many witches! Really, that's what she said. She's back now, in good form, says she is content with her life now that she's seen the end of the island.

My dear husband, Francis, we have sadness to report (wrote Gwened). He has a malady, a "crab," in his intestines.

Theophile's mother, too young, quite sudden—it has left his father devastated. And then America starts in.

I think I feel a lump, Anne says.

Donnie, there's bad news about your father.

Mindy, this is your brother, please pick up. I've been trying to reach you about Mom.

Donnie, looks like a stroke, but your mother is conscious. Sister is talking to specialists. We may go back to the first doctor. This new doctor… The second surgery…

It's to buy time.

🌹

Karrigell an ankou—*wheelbarrow of death, its creaking wheel heard coming to a halt outside your house at night means your time is up, Ankou has come for you.*

✿

Gwened writes the letters from Belle Île. From her we come to expect a dignity and restraint that softens the blow for the amount of time it takes to read of the death of Francis, her beautiful man; Le Vicomte, beloved of Yvonne, hero of Dunkirk; Suzanne, the hardest one to tell about…

Her last letter is brief:

My friends, it was a hard winter, an old adversary returned, and I have been ill… How fortunate I am, Daniel is here with me…

On my faith, this one is a hard Ankou.

Chapter Twenty-Four

A Last Swim in September

The cell phone is on the end table. No bars. I raise it to the skylight and hold it facing the relay tower I know is out there, a couple of miles away over the hill, its crow's nest of satellite dishes poking above a grove of cypresses.

"Stop it!" Mindy snaps, not fooling.

"I'm just getting a signal."

"Stop looking out the skylight. If Madame Morgane sees you…"

Neither of us says anything about the likelihood of that happening.

I sit back down on the edge of the bed and check the cell phone again. We've got bars, but they're going away before my eyes. But not before I see—nothing.

"No messages."

"What *is* he doing?" sighs Mindy. "Okay, call him—no, better text him."

"So now it's okay if I poke my head out of the *vas-ist-das?* Because that's the only way to get a sig…"

"Don't call it a *vas-ist-das*. It's a *chassis Velux*."

"Suzanne called it a *vas-ist-das*. She thought it was funny."

"She did not. She hated the Germans."

"She liked Heinrich well enough."

"She wouldn't sell him her grange, though."

"Of course she didn't sell him the grange. Where else would she go to the bathroom?"

We're in a rhythm now, letting the old familiar patterning of recollection and story ease us back into village life—its characters, rules, and mystery. (*Who owns that cement mixer?*) It's the sort of thing we start up without realizing, then, once we become aware, enjoy spinning out, sometimes for hours.

What is the joke here? That the Germans occupying Belle Île had never seen skylights before. *Vas-ist-das?* they asked when they searched houses on Belle Île for contraband like eggs and butter. *Vas-ist-das* became the name. It was a way, I believe, to point up the invader's stupidity, and to his face, too, while the whole time he'd be thinking it was a friendly overture.

It's possible I'm overthinking this. But remembering Suzanne's gruffness with Heinrich, her neighbor in the adjoining stone cottage for thirty years, I don't think so.

Mindy shifts in the bed and a board groans. "I think it's broken," she says.

My first job upon arrival is always to check the bed for broken slats and, if necessary, to make repairs. But we got in too late yesterday. "I'll get on it," I say, but am provoked by her silent *Oh sure.* "Just as soon as you get off it, slugabed."

I've stalled long enough. After tapping out a short text to Rory, I head downstairs.

❧

From the moment we stepped off the ferry, we were overwhelmed by the rush of old memories and the ever-present beauty of an ageless Belle Île September. Everywhere we turned, people popped up and extended a welcome and an invitation to a drink, dinner, picnic at the beach. Our younger *Bellilois* surf gang, once so wild but now married with children, dragged us into madcap adventures for old times' sake. We walked the moors with Yvonne, the Vicomte's widow, debated the world news with our psychiatrist friends, feasted at the tables of locals and *étrangers*, woke to the quiet of another village morning in our pine-paneled chamber.

Is that a knock on the door? Yes, it's Pierre-Louis, the president of some hyper-learned World Society of Psychoanalysts. He stands there holding a portable electric power drill—says he has one quick job to do—and mounts the stairs. Yes, he's come to fix our once-again-broken bed.

"But how did you know it was broken?"

Pierre-Louis laughs heartily and wags a finger.

How we wish Rory were here. We know it would cheer him up.

❧

Last summer was the first without Gwened Guedel, but her presence was everywhere, especially in the overgrown gardens and laden fruit trees where we wandered in conscious acts of remembrance. This year it's final: her spirit is gone. The sale of her house and land was done coldly and hastily, at a loss, by the son she'd always hoped would take over the place and love it the way she had, the way we did, the way she taught us.

To be clear, Daniel had no choice—he lives in Chicago, he'd lost his job, like us, and had a new baby on the way. *Annus horribilis* 2009 played no favorites, that's for sure.

In a sense we are only now coming to fully appreciate, Gwened prepared everything for Daniel: the house, the village, us, the rest of the cast of characters, controlling as much as she could. Then she sat back and waited, waited, waited for thirty years, for Daniel to come back. And when death approached she made every arrangement with the taxes and title so he could inherit without cost. And all for nothing, it seems. Though he was with her during the desperate treatments and later on in hospice, he simply couldn't build his life around Kerbordardoué the way she had. Poor Gwened. She prepared a snare of love and beauty and belonging, and instead of catching Daniel, all she caught was us.

We, the Americans, whom she lured here, installed here, schooled here and prodded and spurred to finish our house. She chose to put us next door to her, not somebody else, so it was done out of love and friendship, right?

Except that there was also Gwened's unyielding perfectionism—the same controlling behavior that probably drove Daniel away. Because when she needed to bait that snare of love and beauty and belonging, Gwened must've decided she needed something exotic. What better than a couple of American writers for a young man who wanted to be a writer himself? It's not so flattering, maybe, to us, but I can't get the suspicion out of my head that *we were the cheese*.

Yes, she loved us—that we know. But in the back of her mind always, I suspect, was the Plan. I know it would be in mine, if our positions were reversed.

When we heard Gwened's house was up for sale, I emailed Daniel. I know and like him. We pleaded with him to slow down, wait out the economic crisis; good advice which we ourselves were unable to heed in the case of our New York apartment and life. (We would eventually leave, in tears and undignified haste, half of our furniture on the curb as the taxi pulled away.) Though I regret his selling, I know we also considered the same course of action. What Daniel does is really none of my business—except for this matter of the years we spent next door to his mother, watching Gwened wait.

It just feels wrong that we're here when he's not. But we have another, more personal and compelling reason to care about what drove Daniel away—because we have a son, too. A son who hasn't picked up on his cell for the past three weeks, won't answer an email to save his life, doesn't respond even to a goddamned text message written all in $#)$&#$& and emoticons and all the other poetry of the new gen. A son who, if only he knew it, needs this island, too. A son who isn't here with us. Again. For the sixth year and counting.

The losses hit Rory hard. Who can blame him for feeling down? He's an only child. Growing up and living in New York, he didn't see as much of his family or his cousins. At least his grandparents knew it and lavished attention on him when he was with them. His bond with his Aunt Anne was also magical; everyone noticed it. And Gwened—another good witch—gave him so much love, too, and not only because she missed having her own grandchildren.

Now they are all gone, except my mother who's had two strokes. All this and losing his New York City home makes Rory one worried boy. Just turned twenty-one, he seems older. Like so many students at Stanford, he's taken a start-up job on top of his studies. He dug up a scholarship to pay for his junior and senior year tuition. We feel guilty, and tell him to quit the job and focus on his classes, that we can afford it. And we can, theoretically, even after losing our jobs and the economic system's meltdown. But he's wise in his own way. He doesn't listen to us anymore.

So we come to Belle Île alone.

Toward the middle of the stay, we find ourselves alone in the village. The *rentrée* fell early this summer and all the Parisians are gone. Only members of Madame Morgane's extended family remain, spread out among several houses well-hidden by tall hedges. We have our pick of several large gardens heaving up a cornucopia of fat blood tomatoes, stout zucchini and cucumbers, lime-green frisée, runner beans, carrots, parsley and basil and *fenouil*. The trees drip with small red crab apples. The fig's boughs hang low with fruit. Even Gwened's single pear tree by the former dojo produces one perfect little tear-drop Bosc. The owners beg us to take some of this produce off their hands.

We have everything we want, except for who we want.

The empty lanes and long afternoons are made for wandering. Our rusty Renault has died and gone away, so now we sway over rutted moor roads in a tiny opalescent Twingo. We go by eye and whim and memory.

Late September on the last full day of our stay, we're out on the cliffs between Port Kerel and Pointe Saint Marc when we come to a stop at the end of threshed fields that overlook a 300-foot drop. "Isn't this where we first came to swim with Gwened?" I ask. Mindy nods, squinting up and down the coast.

"Yew-Yew? Was that the name?"

"No, Calastren."

"That's a village, not a beach."

"Port Guen?"

We smile at the realization that, yes, Gwened *would* go for a nude swim at a cove bearing her name.

We get out and stare down at the crescent of sand hemmed in by walls of blue-green schist. Remembering how warm and protected it was, how Gwened wanted no other place, even with its difficult scramble down precipitous hillsides full of prickly gorse, we give it a good, long look but don't go there.

Instead we retrace our tracks and worm our way through narrow village lanes and a steep descent under a shady grove. We park and walk into a bowl valley of dense lush ferns that cover every inch of ground in sight. Somewhere down there at the end of the sandy path we'll have our last swim. There will be no postcard awaiting us when we arrive back home in the United States, as there was after our first plunge—*les derniers baigneurs de Septembre*—with just a little scrawl below that followed by a tiny signature: Gwened. But we'll always be the last swimmers of September.

☙

We arrive alone and we leave alone. With an hour to spare after dropping our bags in Theophile's office by the *quai*, we walk back up the boat basins under the overgrown ramparts of the walled town. One of the yellow granite towers is now part of a rest home. As we are heading up the ramp with a bouquet of village flowers, a woman passing says, "She will love them."

We find out that her prescience wasn't all that great: Madame Morgane is the only patient on the second floor. Tiny and wrinkled, shaking quietly in her bedclothes, she lies with eyes closed and lips parted. We assume that what we've heard is true, that she can no longer speak or understand speech or recognize people.

I'm for leaving the flowers and leaving, but when Mindy says her name, Madame Morgane's eyes open, blink slowly. She stares into Mindy's face as we gently remind her who we are. Then she knows us. "*Les Américains.*" Yes, that's us, all right. We discuss the old familiar village sights, how dry the summer was, how grand the gardens.

She listens. Then she slowly opens her mouth. "The village is not the same," she says. "Everything has changed."

Mindy gently agrees that it must seem so and says she knows Madame Morgane must miss Suzanne. This draws out a beautiful smile. So does mention of Mindy's chocolate football, which she pressed into the hands of Madame's daughter as we were about to drive away under Kerbordardoué's tunnel of trees. We have a couple of slices with us, in our packs. We will eat them on the train, knowing that the rest of the cake will not be eaten by the intended. It is an offering, as at *Kala Goañv.*

Mindy finds a nurse, the only one on duty, who digs up an empty jar for the flowers. Madame Morgane's room is all white and doesn't have a TV or even a painting on the walls. But it has a view of the harbor's backwaters and several old wooden boats hauled up on the muddy banks, some to rot, others under restoration. Behind them are the dark green, furrowed hills of the other side.

After we say good-bye, we stand in the parking lot for a moment, overcome.

Back in America we will get the news. But as we climb up the steel gangway into the black hold of the *Guerveur*, it's already over. Now it's just us, and the next generation, and the ones after that.

❧

"You know, when you visited our house in Tours that first time, Don, how the household seemed *dérangée*? I was acting a little crazy?"

Mindy smiled. "You mean when you threw the typewriter out the window?"

Daniel Guedel looked surprised, his wife delighted. *Really?* her look said.

This was in the early winter back in New York City. We hadn't seen Daniel since his mother died. Hadn't seen him at all for a few years. But we'd kept in touch. We cheered his job and marriage and baby and his wife's writing career. He's family. When he called to say he was in New York, we knew it would be emotional. We just had no idea how much.

We settled on the sofa in our apartment after dinner. Our wind-rattled old casement windows looked out over a New York City sunset as it settled scores of doomed battles between light and shadow.

"Very Freudian of me," he said, "seeing as I wanted to be a writer. Well"—the breath he took should have put us on notice that this would be no ordinary story—"what had happened, about a week before you arrived, was that my mother told me I was not my father's son."

Mindy and I just stared. Daniel nodded.

"I had just turned sixteen, you see. She said she thought that I was now old enough to know. She said she couldn't live with the falsehood any longer anyway."

"Did he know? Your father?" I meant the one we knew.

Daniel shook his head. We sat stunned, frozen in place, wineglasses almost touching our lips, hands hovering above the cheese, the chips, the *chèvre* and guacamole.

"Daniel?" But Mindy didn't know what she wanted to ask.

He smiled. "Sorry."

There was of course nothing to apologize for, but in a sense, Daniel understood what a shock this was to us. He'd felt it at sixteen. The perfect woman who is your mother is an illusion.

"But," he continued, implacable, as if it had to be told in one go or he'd lose his courage. "She asked me not to tell my father. It would be our little secret. This I could not believe. She and I were fighting a lot. A lot. You know how controlling my mother could be? It was worse than you could believe. A war. And then this. Why?"

"Why?" echoed Mindy.

"I think she resented my closeness to my father."

"Oh, that poor man," I said, thinking of how Gwened had sold us the story of her upright, bearded husband having taken a mistress.

"Who?" asked Mindy. "I mean, how? I don't mean to pry, but—damn!"

"He was a student, a fellow student in Budapest where she had gone to study. There was a family connection to the Magyars; we are part Hungarian." He smiled as if that explained something. "She was absolutely controlled by her parents and terrified in particular of disappointing her father. But of course she already had, by not being the son he'd always wanted. Right? And when she got to Budapest, well, she went a little wild."

The comparison to Mindy's mother at college, away from Hawaii for the first time in her life, must've popped into Mindy's and my minds simultaneously. I felt an electric surge rewiring the circuitry of my memories: no, not that way, this way. Away for the first time from the adults who'd made her, designed her from the ground up to be a proper little prodigy—that was Dolly. Gwened was the daughter of a prodigy—a dutiful daughter afflicted with insecurity and a sense of not measuring up. This was what she'd told us about her grandfather and father, both university professors, men with serious black mustaches.

We flailed at understanding by making small noises, waving hands, gulping drinks. After regaining our wits, we waited, not wishing to pry but intent on hearing it all, or as much as Daniel was comfortable telling us.

※

To go back to everyday life in postwar Europe after the giddy VE celebrations was an anticlimax, to say the least. Everyone wandered a sepia-tinted, dust-covered civilization: the gray walls; the bombed-out buildings still prominent; the poor food, still rationed; the seemingly continual cold; nobody able to afford heat or take a bath because the plumbing and gas lines were barely functional. For college students in Budapest, the only place to find a little warmth was the café, of course. Poverty was the real source of that romantic café culture we Americans dream about replicating here in Portland and Brooklyn and Peoria.

Gwened had a group of friends. She was giddy and semi-starved, made bold, she said, by at last escaping the great gloomy men whose portraits had glared out of smoky oil paintings on the walls of her dining room. She allowed herself to be seduced by a flamboyant Hungarian music student whose genius was already aflame. Everyone knew Rakel would make it and become one of the imperious, be-caped presences of the international opera houses and symphonies. He represented art to Gwened, art and rebellion and escape. Going to bed with Rakel, a known playboy, in those dangerous days before the pill, was Gwened's refusal to play the hand life had dealt her. She rolled the dice.

Within a couple weeks she knew she'd lost. And with that knowledge came the return of her senses, and the prospect of grim futility and eternal familial disapproval—the very weight of seething wrath that Mindy's mother had incurred from her proper Korean parents.

Pregnant, unmarried, and living with her parents? A recipe for hell. Gwened began to plot. She cast her eye around the group of impoverished students, judging their prospects for the first time by the same bourgeois standards her parents would've employed. Lowering her sights, she chose. They came together as if by chance. The indiscretion seemed all his fault, the bad boy. And now look what a mess he'd landed her in...

Daniel's composure was surreal. But then, we found out, he'd stopped keeping the secret some time ago. As in years ago. We were literally the last to know. *Everyone?* we asked. Daniel nodded. But why leave us in the dark? He smiled. Because she asked.

We got it. All Gwened asked—of life, and in the end, of death and the village—was for *some*body's illusions about her to stay intact until she had time to exit stage left, head held high. That somebody was us.

Chapter Twenty-Five
Village Elders

I n the late summer of 2010, we go back. We no longer live anywhere except, tenuously, in Mindy's childhood home in Hawaii, which her brothers are trying to sell out from under us. If anything we are less secure financially, yet we've hit the road again, traveling light, confident something will turn up. *Still us.*

If Hawaii sells us out, Belle Île will be our home. We've already considered moving here if things get much worse. Maybe that's what the house has been waiting for. But our main concern, this year and every year, is still our son. A new Rory has risen from the ashes of a bridge-burning adolescent. He's settled himself in New York with a girlfriend. And has boldly announced that he's coming to the island for the first time in seven years.

As we wait to see if Rory really will show, we wonder at the changes in our now-subdued village. We don't know what will be done with Madame Morgane's house and farm, but her family is very visible, working on a new wall, waving hello, and even—good heavens—chatting with us. Our new next-door neighbor, the nice lawyer and his judge wife, have reversed last year's decision to sell and buy a larger place. Kerbordardoué is just too friendly and there are so many children for their two girls to play with.

A nephew who inherited Suzanne's ruin is restoring it into a very proper Breton house, we're happy to see. The stonemason with the German shepherd tattoo has nearly finished his renovation, too. *After ten years*, he moans, *what will I do with myself?* One thing he won't do, we're fairly sure, is talk to the dentist across the lane, who hasn't spoken to any of us since the village shot down his plan for a McMansion. (Fifteen years and counting. We'd hate to see that streak broken.)

But now the cell phone is ringing. It's Rory at the *quai*, wondering in a cranky voice why we aren't there to pick him up. "Is Kaitlin with you?" we ask.

"Yes, and a couple of others."

We recognize that tone of voice.

"How many others?" we ask, trying not to sound anxious. Don't want to scare him off, after all. Even if there are only four beds in the house.

"Ten," he says.

We try not to gasp. If Rory is bringing a village with him, this village will make room for them all—as it did for us.

❧

In storytelling, the teller of the tale sets the rules, chalks the lines of the game. This is the way we go—down this path, not that one.

Thus we have always made this story about us, about our impulsive decision that seemed like idiocy, but which over time increasingly was spun as daring, rash romanticism. (*Oh those kids!*) And why not? It's all true.

But it's our truth. There are other truths. There is Suzanne's and Madame Morgane's. I think we're all grown-up enough to admit to the notion of other people's truths.

But there is even another truth, a nonhuman truth, from the point of view of what historians call the *longue durée*, or long cycle of history.

Taking the *longue durée* in this case would be to look at things from the point of view of the house and the village, exactly as if they were characters. Because the house is not us, and its place is where it was born—in the village. We can't take it with us, the way we can a child or a souvenir or a suntan, can we?

So what is the village story? That the house was crumbling away, returning to the earth. We bought it. We never had the money to renovate it, so we never went down that path. Our goal was pragmatic—not changing it would cost the least. Since we didn't have the talent, time, or inclination to do the restoration ourselves, we paid others, local artisans, many of them older or near retirement or even newly retired.

Based on this telling, our role is minimal, close to being caretakers. We handed money to the real artists. We did enter into the spirit of the place, the village, Belle Île; I am proud of us for that. Absentee owners often deserve scorn.

A couple of people did inform us we were depriving someone else—a French person, to be exact, someone like themselves—of their right to our house in our village. Sometimes we found ourselves on the defensive, almost agreeing, although never openly, with the criticism. Long ago we'd asked for a *saine* house, and Denis LeReveur put those characteristics into the *devis*; but did we also have a *moral* house? Did we have a right to be here? Who could say?

As time has gone by, the question ceased to be an idle or self-indulgent one. In both our Chelsea neighborhood in Manhattan and in Mindy's old-timey Hawaiian neighborhood where her mother lived, the new money is scouring away all traces of the past, including washing away the people who made both places unique, functional, more than decorative, more than districts where the global rich or hard-bargaining time-sharer who bought a place would spend exactly two weeks out of each year. How were we any different? Did our four weeks a year really make us so superior?

Whether we were preservers or destroyers was the question we put to ourselves and couldn't answer. There are sterile villages on Belle Île, places where foreign buyers swooped in and snatched up properties and installed colonies of Germans, Belgians, English. Not that there is anything wrong with these nationalities in the singular, but en masse they upset the balance. (As do, it should go without saying, too many Americans.) You drive through these villages and feel nothing. The renters are there for sun and beach and sausages, and because it is cheap—they probably resent not being able to afford Provence.

But I think most who come here and buy a place do so because, heaven forfend, they visited and loved the island to distraction. In them we see ourselves, even if they point at our skylight and ask: *Vas-ist-das?*

Our doubts about a moral house probably seem overdone. Yeah, conservatives have it easy: liberal guilt is hell. But we can't change who we are.

⚘

What vanquished our guilt about taking a house out of circulation for eleven months of every year was the way Suzanne's cat kept jumping in the window. We kept tossing him out, until one day we capitulated and invited Grizzou to join us for a saucer of milk. He acted like he owned the place. Which, we realized suddenly, he did.

Now we knew why Suzanne knitted lace for all the windows. Not for us—but so she and Madame Morgane, childhood friends, could sit in the kitchen of Tante Jeannie as it was when they were little girls. There they could look out the window through the lace, the lace framing the Belle Île view, their view, of village life going on its slow way, uninterrupted. For years they'd had this place to themselves, only surrendering it at the end of August when we arrived.

Silly us. We thought it was our house when it was theirs.

Still, a few people, in France and America, have since tried to take us down a peg for "wasting" it. Americans especially wonder why we haven't turned it into a rental and made it pay for itself like a beast of burden. But that would have meant tricking it out to tourist expectations: TV, phone, Internet, frilly curtains, bright colors, cute lamps, and generic paintings. Perhaps even painting the *salle de cuisine*.

Most of all, it also would have meant finishing it. It's taken us twenty-nine years, but we've finally got our answer down pat:

What's the rush?

And when it is our turn, at the end of our time here, I hope there will be those who stop and point. *Oh look! It's so beautiful!* And then they will see us and make up stories about us. Yes, here they are in their dotage, strolling the village lanes, pockets full of flowers and clippings, brown, shaky, age-spotted hands busily transplanting cuttings into the chinks in the village walls. Seeing our cracked smiles and missing teeth, they will think: *La femme sauvage! L'homme sauvage!*

And then, if this should be you, I hope that you'll go on and pretend not to recognize us. Just turn and go on your way to your own village, wherever it is, and there tend to any ruins that you think are in need of a wise villager's benign neglect.

Leave us to putter and to delude ourselves that our work will one day be done. Because, of course, it never will be.

Author's Note

And if you see him, pick up a tool, not a weapon. A shovel, a plow, a spinning wheel. Ankou only fears honest work by patient men and women.

I picked up a pen.

It's said that we don't know what we are thinking until we put it down in writing, and this is certainly true for this book. My original intention wasn't to bring our old Kerbordardoué back to life one more time. But beginning the writing, I soon realized that if I didn't hurry, Kerbordardoué would be gone and I'd never finish it. That was twenty years ago. So much for deadlines.

To my friends and family who have lived portions of this book and appear here: Thank you. You know I've only borrowed your memories. They're still your own.

When it comes to my memories, I ask that you extend the courtesy of suspending your disbelief. Yes, it's possible to feel simultaneous absurdity and tragedy and, if you're us, to make a joke about it that grows over thirty years into a deeply grooved routine. Yes, you can love your mother and somehow end up living 2,500 miles away from her, with a summer place 5,000 miles away—or, in Mindy's case, 7,500 miles away.

So, yes, I'm saying this happened, more or less as I tell it. Back in the predigital age, there were these things called notebooks, which both Mindy and I carried with us at all times. By some miracle, a box of them and various postcards, documents, letters, and photographs survived our many moves and misfortunes. The famous "Instructions" also surfaced. Finally, decades ago Mindy and I had made a first joint attempt to tell our story chronologically. Although this was certainly premature, it was very helpful.

As I worked and reworked with time and memory, a dozen or so concentrated moments became, for me, luminous as reliquaries. In following my own methodology, such as it is, I did take a special personal inspiration from *The Horse of Pride*, Pêr-Jakez Helias's memoir of Breton country life. How Helias handles physical descriptions and imbues them with psychological traits and depths of mystery stunned me when I first read it twenty years ago. (There is also a film of the book, by Claude Chabrol.) Also, anyone who has enjoyed the films of Jacques Tati, particularly *Mr. Hulot's Holiday* and *Play Time*, will recognize my debt to his rhythms in the beach scenes.

I'm a writer by profession, not an academic, so while I have made my best efforts to get things right, I can't guarantee that I haven't asserted one or two things here as fact that can be dismissed with a wave of the hand by any self-respecting lecturer or assistant professor. For anything I get right in the more subtle interpretations of events and relationships I am absolutely indebted to my wife.

Mindy is always on me to sharpen my thought, my French, my facts, my accounts of events, and I take her advice to heart wherever possible. She could've written this book with me but turned me down, probably knowing we would debate the slightest differing version of the same event until we'd beaten the life out of it. Instead, she fills this book with her humor and wisdom (and an occasional groan of exasperation at Young Strudel).

It will be obvious, to the discerning, that I have changed the name of our village and obscured certain identifying characteristics and found equivalents for the names of our friends. But I didn't alter the names or locations of anything else.

Facts are stubborn things, as John Adams said. But so are experts. University types have a way of being too blinded by the lights along the tenure track to take note of the life going on in the hedgerows and fields around them. In this book, as on Belle Île, I have followed the light of a glowworm on a country lane.

Resources and Attributions

The author's blog has photos and continuing reports from Belle Île at DonWallaceFranceBlog.tumblr.com.

Portions of "The Sole of Solitude" chapter originally appeared, in considerably different form, in essays for the Sunday travel section of the *New York Times*. All photos are taken by or through the courtesy of Don Wallace (copyright 2013), with the exception of pages 273 and 305 by Thomas Rennesson.

Among the more than thirty histories and accounts read as background, the most crucial include the first book written about the island, *Histoire de Belle Île en Mer*, by Chasle de la Touche (1852); *Europe Between the Oceans: 9000 BC–AD 1000* (2008) and *The Ancient Celts* (1997) by Barry Cunliffe; *The Old Regime and the Revolution* by Alexis de Tocqueville (1856); *The Divine Sarah: A Life of Sarah Bernhardt* by Arthur Gold and Robert Fizdale (1991); *Belle Île en Mer: Histoire d'une Île* by Louis Garans (1999); the works of Fernand Braudel and Norman Davies; and the many excellent pocket histories of various facets of island life by the *Société Historique de Belle Île en Mer*.

Quotes on the myth of Ankou are from various journal citations of *La Légende de la Mort en Basse-Bretagne* (1893) by Anatole Le Braz, as well as *The Appointed Hour: Death, Worldview, and Social Change in Brittany* by Ellen Badone (1989), culturebreizh.free.fr, and other websites. As these descriptions of Ankou, La Chienne, and the Breton way of death are drawn from folklore, I believe Anonymous should get the credit.

Fin

$\mathcal{A}$cknowledgments

Although this is a book that invokes the lives of many people both living and dead, I have changed names and altered some identifying characteristics. On the other hand, my wife, Mindy Pennybacker, and our son, Rory Wallace, are mercilessly exposed in these stories. I can only offer in my defense that I come off much worse. And that I owe this book, and much more, to you both.

Similarly, I use portions of the lives of my parents and of Mindy's mother and family, but again out of love and a desire to tell a truthful and human story. I am grateful that both my mother and father blessed my earlier published portrayals of them. They were daring storytellers, never ones to hold back a savory detail out of prudery or propriety, and I think they would be pleased to see me carrying on the tradition. My sister Nancy; my brother Alex; my late sister Anne; and my cousin Marcella have been tremendously enabling of my wild and wicked memoir addiction.

Thanks to my *îliens* and fellow lovers of Belle Île: Adrien, Aidan, Aileen, Alain, Anne, the Two Alexanders, Benedict, Bill, Bridgette, Bruno, Carine, Celeste, Celia, Chantal, Coco, David, Dede, Denis, Didier, Dominique I & II, Dorotheee, Fabrice, Francois, Francoise, M. Grancoeur, Gwened, Gwenn, Guillaume, Henry, Herve, Daniel, Jacques I & II, Jean, Jean-Claude, Jean-Daniel, Jean-Paul, Jos, Julien, Kaitlin, Katrine, Katherine, Leo, Leonore, Man, Marie, Martin, Mattias, Monique, Nancy, Natasha, Noel, Patrick I & II, Pierre-Louis, PJ aka French Spike, Richard, Robert, Rodolph, Sam, Sidonie, Stephane, Stephanie, Sylvie, Theophile, Thibault, Tom, Tomas, Valerie, Veronique, Victor, Will, and Yannick.

To members of the Dream Team and its successors, I stand before you with my hand over my heart. I also must thank the owners and management of Castel Clara, Chez Renée, Crêperie Les Embruns, and the Hôtel du Phare for all the fine meals and companionship.

Great thanks, almost immeasurable, go to my agent Laurie Fox for taking peeks at early drafts and, later, throwing herself deeply into the construction of this complicated thirty-year story. A "genius prize" to Stephanie Bowen, my editor at Sourcebooks, for finally unlocking the sequence—almost as tricky as a genome, in my opinion. The design team at Sourcebooks has done splendidly by the book and Belle Île. Thanks also to Chris Bauerle, director of sales, for his early enthusiasm and to publisher Dominique Raccah for growing such a creative publishing house.

I also would like to thank the editors at the *New York Times* travel section over the years for their support of my storytelling and research jaunts to Brittany and Belle Île. The same thanks go to Donna Bulseco and Ellie McGrath, my soul mates at *SELF*; to Anne Alexander at *Walking* magazine; to *Islands* magazine; and especially to Peter Janssen at *MotorBoating & Sailing* magazine, who repeatedly allowed me to construct reporting assignments in France that took me curiously close to Belle Île. May all writers be blessed with a boss whose sensibilities are still susceptible to the dreams of their underlings. God knows we all need a vacation.

I wish to memorialize my late friend Christopher Burgart, a singer and songwriter in Santa Cruz who, in 1973, long before I ever heard of the island that would so shape my future, came back from a summer abroad and strummed a new song he'd composed on the road: "Belle Isle." Chris, years later, I've realized that you nailed it.

Finally, there is the woman I call "Gwened Guedel" and to whom Mindy and I owe so much. "Gwened," you always knew this book was coming, and I firmly believe you engineered its final surprising revelations. As long as this book lives, you are, in a sense, immortal, which may even have been your intention. All I can say is that you'd love to see how the village that you did so much to preserve and to shape has turned out.

About the Author

D on Wallace was born in Long Beach, California, and has spent most of his life as a journalist and editor in New York City and Honolulu—that is, when not in France. He is the author of four books, including the novel *Hot Water* and *One Great Game: Two Teams, Two Dreams, in the First-Ever National Championship High School Football Game*. His essays, articles, and fiction have appeared in such publications as *Harper's*, the *New York Times*, *SELF*, *Fast Company*, *Wine Spectator*, and *Naval History*. You can visit his website at www.don-wallace.com and DonWallaceFranceBlog.tumblr.com for updates on Belle Île-en-Mer.

Photo credit: Mindy Pennybacker